OTHER RANKS OF KUT

Other Ranks of Kut

by

P. W. LONG, MM
Flight Sergeant, R.A.F.

With a Preface by

SIR ARNOLD WILSON
K.C.I.E., D.S.O., M.P.

The Naval & Military Press Ltd

published in association with

FIREPOWER
The Royal Artillery Museum
Woolwich

Published by
The Naval & Military Press Ltd
Unit 10 Ridgewood Industrial Park,
Uckfield, East Sussex,
TN22 5QE England
Tel: +44 (0) 1825 749494
Fax: +44 (0) 1825 765701
www.naval-military-press.com

in association with

FIREPOWER
The Royal Artillery Museum, Woolwich
www.firepower.org.uk

Printed and bound by Antony Rowe Ltd, Eastbourne

TO THE GARRISON OF KUT

Battle and toil survived, is this the end
Of all your high endeavour? Shall the stock
That death and desert braved be made a mock
Of gazing crowds, nor in the crowd a friend?
Shall they who ever to their will did bend—
From Zain to Ctesiphon—the battle shock
Fall prey to lean starvation's craven flock
And the dark terrors that her train attend?

You leave the field, but those who, passing by,
Take up the torch, whene'er your name is named
Shall fight more stoutly, while your company,
Its task performed, shall carry unashamed
Into captivity a courage high:
The body prisoner, but the mind untamed.

R. W. BULLARD

CONTENTS

LIST OF ILLUSTRATIONS

PREFACE

BY SIR ARNOLD WILSON, M.P.

THIS BOOK speaks for itself. It is from the pen of an eye-witness and is confirmed by half a score of independent narratives. The story has been told in a paper (Cd. 9208) presented to Parliament in November 1918 (before the Armistice): the *Official History* devotes six of its two thousand pages to the subject. Barber, Bishop, Keeling, Monsley, Sandes, Still, and Townshend are among the officers of the garrison of Kut al Amara who have published books dealing with the fate of British and Indian captives in Turkish hands. The public memory, however, is short. The belief, presumably of Crimean origin, that the Turks were clean fighters, who could be relied on to treat prisoners as humanely as circumstances allowed, has survived all evidence to the contrary. The parallel legend of Arab chivalry fostered by Blunt, encouraged by Doughty, and exploited for political and other less worthy motives during and for a few years after the war, seems scarcely less enduring.

Sergeant Long has done a service to the rising generation by placing on record, in the simplest language, the manner in which the Turks and their Arab associates treated their prisoners, as compared with the invariable consideration extended to the latter by German officers and, when opportunity offered, even at great risk, by Armenians, whom those who know neither Turk nor Arab sometimes so lightly speak of with dislike and even with contempt.

It is far from my desire to rake among the dying embers of contemporary history for sparks wherewith to kindle flames of hatred. Yet neither Sergeant Long nor I would have our fellow men ignorant of the profound difference between the attitude of this country to-day towards the suffering of helpless human beings and that of those Eastern peoples with whom we were at war. They were neither better nor worse than other nations with similar traditions and a like environment. Such happenings are a concomitant not only of war but of civil anarchy which may, as I know by experience, entail consequences worse than war to numbers of helpless individuals.

The treatment of prisoners, whether in war or in peace, has in all ages been inhuman, and in many countries still disgraces humanity. Scenes scarcely less terrible were, and perhaps are now, being enacted in other theatres of war.

Sergeant Long and his comrades were "the honoured guests of the Turkish nation." Their fate was long hidden from public knowledge, for the General Staff in Mesopotamia discredited and, when possible, suppressed almost every report of cruelty and brutality till the bitter truth could no longer be hidden, whilst the Government spokesman in the House of Lords on May 16, 1916, was officially inspired to pay the Turks a tribute in respect of their treatment of prisoners "in comparison with other of our enemies."

The representatives of the United States of America in Turkey, notably the U.S. Consuls at Baghdad, Mersina, and Tarsus, did all that was possible, but it was little. Of 2,592 British rank and file taken prisoner at Kut, 70 per cent died in captivity. It is true that the machinery of civilization broke down everywhere: in Turkey it never began to work. If, God forbid, such things should happen to the world again, will the best-laid schemes fare any better? To the historian the perspective of time is as vital as that of distance to the artist, and in human affairs progress must be measured in generations, not in calendar years.

But this story has a brighter side: it is a modest record of endurance and heroism of men of our race which lends point to the proud motto obscurely carved upon the cross bench of the House of Commons in front of the Sergeant-at-Arms:

> "*Numine et patriae asto.*"
> "I stand by God and my country."

It lends point to the last stanza of a sonnet, *To the Garrison of Kut*, published in *The Busrah Times* by Mr. (now Sir) R. W. Bullard, of H.M. Consular Service, which appears on page 5 of this excellent book—the first work upon this subject to be written by one of the rank and file on whom fell the brunt. The author's repeated escapes, and the courage shown by him and his fellows, prove, if proof be wanted, the strength of character and capacity for leadership latent in men of our race even under the fiercest torments and bitterest physical miseries. Let those who proclaim the decadence of the rising generation—a favourite theme in 1913—read this book and ask themselves whether they, in like case, could do and dare as much as Sergeant Long.

ARNOLD WILSON

AUTHOR'S NOTE

WHEN I decided to write this book I had one outstanding motive, and that was to put on record something that had not hitherto appeared in print; a record of the treatment meted out to the "other ranks" of the Kut Garrison during their long and terrible trek into captivity, also something of the life that they led as prisoners in the hands of the Turks during the years that followed.

Several officers had written of their various experiences, and most of them had touched upon the subject of the treatment that we of the "other ranks" had been subjected to, but they could not tell the full story for the simple reason that they were not permitted to accompany us—possibly one reason why we suffered as we did. One book was published as I was writing this, a book that is a compilation of brief accounts told by certain officers and men, with the result that it is a patchwork affair and does not satisfy us of the "other ranks."

For many years we of the rank and file of the Kut Garrison have waited for an author to come along to write the story for us, one who would do justice to the theme and leave us at last satisfied that the story of the annihilation of the greater part of the Indian Expeditionary Force "D" had been fully told. No such author has appeared, so I have, at long last, yielded to the many urgings by both officers and men of that generation and this, to write my story.

Each and every surviving member of the "other ranks," who passed along that trail of death into Anatolia, could tell a similar story to mine of what happened during that long march up-country from Kut. Many could, I have no doubt, tell of incidents more horrible than those I have described, but I know that what I have told concerning the experiences of my own particular party is, in general, the story of them all.

To my mind nothing has been lost by the long delay in making public this story. In the years that have passed since the days of which I write I have been fortunate enough to have been able to revisit Mesopotamia, and have passed over many miles of the route we were made to take as captives. I have fraternized with both survivors and descendants of those peoples who were responsible for adding to the sum of our sufferings, so that I have written my story confident that I have done so in true perspective; not unduly biased against our erstwhile enemies.

To-day I have a great admiration for the present generation of Turks who, led by that great soldier and administrator, Kemal Ataturk, are successfully striving to rid their race of the opprobrious epithet "unspeakable," and who are endeavouring to lift themselves from that position beneath humanity which many years of maladministration and corruption, practised and countenanced by their forbears, had thrust them.

To the many who have asked, and to those who would ask, "What happened to you after the surrender of Kut?" and "How did the Turks treat you?" this book is an answer.

P. W. LONG

MALTA
June, 1938

OTHER RANKS OF KUT

CHAPTER ONE

THE FIRST DAYS OF CAPTIVITY

"I HAVE come to say good-bye, Jerry; we surrendered yesterday and to-morrow we march out."

It was thus that I learned that all our sufferings during five long weary months of siege warfare had been in vain.

Hardly in vain, perhaps, if one took the trouble to sort out the strategical niceties, but so far as the "other ranks" were concerned it was so.

The gallant 6th Division, I.E.F. "D," had fought their way from the Persian Gulf to the very outposts of Baghdad. Hundreds of miles of enemy territory had been won without a single reverse action, and we considered ourselves to be an unbeatable army, as indeed we had proved ourselves to be. Now we had been starved into surrender, but we remained unbeaten.

On office scribbling blocks and calendars and in books of reference can be found this information: "April 29, 1916. The Fall of Kut-el-Amara." Someone will read it and inquire: "Kut-el-Amara, wasn't that in Palestine or somewhere?" Like as not he will receive answer, "No, that was something to do with Allenby's crowd in Mespot."

Even the generation of that period are only dimly aware of what went to make another page of military history. Yet on that day thirteen thousand officers and men of Britain's Imperial Army were taken into captivity, and from then on were treated like the captives of the Old Testament days.

I heard the fateful news as I lay on the beaten earth floor of a mud hut that was graced by the name of No. 4 Field

Ambulance. After several weeks of suffering from acute stomach trouble I had at last collapsed on duty, and had been carried there just as the ill-fated river steamer *Julnar* was making an epic attempt to get food through to the beleaguered garrison.

My pal of many years' standing had brought me the news, and, as he knelt and looked at my seemingly hopeless condition, the tears ran down his sun-blackened cheeks. It was plain that he regarded me as a dying man and that he was saying good-bye for the last time. It *was* our last good-bye, poor old Joe Cresswell died an agonizing death in a labour camp in the Amanus mountains.

The floor of the ambulance hut was covered with men in the last stages of sickness, and only when the dead were removed—which was all too frequently—could we stretch and move with comfort.

After my pal had gone I lay and tried to picture what it would be like to be a prisoner of war, until I was roused by a voice saying, "Come on, Cocky, you're going to the 'General.'" A cheery medical orderly was addressing me and I gathered that I was to be moved to the General Hospital. This hospital was actually the town bazaar, a street of open-fronted shops that had been commandeered for the purpose. Beds occupied the whole length of the roadway, and the shops were one- or two-bed wards.

I was placed on a stretcher and given in charge of two Indian orderlies and we set off on our way.

We had not proceeded far when our way was blocked by a yelling crowd of Arab townsfolk. My stretcher was lowered to the dusty road and the orderlies craned their necks to see what the excitement was all about.

Wearily, I turned my head to peer between the legs of the Arabs, who were crowding right up to my stretcher, and I saw the cause of the excitement.

A ragged company of Turkish soldiers was parading the

town led by a gaudily dressed officer mounted on a sorry-looking Arab pony. The company was headed by two men who shrilled out a discordant wail on reed pipes. The soldiers were a most miserable-looking lot, sun-blackened and gaunt and altogether unlike a conquering army.

I closed my eyes and waited patiently for the Indians to pick me up and resume the journey to the "General."

I remember little of the rest of the journey until I heard a voice say, "Shove him in here."

The Indians carried me into a one-bed booth and lifted me on to a bed that had only a blanket covering the springs.

"Kutch nay mattrish, sahib?"* queried one of the Indians.

"Kutch nay,"* was the answer.

What did a mattress matter anyhow? I was almost beyond feeling, and was content to lay and dream of home and food, mostly of food. I soon drifted off into unconsciousness.

How long I was left alone that day I do not know, but I was awakened by someone saying, "Do you know me, Jerry?"

I opened my eyes and saw a horribly distorted face close to mine. It was fully a minute before I recognized in this piece of human wreckage a man of my own battery, one who had been in hospital for months, and was bent double from the effect of a shrapnel bullet that had travelled the length of his body from shoulder to ankle.

I mentioned his name and he said, "Blimey! you look rotten; what's the matter with you?"

"I don't know and I don't care so very much," I replied.

"Hang on, and I'll find out," he said, and was gone.

Sometime later he returned with his information.

"You're for it, Jerry," he commenced. "Enteritis, that's what you've got, and that's a posh name for cholera," he concluded.

We were a cheerful crowd in those days and called a spade a spade.

* Lingua franca of British and Indian soldiers. Lit. "No mattress, Sir?" "None."

He stayed with me for a time and told me what was happening outside, and we discussed the possibilities of getting exchanged as sick prisoners.

"Turkish medical bloke coming round to-morrow, and I'm on the list so I expect that I shall be inspected," he informed me.

I vaguely wondered whether I, too, should be "inspected."

He told me of the looting by the Arabs of the town and by Turkish soldiers. Of how a Turkish soldier had stolen the field boots of General Melliss from under the bed on which that gallant officer lay sick and helpless to prevent him. And how the general had got out of bed to give chase, luckily meeting a Turkish officer outside who was in time to catch the thief and administer summary justice—Turkish variety. How the Turks were hanging Arabs by the score, and many other gruesome details that he thought might interest me.

It was only an hour or so after he had left me that I witnessed for myself an act of looting.

Out in the roadway opposite my bed-end was a bed containing a badly wounded patient who was covered by the regulation red hospital blanket. His pillow had been raised by putting underneath it his folded overcoat. I was disturbed from my dreaming by a loud scream from this patient, and opened my eyes in time to see an Arab, who had the red blanket over his arm, snatch the overcoat from under the poor fellow's head. Several patients came hurrying up in answer to his scream, but of course they were too late to catch the thief.

The next day the Turkish medical officer duly arrived, and one of the over-worked hospital orderlies came and told me that I was on the list for exchange and would be examined by him.

I remember that I was vaguely disturbed by this news as I had an idea that I should be deprived of a new experience if I were exchanged. There was no need to have been alarmed, as I was to get more than my share of new experiences.

In due course the great man arrived at my bedside accompanied by one of our own doctors and several other Turks. He stood at my bed and looked at his list, and then said something in French to our medical officer before bending over me. Lifting up each eyelid in turn he gazed for a few moments into my eyes. Then he felt one of my arms above the elbow—why, I don't know, as there was only a bone there! That was the extent of his examination and he crossed my name from his list. Ever since, I have admired that man's judgment as, after such a brief examination, he considered that I still had the makings of a soldier in my starved and sickened body.

The rest of that day I spent in a dream world of my own, from which I occasionally returned when someone was prising open my mouth in order to give me a drink.

I must have been very near to death.

How long I remained in that state I do not know, but it must have been a day or two.

The next thing I remember was feeling something cool on my head and hearing a voice saying, "Are you awake, Long?"

I made an effort to open my eyes, and saw that it was our medical officer who had his hand on my forehead.

Without waiting for me to answer he said, "The padre is here to see you." He moved away and his place was taken by the Rev. Harold Spooner, our Church of England chaplain, who asked me if I should like any messages sent home.

Whether I gave him any or not I have no idea, but I was conscious of his voice, which sounded a long way off as he continued to speak.

I was back in my dream world when across my mental vision came these words, written in letters of fire: "O Lord, prepare this man's soul for heaven."

I was vaguely troubled, and another sentence came into

my mind: "To get to heaven you must die." To my tortured
mind those two sentences became demons and were fighting
a battle for the possession of my soul.

How long the torture lasted I have no knowledge, but
when next I became conscious I found myself lying in the
roadway with several faces dancing above me in the light of
a guttering candle.

"How the hell did he get here?" queried someone.

"Blimey, the padre said he was going west," said another
as they carried me back to bed.

I must have fallen straight to sleep, for when I opened my
eyes again it was broad daylight and there was a lot of bustle
going on in the hospital.

From that day I commenced to get well. I was fed with
sips of arrowroot—well watered to make it go round—by one
or another of the convalescent patients, as I was unable to
lift a hand to help myself.

The springs of my mattressless bed began to make themselves felt, and I became conscious of other bodily discomforts, a sign that I was coming back to normal.

Came the great day when I had enough strength to lift my
hand and wave away the flies that persisted on swarming
around my eyes and mouth. Then one fine morning I was
carried out on a stretcher to the riverside, in readiness to
embark on the *Julnar*, which was to convey the sick prisoners
to Baghdad.

It was wonderful to see the sky and the waving palms again
and to listen to the shouting and bustle that was going on.

I had not long to wait before I was being carried up the
gangway of the boat. Before my stretcher-bearers had been
allowed to pass they had been stopped by an ancient Turkish
officer whose job was apparently to search all kits going
aboard. To prove to the world that he was doing his job he
took my ground-sheet and threw it into the river. Why he
chose that article I have no idea, nor perhaps had he.

I was placed on the deck in line with other patients and in a very short time the whole of the deck space was covered with sick and—in some cases—dying men. My kit became my pillow and a folded blanket my bed.

I soon discovered that I was very fortunate to have any kit at all as the men around me told me how theirs had been stolen.

When the full complement of sick were aboard, the shot-riddled *Julnar* got under way and began to puff and clank its way upstream.

So far I had not fully grasped the significant fact that I was a prisoner of war. It was very difficult to do so as we were being tended by our own doctors and orderlies, and there was no intrusion by the Turks so far as I could see.

I remember having a feeling that the unbeatable 6th Division would be all right in the end, and that we should soon be celebrating in Bombay.

Meanwhile, I took stock of my comrades in misfortune. The men on either side of me looked in a bad way, and did not answer me when I spoke to them. Some of the others near by were able to sit up, but they were mere ghosts of men. Gaunt and fearfully emaciated, they presented a very sorry spectacle, and I was unable to recognize any of them, yet I discovered later that many of them were old acquaintances of mine. They were unable to recognize me either, so I suppose I looked pretty bad.

Day after day we chugged along against the swiftly flowing but now shallow Tigris. Progress was slow as the old paddle-steamer was heavily loaded and we often ran onto sandbanks.

Occasionally we stopped, and a party would go ashore to bury our dead, for deaths were a daily occurrence among us.

For the most part we lay or sat watching the desolate scene on either side.

A few months before we had passed this way as we

pursued the Turks to their position at Ctesiphon, the scene of our last battle, and our turning-point.

As we neared the village of Baghala we were greeted by the blood-curdling keening of the Arab women who lined the river banks, and as we drew broadside with them they shrieked and yelled and the males among them began to chant and prance up and down the bank top. Louder and more excitedly they chanted and pranced until, reaching the pitch of the frenzy, they commenced to fire their rifles into the air and brandish their wicked-looking knives. I was thankful that we were out of their reach.

We drew alongside at Baghala and made fast for the night as we were out of oil-fuel for the engines and would have to wait until a fresh lot was obtained from Baghdad. Turkish soldiers lined the boat to prevent the Arabs interfering with us.

Shortly after we had made fast another small steamer with a freight of captives passed us, and we exchanged cheers as lustily as we could.

Next day we recommenced our journey and I attempted to use my legs. Space for walking was non-existent, so all I could do was to hold on to a stanchion and mark time. This I did several times that day and the next before I finally ventured to pick my way among the feet of my comrades.

Officially I was on milk diet, and that meant that twice a day I got half a pint of well-watered tinned milk. What the poor devils got who were on ordinary diet I cannot say, but it wasn't very much whatever it was, judging by our ration.

Just north of Azizieh we stopped to bury more of our dead, and I went ashore with a party of our own officers to act as interpreter as they purchased fruit and fish from some villagers who had collected to watch the burials.

I received some fruit for my trouble, but it was only sufficient to whet my appetite for more and I had no money to buy any.

Then I conceived a notion.

Why not sell some of my kit and get the wherewithal to buy food for myself?

It was in the middle of May and becoming uncomfortably hot, so the first thing that I tried to sell was my British warm. After much haggling and cursing on both sides I managed at last to sell it to a member of the crew of the *Julnar* for a mejidieh—a miserable 3s. 8d., but I was perhaps lucky to get anything at all.

I found that the crew had fish to sell, so I bought a large portion already cooked. Needless to say that I did not inform the doctor that I had put myself on a different diet!

The fish did me a lot of good, I believe; in any case it was food, something that I had almost forgotten the taste of.

From that day until the end of the voyage to Baghdad I was never without fruit or fish, but it took nearly all my kit to pay for it.

It was near Baghala that we who were too sick to march to Baghdad realized how fortunate we were in comparison with the main body of the Kut garrison.

We had left Baghala astern when there was a cry of "The column!"

All who could sat up and gazed across the dusty wastes towards the east. Far away in the distance we could see a cloud of dust that hid the marching column of prisoners. Occasionally the dust would be blown clear and we had a momentary vision of a long line of slow-moving men, recognizable as our men by the helmets and pugarees that they wore.

As we watched we saw the head of the column change direction and make for the river. Then all was bustle aboard as we were made to move up closer and make room for any very sick that might be unable to continue the march.

Gradually the column drew nearer, until at last they arrived at the river-side, and we pulled into the bank.

No words can adequately describe the appalling misery of that scene. Here were men who had suffered and fought through the long months of the siege, although they were gradually starved, and were not fit to do a day's march, yet they were being driven across the pitiless wastes under a scorching sun, herded along by a brutal and callous escort of Arab conscripts. Limping and staggering along they all finally arrived, some of them being assisted along by their comrades who themselves were in dire need of assistance.

Our medical officers went ashore and had the most heart-breaking job of their lives in deciding who of the sick could be taken aboard. Space was very limited, so that they had to be very careful in their choice. The fortunate ones—or unfortunate, according to how one viewed it—came limping aboard and dropped down in the places allotted them. Some were barely conscious and were carried aboard, others were crying weakly, all were in an appalling state of exhaustion. Several who had been forced to march with leg wounds scarce healed upon them were in great pain, and many of the wounds had burst open under the strain, as blood-soaked garments plainly testified. The medical officers and orderlies did all in their power to relieve their aches and pains and to make them comfortable. We shouted greetings to the party on the bank and asked after the fate of "old so-and-so" or "poor old such-an-one," pals who we knew were hardly likely to have survived such a march.

As we once more got under way it was pitiful to see the looks of dejection on the faces of those who were in a very bad way but were unable to be embarked owing to lack of space.

The next day we chatted to those of the new-comers who had recovered somewhat, and heard most frightful tales of the brutality to which they had been subjected. They told us that their escort were Arabs who were mounted and had driven them along like cattle. Some of the party had collapsed early in the march, suffering from dysentery and kindred complaints, and these had been tied by the wrists or ankles to the pommels of the escorts' saddles and literally dragged to death. Others had been clubbed and beaten as they stopped by the wayside to answer Nature's urgent call. Many were the horrible tales we listened to that day, and we began to wonder what fate awaited us on our arrival at Baghdad.

It was very difficult for us to believe all we were told, yet we were soon to have our share of like treatment and made to realize that we were no longer free men.

The *Julnar* continued to chug its way upstream, and one day the gaunt ruin of Ctesiphon Arch appeared on the skyline and we knew that it would not be long before our journey to Baghdad was ended.

As we passed the famous ruin I thought of what my section officer had told me after the Battle of Ctesiphon, when the scattered remnants of our force had collected behind the remains of the walls of that ancient place. He told me that immediately opposite—on the other side of the river—was the site of old Selucia, where the Romans had been compelled to give up their dreams of the conquest of India.

Well, *we* had given up *our* dreams of conquering Baghdad, but at least we should see that almost legendary city.

At long last we reached the palm groves that heralded our close approach to Baghdad. I shall never forget the beautiful picture that came into sight as we rounded a bend in the river near Karradah, a suburb of the city. Turquoise-blue domes and slender minarets peeped above the dark green palm fronds and formed the background. The steely-blue sky was mirrored in the waters of the Tigris and in the foreground was an island, reed-covered, and the hunting-ground of a flock of long-legged herons.

As I gazed at the scene, whilst storks clacked their way overhead, I forgot for the moment that I was a prisoner, and ceased to muse on the probabilities of the future.

The navigation of another bend broke the spell, and I gazed with interest at the riverside houses. Most of the upper balconies were crowded with women and girls, for the most part unveiled, a rare and refreshing sight for us. In all probability they were Armenians or Chaldeans, as many of them dared to smile and wave their hands at us.

We passed a hospital and the patients lined the waterfront to watch us pass. In all probability they were some of our victims. It was strange to think that.

Some of them shouted "Bon jour," others "Good-morning," but I did not see any looks of hatred or hear any abusive remarks.

We passed from Karradah into the wide sweep of water that divides the city of Baghdad.

With much shouting by the crew and shore gangs, and much clanking of the over-worked engines, captured ship and captive troops were brought alongside a broken-down landing-stage on the left bank, near to the bridge of boats.

Without loss of time we were disembarked and went ashore, carrying what goods we possessed in bundles. As we came off the boat in single file we were counted by a dozen or more officers and soldiers, but apparently their totals did not agree for we were counted again when everyone was ashore. Still the number was not correct, so we were made to pass slowly between two officers who counted us again, touching each of us as we passed by. At last they were satisfied—at least, there was not so much arguing over the result—and we were told to pick up our kits and form up in fours.

I had very little to carry as I had sold most of my kit on the way up. Perhaps it was just as well as I was still very weak, and discovered long before we arrived at our next destination that I had all I could manage.

Led by several strutting Turkish officers and guarded by tough-looking soldiers we moved off and crossed the bridge of boats to Baghdad West. Leaving the bridge-end we passed

BRIDGE OF BOATS, BAGHDAD

[*See p.* 26

THE MOSQUE
AT KUT-EL-AMARA

AUTHOR LAYING A WREATH
AT THE NEWLY ERECTED
PERMANENT MEMORIAL IN
THE "KUT PLOT," BAGHDAD
CEMETERY

into a filthy bazaar which was crowded with curious sight-seers. Bearded Arabs in flowing kaftans and red-fezzed youths gazed at us in amazement and disgust. No doubt they thought we were a sorry-looking crowd and not at all like the powerful "Ingleezi" they had heard knocking at the gates of Baghdad a few months before.

Groups of veiled women chattered at us as we slowly passed along, whilst other groups of unveiled women, with tattooed faces and ragged clothes, shrieked at us and spat on the ground to signify their contempt.

The crowd grew denser and eventually we came to a halt.

I was on the outside of my section of fours and, as I turned to look at the crowd, one of the tattooed ladies came close to me and spat full into my face. Entirely forgetting the fact that I was a captive I clawed weakly at the hag's throat. Behind me the nearest soldier brought the butt of his rifle crashing down between my shoulders, and I was knocked sprawling into the filth of the roadway. I rolled on to my back in time to receive the point of his bayonet through my bottom lip as he made a vicious lunge at me. Luckily for me it was a bayonet of the type we knew as "needle," a long three-sided affair, otherwise I might have sustained a very nasty wound. As it was the blood flowed freely down the front of my chin and on to my ragged shirt, giving me a ghastly appearance.

The spectators among the crowd cheered wildly at this little side-show, and the women shrieked, "Kaffir, kelb ibn kelb!" ("Unbeliever, dog son of a dog!") at me as I staggered back to my place in the ranks.

The column moved on again and, picking up my small bundle, I reeled along with it feeling very sick, and praying that I should be able to keep on my feet till we reached our destination.

Although I had received a nasty jab in the mouth the blow with the rifle butt had occasioned me more pain, and it was several days before I could swing my arms with comfort.

It was not long after this incident that we came to Baghdad railway station, and on a dusty open space before it we were to camp.

British and Indian we numbered, I should think, about three hundred, and beyond a small roof of reed matting, which would give shelter to about fifty, there was no provision whatever to shelter us from the sun, which was at this time of the year uncomfortably hot.

As we were within a few hundred yards of a palm grove I thought that it would be an easy matter later on to find shade. I had yet to learn that the movements of prisoners of war were very much restricted, and depended a good deal on the amiability of their guards.

The short journey from the boat had proved too much for several of the party, and many others were already feeling the heat pretty badly. These we moved to the shade of the mat roof, and it was one of our self-imposed tasks to keep moving them in time with the movement of the sun as there were no side walls to the shelter.

It was not until late that afternoon that we received permission to get water from a tap near the station, and even then we were not provided with any receptacle to get it in, but had to fill up water-bottles or mess-tins. As very few of us had either of these things and all of us were continuously thirsty, that first evening seemed to be spent in journeyings to and from the station tap.

Shortly before sunset we had to fall in, and were again counted innumerable times before we were handed over to an Arab guard. It seemed to be a very serious business for the young officer who was in charge, and he followed in the wake of the two sergeants who were counting us, himself counting and touching each one of us as he did so.

When he came to me he saw the blood on my clothes, and asked in Arabic how it came to be there. Fortunately I was able to understand and answer him. I told him briefly of the incident in the bazaar, and pointed to the hole in my bottom lip.

I was startled by the effect of my story. Dashing down the ranks of prisoners he screamed out for one Achmet Chaoush (Sergeant Achmet). Achmet Chaoush was the N.C.O. of the Turkish escort, and was one of the two who were counting us prior to handing over to the Arab N.C.O. He came dashing up to the officer and received orders to fall in the escort, those who had brought us from the boat. In a very few moments they were standing to attention before us and, I have no doubt, wondering what was afoot.

The officer—a Mulazim Awl (Lieutenant)—asked me if I could identify the man who had struck me. This I was easily able to do as he had never left my side from the bazaar to the camp, probably thinking that I was a desperate character that required watching.

The Mulazim was carrying a peculiar type of rawhide whip, which we quickly found was in popular use throughout those regions under Turkish dominance. Not strictly "hide," but made of a certain portion of a buffalo's anatomy, this whip could be a very nasty implement in the hands of a violent man, as many of us have cause to be aware.

Without waiting to hear the soldier's version of the story the Mulazim made a vicious slash at him with his whip that caught him right across his face, raising a livid weal at once to the surface. This was a prelude to a terrific beating, one such as I had never witnessed but which was slight in comparison with others I saw subsequently. As it was I felt physically sick at the display of barbarity given by the Mulazim, and was sorry that I was the innocent cause of it.

The rest of the escort stood rigidly to attention, and appeared to take very little notice of the awful punishment being given to one of their number.

When it was over the old escort was dismissed, and the two

sergeants continued to count us as though nothing had happened.

At last it was found that our numbers were correct, and Achmet Chaoush disappeared into the palm grove and left us to the tender mercies of the Arabs.

As the Arab Chaoush had discovered that I understood Arabic I was instructed to tell the party that they were forbidden to go for water during the night and could only move as far as the latrines—trenches dug close to the railway embankment and screened on the camp side by reed matting.

Shortly after this our own medical orderlies appeared from the direction of the palm grove, bringing the first food that we had had since dawn. This consisted of watery milk for the sick men and very thin rice soup for the remainder, supplemented by a ration of coarse, black, and gritty bread from the Turks.

It was little enough, but we were very pleased to get it nevertheless, and, unpalatable as it was, could have eaten much more of it.

Darkness fell and the sentries began to make themselves comfortable for the night by making down their beds on their "posts." This completed, they either sat down and smoked or curled up on their beds and went to sleep or made the night hideous by shrieking out some love ballad in a high falsetto voice. Their job of sentry did not seem to bother them unduly, and neither officer nor N.C.O. came along to worry them.

For our part we disposed ourselves as comfortably as we could on the ground, those who had any kit of value using it as pillows, and all of us sleeping in the few rags we wore.

Everything seemed peaceful as we lay down and, after chatting for a short while, dropped off to sleep. It was soon to be proved that the peace was only seeming.

It must have been near to midnight when we were roused by screams coming from the direction of the latrines. Several of us jumped to our feet and hurried over to see what was wrong. Just outside the latrines we found two Englishmen lying groaning on the ground. They were stark naked, and one of them had several knife-cuts on the hands and arms. Weak as we all were it was a difficult matter for us to drag them to the main party.

I roused the nearest sentry and asked him to come and see the men and get a doctor for them. After much cursing and grumbling he at last got up and came over to see them.

It occurred to me at the time that it was peculiar that none of the sentries had been disturbed by the screams, and that none of them troubled to see what the excited chatter of the prisoners was all about.

We found that one of the men had several very nasty cuts and these we washed and bound up with odds and ends of rags that some one of us or other produced. The other man had one ugly cut on the head in the centre of a huge bruise.

From what they told us it appears that they had gone to the latrines and while they were there three or four Arabs had suddenly appeared over the embankment and had attacked them without warning, stripping them of their clothes. One had been clubbed by a knobkerrie and stunned into help-lessness, and the other had received his cuts whilst struggling to keep his only clothing. He it was who had screamed and roused us.

As the majority of our party was suffering from various stomach troubles it was absolutely essential that we should have safe access to the latrines, so here was a problem for us to solve.

The only help we got from the sentry who had come over to the injured men was advice to wait until daylight before using the place. As these sentries were Arabs we did not expect them to co-operate against their own kind to any great extent. Why should we? We had been long enough in Meso-potamia to know that the only friendly Arab we should ever meet would be a dead one. Hadn't they robbed our dead and multilated our wounded on many occasions during the campaign?

Well, here they were robbing our sick whilst their brother ghouls played at being on guard over us.

Among the English prisoners we decided to provide an escort from those who were most able to do the job, and accompany all those who were compelled to use the latrines during the night. We decided also that both escort and escorted should go completely naked!

For the remainder of that night we carried out that procedure, and there were no more raids. The next morning I told several Havildars among the Indian prisoners what we had done, and they said that they would do the same among their men.

I may mention here that the Mahommedans among this party had collected apart from the Hindus, and anticipated preferential treatment from their co-religionists the Turks, and were extremely servile—not to say grovelling—in their manner towards their captors. This attitude they maintained throughout the long march up country, and their studied contempt of, and insults to the English of my particular party not infrequently resulted in blows being struck.

During the second day in this camp the Mahommedans were visited by several deserters—of the same religion—from our force. The Turks had dressed them in a very conspicuous uniform, and they were quite easily recognized as deserters by reason of it. This uniform consisted of baggy black trousers and shirt tunic and a green astrakhan fez. If they were N.C.O.'s they wore chevrons of yellow braid that conformed in pattern and manner of wearing to our own, which was quite unlike that of the Turks

I have always admired the action of the Turkish staff in thus attiring these despicable men, for they were recognized for what they were by everyone.

It was during the late morning of the second day that we got our first meal of that day, and it was very much like that we had received overnight.

One of our own doctors had visited us and had done what he could for the more seriously sick.

Several died that day and two more were smitten with sunstroke. These latter we held under the water-tap at the station until they recovered somewhat.

I was so hungry that I decided to sell the remainder of my belongings in order to buy food.

Village women were permitted to sell fruit, eggs, flaps of bread, *libn* and *roba* (sour and curdled milk) to those who had the wherewithal to buy.

A complete battalion of Algerians (who, we were told, had surrendered without the slightest resistance) were camped near by, and many of them came among us during the days that followed in the hopes of buying our kit cheaply.

For some peculiar reason they claimed to be our friends. Perhaps because they had been French soldiers and were now prisoners of the Turks. Seeing a good deal of evidence to prove the truth of the story we had been told concerning their surrender we did not accept their overtures, more especially as they drove a much harder bargain in the purchase of our kit than even the Arabs, and we were not sorry when they ceased to visit us, gone, we were told, to fight the Russians on behalf of the Turks.

I quickly disposed of all the saleable kit I had and felt myself getting daily stronger from the effects of the better food I was able to buy with the proceeds.

This business of selling kit caught on very rapidly and I undertook to sell anything for any of the English members of the party. Understanding Arabic I was able to get a good deal more than they would have done, and I was quite content to receive halfpennies and pennies (that is, the equivalent in the local currency) for my services. So that after all my own kit was gone I was able to continue to supplement the starvation rations we were receiving for so long as anyone had any kit to sell.

One day the sentries appeared all excited and told us that Enver Pasha was coming to visit us. We saw nothing to get excited about and merely passed rude remarks about the great man. For all that we were made to fall in and stand in the sun for a couple of hours to await his arrival.

At last the Pasha arrived accompanied by a large number of Turkish officers. As the party of officers were dressed after the fashion of comic opera, it was difficult to know which one was the more important and likely to be the Pasha, and as no one pointed him out to us I do not know to this day whether he was really there or not, though I was assured afterwards by one of the sentries that he was. Someone addressed us in English—it may have been Enver himself—and praised us for our gallant defence at Kut, etc. Then came the declaration that, in various forms, was heard by most of the unfortunate Kut garrison, a declaration that should go down in history as the most ironical ever made. This is how we heard it that day:

"Your troubles are over now, my dears; *you will be treated as the honoured guests of the Sultan.*"

Some of us hoped that things would improve for us after we heard that. It took just twenty-four hours to dispel those hopes!

Before nightfall on the second day we managed to cut sticks from the palm fronds in order to arm ourselves for our latrine guard. It was as well that we did so as we received another visit from the looting Arabs during the night, and we were able to rout them completely.

The third night brought a new kind of attack.

Finding they were baulked at the latrines the Arabs crept stealthily among us in the darkness and snatched blankets, overcoats, or kit from the sleeping sick. The looters had copied us by removing all their clothes before they came among us, so that even had we been quick enough to have caught them we could not have held on to them. In any case they were too fleet of foot for us.

Thus our days and nights became filled with suffering and fears.

Rather than have my blanket stolen I sold it, together with my boots—or what was left of them—so that I had no fears during the night.

My feet I covered with the legs of my trousers, which I cut off for the purpose, leaving me with a pair of ragged "shorts" and a threadbare, blood-stained, buttonless shirt as my entire wardrobe.

At no time did I regret selling my possessions, as I believed then, as I do now, that the food I got in exchange saved my life by giving me strength to withstand the hardships of the years of captivity that followed. And another advantage was that I had nothing to carry during the hundreds of miles I had to march to the railhead at Ras-el-Ain. Many a poor devil humped his kit along for many weary miles until he was robbed of it or was too ill to carry it, in which case the escort promptly pounced on it. Many others died before they got any benefit from the kit they had so painfully and laboriously borne to the end of the journey.

For about nine days we were camped in the open near the station at Baghdad West and, despite the attentions of our medical officer and nursing orderlies, sickness, disease, and death increased among us.

When things became so bad that we none of us expected to live, we were moved to the shelter of the palm-groves on the right bank of the Tigris, not many hundreds of yards from the open camp. Bell tents were provided, and we were permitted to bathe in the river, which also became our water supply, filthy as it was at that point. Rations were increased by daily additions supplied from the American Consulate for which, no doubt, the Consul was duly paid by the British Government.

I spent many hours sitting on the river bank, chatting with any Arab who was at all amiable. In this way I greatly improved my Arabic, and often received tit-bits of food.

One day I was thus engaged when I witnessed a little drama that brought home to me very forcibly how lightly life was held among the people of that country.

Within five yards of where I was sitting a group of Arabs, four of whom were dressed in national costume and one in uniform, were having a very wordy argument. They were all armed, as indeed was everyone in those days. The one in uniform seemed opposed to the remainder though I could not follow their argument. Suddenly their voices rose and they all began to gesticulate wildly. Then he of the uniform reached for his revolver, which he wore suspended from a belt and resting on his right hip, a ridiculous position I thought at the time. In an instant he was seized by the other four and he commenced to struggle violently, until all of them were floundering about up to their knees in the river. I sat idly watching, and was not prepared for the sudden end. One of the four robed Arabs succeeded in wresting away the revolver, and in a flash he rammed the muzzle into the back of his victim and fired twice in quick succession. At once the others flung the shot man into the river, and the murderer flung the revolver after him before they all turned and fled.

All this happened in a few minutes, much quicker than I can write it, and all the time I sat calmly watching it whilst no one else seemed to have noticed anything. Strangely enough I had no feelings one way or the other about it, so callous was I becoming at the daily sight of suffering and death.

Within a few days of our occupying the new camp all the more seriously sick had been removed to a hospital in Baghdad; yet there were many deaths among the remainder, mostly from enteritis. Men who in the morning seemed to be quite normal would become stricken with this dread disease and in a few hours would be dead.

One day we were surprised to get a five-piastre note each (Turkish = 1od.) and were told that as prisoners of war we should be paid by the Turks at the same scale as our equivalent ranks in the Turkish army. This worked out for me at tenpence a month if paid in cash, and rather less than a penny if I received paper!

It was the first and last pay I ever received from the Turks, and as the soldiers of the Sultan were about two years in arrears for pay I consider that I was lucky to have been paid once!

During the last week in May those of us who were getting fit were listed to proceed north as soon as a large enough party could be formed. I was very thankful that I was among the first to be chosen as I was heartily sick of the enforced inactivity, and was becoming afraid that I, too, might become a victim of enteritis.

A party was formed in early June and, bidding good-bye to those we were leaving behind, we marched out of the camp and across to the railway station.

CHAPTER TWO

ADVENTURES AT SAMARAH

AT Baghdad West station we entrained into steel goods wagons and were locked in to await the train's departure.

We were packed like sardines and in a very short time the interiors of those wagons were like ovens and the condition of the human freight can be imagined.

At last we felt the train slowly drawing out and, gradually gaining speed, we left behind Baghdad, the goal of the 6th Division, I.E.F. "D." We had reached our goal, not as victors but as captives more wretched than the Israelites who were in Egypt.

For a further two hours we had to endure the stifling heat of those steel wagons as the train clanked on its journey until, at the first stopping-place, all the doors were opened.

A Turkish soldier was put into each wagon and we continued on our way.

With the doors open things were not too bad and we were able to see what kind of country we were passing through. If anything it was worse than that we had left behind, south of Baghdad. Then we had perforce to be within reach of the river and there was usually a clump of palms or some vegetation around the riverside villages. But the railway had no need of the river and passed through a land that was well and truly dead. Occasionally we glimpsed palms far away to the east, but to the west was a vista of dead, dreary waste.

The following year was to see our avengers fighting for the possession of that same waste. Ye gods! The madness of civilized peoples who permit war is incomprehensible when one thinks of the young manhood of both sides that was sacrificed on those grey, arid wastes.

It was late afternoon of the same day when we arrived at the end of the last ride we were to get for many a long day.

As we detrained there was much shouting of "Yellah, yellah," from an Arab escort awaiting us. That word *yellah*, together with *haidi*—meaning "get a move on"—was to bite into the very soul of every Kuttite of the "other ranks" who trod the road of death to Ras-el-Ain. I have seen men wince at the very sound of it, as too often the word was accompanied by blows.

The Turkish soldiers who had been with us remained in the train as our Arab escort herded us along to the river-bank, where we were to stay the night.

The setting sun shone on the golden dome of the mosque of Samarah and the slender minarets that seemed to guard it as we reached our camping place, and I regretted that it was on the other side of the river, for I should have liked to have seen the whole structure. I need have had no regrets had I have been able to have seen into the future.

Before night fell we were given each a small black loaf of bread and told to conserve it as we might not get any more for a day or two! That was a cheerful bit of advice, but it did not prevent the majority from eating the small whole of it there and then.

Thinking of what the morrow might bring I curled up close to my companions and slept.

Next morning I awoke to the sound of "Yellah, yellah. Goom, goom" ("Come on, come on. Get up, get up").

Sitting up I discovered that I could not see. My eyelids were stuck down! In vain I rubbed them with my wetted fingers.

What fresh malady had got me now I wondered.

I asked someone to lead me down to the river, where I bathed my eyes. It was no good, all the water in the Tigris could not remove the film that covered my eyeballs. I became frantic and clung to the friend who had helped me down to the river. He advised me to tell the Arab N.C.O. who was in charge of the escort. Fearing that I might be sent back to Baghdad I would not do that so he did it for me.

Stumbling along and in deadly fear I was led away from the party, I knew not whither. In a few minutes I was told to sit down and someone queried, "What's up, chum?"

"I dunno, I've gone blind," I answered and then asked, "Where are we?" and "Are you sick too?"

I was told that he was one of two Englishmen and three Indians, all of whom were suffering from a bad attack of diarrhoea and could not continue the journey. Also, the speaker said, we were all being sent to Samarah where an English medical officer was in charge of a hospital, or so he had gathered from the sentry that he said was mounted over us.

This proved to be true and several hours later we were put into a *gufah* (the Arab coracle) and ferried over the river.

I was assisted by the man who had spoken to me, a man of the Dorsetshire Regiment, and as we ascended the river-bank on the Samarah side he warned me to lift my feet as the road to the town was made of cobble stones. I was soon made aware of this, as I stubbed my rag-covered toes against them all too frequently.

We had not gone far when my battered sun-helmet was violently knocked from my head. At the same time I received a blow in the back.

"What was that?" I asked, as I stopped to grope around for my helmet.

My friend pulled my arm and said, "Come on, chum, the bastards are stoning us."

True enough, for again I was struck, this time on the bare shin, so I did as I was bid and hurried on as well as I could to the tune of "Yellah, yellah" from the Arab who was escorting us.

"We are inside Samarah now," said the man of Dorset,

and he explained that the town was walled and that we had passed through a gate and had left outside the rabble who had stoned us.

It was a terrifying experience to be stoned, more especially as I could not see, and I was very thankful to know that we had got away from the brutes who took pleasure from stoning sick men.

We had not far to go before we reached the hospital, and I was led up some stone steps and into a room where an English voice told me to be seated. I sat down gingerly on to a stool that was placed for me. I remember how queer it seemed to be sitting with my legs hanging after squatting on my haunches for weeks.

The doctor—a medical officer of our garrison—asked me a few questions to help in making his diagnosis, but I had nothing to tell him that could help. The night previously my eyes had been perfect, now I was blind, and that was all I could tell him.

"I have very little here," he told me, "and it's the devil's own job to get anything out of the Turks too," he added, referring to medicines and drugs, of course.

After a time he found something which he said would hurt me but might do the trick.

"Tip your head back and open one eye," he ordered.

Anticipating the pain I did so. I was not disappointed. The first drop on to my eyeball and I squirmed and gasped with agony. It was terrific, but I had to endure it. The other eye was punished in a like manner and then I was led away to my "bed," which was a reed mat on a stone floor in a cell-like room occupied by two other Englishmen.

These other two had been several weeks in the place, having fallen sick from the main party. One, a bandsman of the Dorsetshire Regiment, was unaware of his complaint beyond the fact that he was too weak to continue the journey north. The other, a man of the Oxfordshire and Buckinghamshire Light Infantry, was suffering from an old bullet wound in the ankle.

All that day we talked and talked, I giving them news of the fate of the sick convoy from Kut and they telling me of the horrors of the march from Kut to Baghdad.

At sunset we each received a tin bowl of *chourba* (rice soup) and this, I was told, was the stable diet and issued twice daily. I shouldn't get very fat on that ration, I thought, and prayed that I should soon recover and be on the road again.

The following morning I found that I could see just a little, although very mistily. The doctor was as pleased as I and gave me a second dose of his "kill or cure" treatment.

In three days my eyes were clear and my sight as good as ever, and I have never had a recurrence of the mysterious trouble.

I have never known what the trouble was and the doctor was unable to tell me, but who wonders for long at any pestilence that comes out of the vileness that is Mesopotamia?

Now that I could see I was able to take stock of my surroundings. The building was originally a caravanserai and had been brought into service as a hospital since the first battle of Kut in 1915. It was a rectangular, two-storied building surrounding an inner courtyard. The ground floor accommodated the Arab staff, kitchens, stores, and stables, etc. The second floor, which was balconied, comprised windowless cubicles along the entire length of both sides and several larger rooms with windows at each end. I have no doubt that the cubicles had given lodging to many hundreds of Moslem pilgrims who had come to visit this holy city of Samarah; now they contained sick infidels, British and Indian, all of the Kut garrison. Of the larger rooms, those over the main entrance were occupied by the doctor for his quarters and surgery, whilst ten Russian prisoners from the Khanikin front occupied one large one at the opposite end.

It was forbidden for patients to go down to the ground

floor, and if anyone required water or anything else they had to shout out their requirements to the Arab orderlies below and then await their tardy pleasure before they got it.

Two or three times a week the Turkish Commandant used to have a table laid for two in the middle of the courtyard, when he would invite the doctor to eat with him. Very nice for them, but a species of torture for half-starved patients to watch.

It was on one of these occasions that an incident occurred that was to add to the uneven tenor of my life at Samarah.

The orderly detailed for duty on my side of the hospital was a more than usually churlish beast whose great delight was to make us wait a long time before he would refill our very small earthenware waterpots. This was a particular hardship for those who suffered from recurring bouts of malaria, though it was hard enough for all of us now that the shade temperature stood above a hundred degrees.

The bandsman of the Dorsets had been in very low spirits most of this particular day and had been constantly crying out for water. The evening meal of *chourba* had been served and the doctor and Commandant were dining in the courtyard when he again asked for water, the pot being empty. I shouted out to the orderly to bring water, well knowing that he dared not delay now that the Commandant was in the building.

I was sitting on the balcony eating my *chourba* when he arrived and, after he had filled up the pot, he cursed me for disturbing him and then spat on me. Such an act was a vile insult at any time, but is considered to be doubly worse if the recipient is eating at the time. It was too much for me to take without resentment, so I jumped to my feet and hit the filthy brute as hard as I could between the eyes; then I ran to the balcony rail and loudly protested in Arabic to the Commandant.

That great personage was furious, but not on my behalf.

He wouldn't have cared what insults had been offered to any of us, but he had been disturbed during his dinner, an unpardonable affront to his dignity. He called the orderly to him and soundly smacked his face, cursing him obscenely as he did so.

I chuckled to myself as I considered that for once I had got the better of our orderly, but I chuckled rather too soon as there was to be a sequel to the incident, and one that might have had serious results for me.

Night fell and we had nothing else to do but to curl up on our reed mats and try to sleep.

I was becoming used to the hardness of the stone floor, but the lack of something to use as a pillow caused me to turn and twist all night. I had tried using the step of our cubicle, but it was rather too high for the purpose. I eventually got over the discomfort by using my rolled-up shirt, though it meant me lying practically naked.

I had discarded the rags from my feet in order to get the soles of my feet hard, and I had reason to be very thankful for this when I got on the march again.

To return to the particular night following the spitting incident. I had fallen into a light sleep when, somewhere near to midnight, I was roused by screams from the Dorset man. I opened the cubicle door to let in the moonlight and then asked him what was the matter. He would not answer me, but continued to scream and cry out for his mother. I ran along to get the doctor, as I had no idea what was wrong with the man. The doctor returned with me, carrying a hurricane lamp, and it did not take him long to see what was the matter.

The man was in hysterics and after the doctor had smacked his face and ordered him to be quiet, he became calmer and lay quietly sobbing. After he had administered a sedative the doctor instructed me to take no notice of him should he start shouting again.

Easier said than done. When three men are sharing a room eight feet by six, it would be a bit of a job to disregard one who was yelling his head off in hysterics!

When the doctor left us the man of the Ox. and Bucks. and I sat quietly chatting, as it was hopeless to try and get to sleep again. We were occupied thus for about half an hour when we suddenly noticed how quiet the Dorset man had become. We listened intently but could not hear him breathing so I crawled over to him and felt his pulse. It had stopped!

Again I went for the doctor, who brought along his stethoscope this time.

In silence we watched the doctor examine the unfortunate bandsman. At last he got to his feet and said, "There you see a man who has died of a broken heart! We shall have to let him stay where he is until morning," he continued, and, after bidding us good-night, returned once more to his room.

Just one more of the "other ranks" of the Kut garrison who would not return to England. Dead, of a broken heart.

Had the doctor not have said so I would never have believed that a man could have died of such a thing.

The two of us who were left sat and chatted until day came and the corpse was removed for burial.

During the morning the doctor sent for me.

"Well, Long," he commenced, "I have something serious to tell you. All the orderlies here have sworn to get you before you leave this hospital, owing to the trouble last night. Personally, I think you were foolish to have made such a fuss about a trifle. However, I am warning you never to be alone at any time, not even at the latrines."

I was not unduly alarmed, but I asked the doctor how long it would be before a party would be ready to leave.

"That I cannot say," he answered. "The Commandant may decide to form a party to-morrow or in three weeks' time, but you can rest assured that you will be of the party whenever it forms."

With a final warning to take heed he dismissed me.

There was only one score on which I was worried after hearing this news. Every Saturday morning it was the custom for the convalescent patients to be taken to the river in order to do the week's washing for the remainder of the patients. When this task was over and the clothes were drying on the rocks, they were then permitted to bathe. From this time forward I should be barred this one day a week glimpse of the outer world and a glorious half-hour swimming in the cool water.

For the next two weeks I was like a caged animal. I took every precaution possible against attack, but I saw nothing to warrant those precautions. Life was terribly monotonous, and the more I thought about the swim I had missed the more I chafed.

On the third Saturday I threw caution to the winds and joined the washing party.

I thoroughly enjoyed the impossible task of trying to wash dirty clothes with the awful yellow soap provided.

As usual there was a crowd of Arab boys to watch us and to skylark about in and out of the water.

The washing done I took a header into the water and revelled in the delicious coolness of it. It was a great treat after the long days of stifling heat in the restricted space of the hospital.

I was thinking what a fool I had been for not coming down to the river as usual when I felt something grip my ankle. Kicking free I dived in time to see a body streaking away under water. I rose to the surface, thinking that it was probably one of the Arab boys having a lark at my expense. Then I saw that a dozen or more young men were in the water around me. In a flash I remembered the doctor's warning and I dived again, striking out for midstream, swimming under water. I rose to the surface only for breath before diving again and as I went down I saw bodies underneath coming towards me. It was a great game, but the odds were against me and the end likely to be tragic, so diving, turning, and twisting I managed, after a few minutes, to elude my pursuers sufficiently long enough to reach the rocks and clamber out among my comrades.

They had sat watching the drama, powerless to help me however badly I may have needed their help. Indeed, they were very wise not to have interfered.

The two orderlies who had escorted us to the river did not look too pleased to see me scramble out of the water, and curtly ordered us to collect the washing and start back to the hospital.

Carrying my bundle on my head I kept in the middle of the party as we ascended the cobbled road that led to the city gate followed by a jeering rabble of youths and boys. When we were within thirty yards of the gate we were received by a hail of stones from a crowd of youths who had collected on either side of the road.

We hurried on as fast as we could under our loads of washing as the stones continued to be thrown.

"Hadtha huwa" ("That's he"), I heard them shouting, and knew that they meant me.

It was a great relief to get inside the gate with nothing more serious than a few bruises among us, and I decided that it wasn't healthy for me to go out washing!

Another week passed and then, to my great joy, we were told that a party would be leaving on the morrow.

The following afternoon a hundred and fifty Britishers and Indians and the ten Russians were sitting in the courtyard ready and waiting to commence the journey into—for us—the unknown.

We were waiting for the escort and, when at last they did arrive, they looked as villainous a party of Arabs as one could imagine, and all of them were mounted on wiry-looking ponies.

A diversion was caused just before we marched out by the cook, who dashed up and demanded that all of us be searched as he had lost one of his small ration tins. After much argument between the cook and the Onbashi (Corporal) of the escort everyone was ordered to open up their bundles for inspection.

I hadn't one so I looked on as the search party rummaged through the kits of the others, without finding the missing tin.

Several days later I saw that tin being used by an Indian and he told me that he had put it upside down on his head before winding on his turban, and they hadn't thought of searching the turbans! Very neat, I thought.

The search ended and bundles once more tied up and we were again ready. To the oft-repeated "Yellah" of the escort we marched out of the hospital and through the city gate and, heading north, we commenced the journey that was to prove the last for most of the party.

CHAPTER THREE

HORRORS OF THE MARCH

AT the foot of the ancient spiralled tower that marks the site of the old city of Samarah, capital of Mesopotamia for three centuries during the reign of the Caliphs, we halted, whilst the Onbashi counted us to make sure that we had all come out of the town safely. It was here that I picked up a cudgel that was to prove a good friend to me. Many of the Indians had sticks that they had carried all the way from Kut.

The counting over we recommenced the march, goaded on by the continual shouting of "Yellah, yellah."

Before long it was dark and we trudged on in silence mile after mile and none of us knew whither.

It soon became evident that a number of the party were not really fit to have started, and in any case there were very few who were at all strong. I was in excellent shape and only suffered from fatigue due to the unaccustomed exercise of my legs. The road was inclined to be rough and stony and my bare feet gave me trouble over the worst patches.

After the first hour we halted to allow the stragglers to catch up and we could hear an occasional cry of pain as one or other of these unfortunates was beaten into a quicker pace to the shout of the infernal "Yellah."

When we started off again I noticed that the Onbashi and five of the escort led the column and only one brought up the rear. I had chatted to the Onbashi when we halted at the ruins outside Samarah and he had appointed me *Terjiman* (interpreter). He had seemed an amiable sort of chap and certainly did not goad us unduly.

It was the *askar* (soldier) who brought up the rear who was going to prove the great thorn in our side. He it was

who had commenced whipping the sick and, after the first
halt, had flogged the tired stragglers to their feet as soon
as the Onbashi gave the word to resume the march.

On two occasions I had felt the weight of his whip as
I stayed behind to help one or other of the Englishmen who
had been compelled to stop to answer the call of nature,
suffering as they were from diarrhoea. I burned with an
intense hatred of this brutal fiend as I trudged along in the
darkness. Scores of mad plans of vengeance formed in my
mind, for as yet I was not broken in to the harsh rules that
govern the life of a captive. Nor was· I ever to be but I
learned to take things more calmly and to suffer blows
without always thinking of murder.

The night wore on and at last we heard the barking of
dogs and knew that a village was near.

We all badly needed water. Those who possessed water-
bottles had long since emptied them. I had nothing in which
I could carry water and had not had a drink since we started
and was, by this time, choking with thirst.

We drew nearer to the village and were soon passing over
cultivated ground and through some sort of green crop,
through which ran an irrigation ditch full of water. Here
the Onbashi called a halt. How we drank and drank of the
muddy water of that ditch. To me it was pure nectar.

It was nearly a quarter of an hour later that the last
straggler staggered in under the lash of the foul Arab who
brought up the rear. Quite a number of them were in a very
bad way and they implored me to ask the Onbashi how
much longer it would be before the first march ended. The
only answer I could get to my queries was "Yakin" or
"Gureeb" (near or close).

It had been increasingly difficult to get the worst sufferers
started again after each successive halt, and I knew that
after this one, where we had all drunk more dirty water
than was good for us, it was going to be still more difficult.

We had each been given a small, flat loaf of bread before we left hospital and I sat and ate mine now that there was water to wash it down. Little did I dream that I was eating the next day's ration!

It was not long before we were ordered to get on the move again and groans went up from the stragglers who had only been resting a few minutes. As before, the Onbashi and his five companions led the way, leaving the sixth *askar* to get the others up. He commenced his cry of "Goom, yellah" ("Get up, get on"), lashing the still prostrate figures on the ground.

It was too dark for me to see him from where I sat but I could hear him plainly enough, as I could the poor devils who were unable to rise to their feet quickly enough to suit him.

Again I grew hot with passionate hate and I determined to attempt a mad scheme that came to my mind. I hoped that the darkness would frustrate recognition should I fail in what I was about to attempt.

Grasping my cudgel firmly I crouched down on one knee as the Arab drew closer, leading his horse as he searched for his sick and tired victims.

"Yellah, yellah. Goom!" Swish! Thwack! fell his whip as he came nearer to me. Now he had seen me and, no doubt thinking that I too was too ill to get up, raised his whip to strike me.

Springing to my feet I brought my cudgel crashing down onto his head. He fell to the ground and his horse snatched loose and stood snorting. Again and again I struck with all the force I could muster, using both hands to my stick and feeling the shock of impact tingling up my arms.

Trembling and sweating, I stopped at last and stood listening. The horse was quietly cropping and snuffling nearby.

Hastily washing my cudgel in the water I stepped over

to the horse and caught him a crack over the rump. With a snort he galloped off in the direction of the party. I hurriedly followed.

The whole incident had been swift and it was not long before I had overtaken the rearmost of the column.

Hurrying forward I commenced to shout for the Onbashi and continued to shout until he heard me and halted the party.

Still gasping from my exertion and hurry I told him that one of the escort had been kicked in the head by his horse and was lying unconscious on the ground at our last stopping-place.

As if to back up my story the horse itself appeared, whinneying to the other mounts. At once the escort made a wild rush to seize it. Saddlebags were off and rifled in a twinkling.

For a few moments I was unable to grasp what was happening, then it dawned on me. They were looting the belongings of the ghoul who would no longer shout "Yellah, yellah" to his hapless victims.

The escort neither knew nor cared what was happening to the owner of the horse, sufficient for them that I had said that he was unconscious.

The Onbashi gave away the saddlery between the *askars*, and he kept the horse and led it away into the darkness as we once more got on the march.

I trudged along quite happily now, wondering at the amazing stroke of luck I had had and musing over the extraordinary life I was now living. A life that was to seem, in after years, like some weird fantasy that I had dreamt.

At dawn we reached a riverside village called Duer, and here we were to remain until evening when we should continue our march. We were herded into filthy mud huts, which were inches deep with sheep droppings, and told not to go outside on any pretext. In a very few minutes we were all asleep, the majority of us thoroughly exhausted, though the march was not a particularly long one as distance goes; probably twenty-five miles.

I was awakened just before noon by one of the Britishers who complained that his kit had been stolen as he slept.

We went in search of a sentry or one of the escort, but there was not a sign of a uniform anywhere. I shouted to a small Arab boy to go and bring the Onbashi or any *askar* he could find. Off he ran and in a few minutes he came back with one of our escort, who was none too pleased at being disturbed.

As I was telling him of the theft, several more of the party came up and reported losses. One of them had used his kitbag as a pillow and had secured the end of it to his wrist. The thief had deftly cut a hole in the kitbag and had removed more than half the contents without wakening the sleeper!

The *askar* became furious as, one after another, complaints were made, and he threatened to whip the victims if they said any more about it. That was all the help we got from him.

There was nothing more to be done, so I advised everyone with kit to pay particular attention to the security of it before they slept in future.

I was greatly refreshed by my sleep and went down to the river to bathe my feet, which were covered with huge blisters. These I pricked and, after washing them thoroughly, I bandaged them with a strip of linen torn from the tail of my ragged shirt.

By this time I was famishing, but there were no signs of rations to be issued so I decided to go on a foraging expedition into the village.

From one mud hut to another I went, begging food, but I received more curses than anything else. One old harridan chased me away with a stick. Here and there I received a small piece of stale *chupatti* (unleavened bread), and one woman gave me a bowl of *libn* (sour milk), which was very acceptable.

The village pariah dogs snarled and barked at my heels all the time, but I had only to make a motion as though I was going to throw something at them when they would run away, yelping as though they had been whipped, to return again immediately I turned my back. This was the usual practice of the Arab dogs, but the dogs belonging to the Kurds, further north, were of vastly different calibre.

I was on my way back to the party when I came across the Onbashi and his men, sitting in the shade of a courtyard wall, smoking and drinking coffee.

"Taal hena, Terjiman" ("Come here, Interpreter"), he cried.

I went to him and, to my surprise, he gave me a cigarette and told me to sit down.

For the next hour I was kept busy answering questions, mostly about the life of a British soldier. When I enlarged on the privileges and pay of Tommy Atkins there were many expressive "ah's" and grunts from the audience of villagers that had silently collected as I talked.

The Onbashi commented that we were not very good as soldiers, at least not so good as the Arabs, and would soon be driven out of Mesopotamia by the Osmanlis (Turks).

I thought discretion the better part of valour on that point, so I did not contradict him. During a lull in the conversation I asked the Onbashi how far we were likely to march that night and how soon it would be before we received rations. He assured me that six or seven hours on the road would bring us to Tekrit, our next stopping-place, and there we should get rations.

Neither the Arab nor the Turk will give the length of a journey other than by days or hours, and they compute this by how long *they* would take, whether mounted or on foot. To indicate a mounted man they would open the first and second fingers and, pointing them downwards, state the destination and number of days. We learned to judge the distance by doubling the number of hours given, multiplying the answer by three, and calling the result miles! More often than not we were about right.

Getting abruptly to his feet the Onbashi said that we must get back to the party and see that everyone was ready to march.

On arriving back to the huts we found a game of barter and exchange going on. The starving prisoners were bargaining for food with the villagers, using articles of kit and clothing as a medium of exchange. The Russians, who had nothing but the scanty clothing they were wearing, were interested spectators.

I asked the Indian Havildars whether all the Indians would be able to continue the march that night and they reported that four or five of their men were very bad. One or two Englishmen were in a like state. I discussed the position with the Onbashi, who said that they could be left at Tekrit —our next stopping-place—if they could manage to reach there, otherwise they would have to remain where they were and get to Tekrit as soon as they were able.

To have abandoned them to the tender mercies of the villagers of Duer could only have had one ending, so we decided to get them along with us somehow. So at sunset, when we were ready to move off again, I explained the position to the party and between us we agreed to take turns at supporting those poor fellows.

Once more we were off and, shortly after nightfall, we saw, far away in the distance, a light, which I was told was a beacon at Tekrit.

Long before that agonizing march was over I could have sworn that that light receded as we advanced, and it was well after midnight before it appeared appreciably nearer.

Although the escort urged on the stragglers with the

everlasting "Yellah," there was no beating and halts were frequent.

Several of the stragglers lost their kits, however, as villagers from Duer had followed us in the darkness for an opportunity to rob whom they could.

A few hundred yards from the river, on the opposite side of which stood Tekrit, we had to pass between banks of high reeds and from out of these sprang an Arab who snatched the bundle of kit from the head of a sepoy. The sepoy managed to grab the bundle before the Arab got away and struggled to retain it. In a flash the Arab drew his knife and slashed the wrists of the unfortunate Indian. His cries gave us the first indication of trouble, and when we found him he was crying pitifully and holding his hands, dripping with blood, in front of him. The right hand was almost severed from the wrist and blood was spurting from severed veins in both wrists. Using the man's *pugaree* (turban) we improvised tourniquets and rendered what first aid we could. This sepoy was left behind at Tekrit and what happened to him subsequently I have no idea.

There was a shingle beach opposite Tekrit, and here we halted whilst the Onbashi fired a shot at the cliff facing us across the river. This was probably to waken the sentries! The resounding crack of the shot set hundreds of dogs barking in the town and in a few minutes there was much shouting and arguing between the Onbashi and voices on the other side, so that a small pandemonium resulted. This gradually subsided and we were told that we would have to remain where we were until daylight.

I shall never forget the misery of the next few hours, as, tired and hungry, I tried to sleep on the pebbles of that beach. The dew that fell before dawn speedily soaked the few rags that I wore and as I lay and shivered I longed for the rising of the sun, forgetting that its terrific heat was almost as unbearable.

The morning was well advanced before a raft was poled over the river and the ferrying of the party commenced.

Tekrit is built in a cleft of rock on the right bank of the Tigris and is at the southern end of the Fatha Gorge which contains the river for many miles. It has always borne an evil reputation since the days of Saladin and is reputed to stand on the site of an extensive Assyrian city.

Our party was received with jeers and curses from the crowd of idlers assembled on the waterfront, and many of them spat upon us as we clambered up to a ledge of rock upon which we were to spend the next two days.

A posse of Gendarmerie took over from our escort and I was introduced to them as the Terjiman and Chaoush (Sergeant) of the party. Our Onbashi had apparently considered me worthy of promotion even if my late Commanding Officer had not! To the end of our journey I was considered to be in charge after this, and was referred to by our various guards and escorts as Terjiman Chaoush.

When our escort had gone I was told to collect a blanket and three or four men and to follow one of the Gendarmes. This I did and we were led through the narrow, winding streets of Tekrit until we came to a *serai*, which appeared to house the Gendarmerie.

We entered a courtyard and crossed to a small room that was the ration store. Here, a carefully checked number of measures of coarse flour was tipped into our outspread blanket. This, together with a very small quantity of crude salt, was all the rations we were to receive for the day. I was told, before we left, that if we behaved ourselves we should receive a like quantity the following day.

Thankful for small mercies, we humped the stuff back to our comrades, and I performed a task that was repeated every time we drew rations from that day forward, a task that I loathed because of the bickering that invariably followed.

First, I had to measure out the flour on to another blanket, using a battered tin mug for the purpose, each mugful being shaken down and scraped off level with the top—a dead measure. Each measure was carefully counted by a Hindu Havildar, a Moslem Havildar, and myself, the Russians being content to be one with the English. The total number of measures was divided according to the number in each party, English, Hindu, and Moslem. The total was not always the same as sometimes we were treated more generously than others and got a pound or so extra weight; at times we got less than was our due. When each party had got their share in bulk it still had to be divided equally among the individual members of each party. It was a very serious business as no one man must have the tiniest bit more than the others, so little did each receive. At the end of the business a man was possessed of nearly half a pint of flour, a pinch of salt, and the job of making a meal of it!

We became experts at making a *chupatti* on a fire of bracken, straw, or dried dung. Fuel was usually as scarce as food, and none was ever issued to us however scarce it might be. Sometimes I borrowed a mess-tin and boiled up my flour into a sort of porridge, but only when fuel was more easily obtainable.

The difficulty of obtaining fuel was so great on the plains that I very often collected camel dung on the line of march and carried it in my shirt front—for the lack of anywhere else to carry it—for miles, so that I should be able to cook my rations when I got them, without the fatigue of having to search for fuel. On one occasion, when we passed a village at night, I stole a cake of dung fuel from the wall of a house where it was stuck to dry, and this lasted me for three days. What was left after the first and second days I used as a pillow, mostly to prevent it from being stolen!

Here we were then with our first uncooked ration.

The Gendarmes had already lit a fire on the ledge of rock

to cook their own food and after they had finished they allowed us to use it. A great task for a hundred and fifty men, but they would not permit us to build others.

Before I could cook mine I was told to get all the very sick together and go with them to the hospital. This was another task that fell to my lot each time we arrived at a place where there was a hospital or sick quarters.

Once more I ascended the narrow streets of the town until we came to a low building built of pebbles and mud, resembling more than anything else an ancient cow byre. At the doorway of the place sat a Turkish medical officer at a low makeshift table. My party of sick—three Englishmen and five Indians—was made to sit in the roadway, some ten yards from the officer, who apparently did not intend to risk contagion by any closer contact.

I explained the circumstances of each case, mostly chronic diarrhoea, and asked that some sort of conveyance be provided for them if they had to continue the march with us.

It will be as well to mention here that only the most desperately sick men ever reported sick during the march, as their fate was problematical if they were compelled to remain behind.

These eight men were in a very bad state and would never be able to continue even if they received the best of attention from the doctor, and that was very doubtful. After much talk with an assistant the doctor said that they could remain in the building until our party left Tekrit. He promised that he would give them medicine and milk and then they would be able to continue with us.

I left the sick men still sitting in the roadway and made my way back to the main party. When I arrived back, I found that a Sergeant of the 1/4th Hampshire Regiment had very kindly cooked my flour for me, so that I was able to eat without further trouble. After that he and I were pals for many weeks, until he died of dysentery at Adana, Turkey in Asia.

All that long day the sun beat down upon us and its terrific heat was intensified by being reflected from the granite rocks upon which we were billeted.

We had only such water as those who had containers had brought with them from the river and the guards would not allow us to leave the rock in order to get any more. In fact we were not allowed to leave our place for any purpose whatsoever. The result was that we endured agonies of thirst, made worse by the sight of the river flowing at our feet, and many of our number collapsed from heat exhaustion.

It was only after sunset that the guards—who had sheltered all day in a small wooden hut built at the end of the ledge—would allow a party to go for water. Even then the party was restricted to six men, who were permitted only one journey.

I was one of the party and, with water-bottles slung all over us and half a dozen mess-tins in each hand, we made our way down to the river, accompanied by one Gendarme. We waded into the river to waist-height and drank our fill and soaked our bodies in the cool water. The Gendarme immediately commenced to shout "Yellah," but for all we cared he could shout his head off, we intended to make the most of our opportunity to get really wet and cool. Very slowly we filled our bottles and tins and when all of us were ready we staggered out of the river under our load of water.

A crowd of boys had collected on the beach, and laughing and shouting they began to throw pebbles at us. Unfortunately we could not hurry, loaded as we were, and ammunition was plentiful for these brats of the devil.

I learned subsequently that every party of prisoners that stopped at Tekrit were similarly treated. How I wished that I had been a Tamerlane or Ghengis Khan, then Tekrit would have been more desolate than the ruins of Babylon, and another pyramid of skulls would have adorned the landscape!

We delivered the water to our thirsting comrades and then sat and rubbed our bruises. One of us, a sepoy, had received a nasty cut on the cheek, and he looked very ill as his friends bathed it for him. An occasional stone was thrown at us on the ledge, but as the guards were likely to be hit they soon put a stop to it.

Darkness fell and we sat and contemplated our fate with hunger gnawing at our vitals, for we had had only about eight ounces of food in three days.

My new-found friend, Sergeant R., told me that he suffered from recurring bouts of malaria and he wondered what would be his fate should a bout come upon him during the march. I tried to cheer him up, but as I was none too cheerful myself I am afraid that I was not very successful.

We eventually dropped off to sleep, he covered by an old sack he had had the good fortune to find at Samarah, whilst I curled up close to him for additional warmth.

I was very sore in those naked parts of my body that had been exposed to the blistering sun all day, and I turned and twisted a good deal before I managed to fall off to sleep.

The following day was a repetition of the first and it was with intense relief that I saw our old escort arrive to take charge of us again.

I asked the Onbashi to find out how the sick men I had taken into Tekrit were faring and he sent off a man straight away. When he returned I was told that they would not be coming with us as they were too ill to march. I was not allowed to go and see them before we left and to this day I have never known what happened to them subsequently. From my experience of Tekrit I did not envy them their fate.

At sunset we were ferried back over the river and again had to sleep on the pebbly river front.

When I was told by the Onbashi that we should have to wait for daylight before moving off I at once protested, for two reasons. One was that until we reached our next stopping-place we should get nothing to eat so the sooner we got there the better, especially in view of the fact that it would be at least twenty-five miles' journey. The other reason was, that we should be marching through the heat of the day, which would spell disaster to one or two of the party and terrible hardship to us all.

The Onbashi listened to my protests and then told me that the previous parties of prisoners had travelled up from Tekrit on the right bank of the river, and he knew that road well enough to travel by night. Our party, however, was going to Kirkuk and he was not sure of the way, therefore we must travel by day!

Against that information I had no argument so there was nothing for us to do but lay down and try to sleep and hope for the best on the morrow. I was somewhat consoled when the Onbashi told me that the Commandant at Tekrit had informed him that there were plenty of ration depots on the road. I was yet to learn not to believe anything that I was told when it had to do with the treatment of prisoners of war by the Turks.

Dawn found us wet through with dew and shivering as we got to our feet, roused by the usual "Goom, yellah," and none of us were at all sorry to get on the move once more.

The first few hours were not very arduous, but when the sun climbed higher and the heat become really fierce, each mile we covered was an age of torture. The escort, who were riding, spent their time singing in the shrill, discordant manner that is not appreciated by the average Western listener under the best of conditions; to us it sounded like the howling of a thousand fiends.

The terrain was, for the most part, stony and hilly and entirely different from the alluvial plains below Samarah, and by noon our pace was very slow; made slower because of the many who were now being assisted by their comrades. So far we had seen "neither man nor beast nor any living thing," nor had we passed water of any kind.

On we went, reeling and staggering along a track that was like a red-hot grill. The rocks and stony way shimmered with heat, and, when a halt was called to allow the stragglers to catch up, it was more comfortable to stand than to sit, though many dropped from sheer exhaustion.

It was evident that our number would be greatly decreased if we had always to march in the daytime and I pointed this out to the Onbashi. He had become very churlish now, exasperated by the slowness of our pace, and said that we were women, not soldiers, and that one Arab was worth twenty Englishmen. The *askars* of the escort were becoming impatient also, and their cries of "Yellah, yellah" became more insistent and threatening. We foresaw trouble ahead if we could not get along quickly enough to suit them.

Those of us who had neither water-bottle or other means of carrying water were suffering agonies of thirst. Fresh blisters had formed on my heels and I began to limp painfully. My head ached terribly and I was compelled to wear what was left of my shirt bound turbanwise around it. This left the upper part of my body exposed to the sun and it was not long before I became badly burned. How I did not succumb to sunstroke that day I have no idea, as I had never been used to going without a helmet.

During the afternoon a sepoy, who had been helped for several miles, finally collapsed and could not rise again, not even when the Onbashi tried kicking him to his feet. He was a Hindu, and a *Naik* (Corporal) of his regiment, pleaded to be allowed to stay with him. I knew a fair amount of Hindustani and interpreted his wishes to the Onbashi, adding on my own behalf that the Naik would follow on and catch us up later.

The Onbashi would not hear of it and ordered us to leave the sick man and get on the march again. The poor fellow was left where he had fallen and we all hoped that death would soon put an end to his sufferings. That was nine gone from our party of one hundred and fifty in only three days. It augured ill for the remainder of us.

Not long after this incident we saw dark patches shimmering in the heat haze a long way to our left front. The head of the column was turned in that direction and, just before sunset, we came to a squalid village near the river. The dark patches proved to be the goat's-hair tents of a party of semi-nomadic Arabs, and long before we reached them the Arabs streamed out across the stony plain to meet us. Prancing and yelling and snapping their fingers in time to a kind of chant, they accompanied us to the place on the riverside that we were to occupy that night. They were evidently delighted to see us, beaten, sick, and exhausted as we were, and it was just as evident that they would have delighted to have slit all our throats.

At the riverside, Arab boys had taken charge of the horses of the escort whilst they had gone to the village, no doubt to demand food for themselves. We were left to our own devices.

The river at this point was very shallow and we had to scramble down the sun-baked bank to reach it. This was too much for many of the party, so we that could had to carry water to them, an effort that strained—for the time—our comradeship, as we were all in a very bad condition.

During the march our need for food had given way to our great thirst, but once that had been slaked we were urgently reminded of our hunger. We waited anxiously for the return of the Onbashi, hoping that he would manage to get rations for us. As darkness came on our hopes died for there was no sign of either Onbashi or food. Instead, we were surrounded by a crowd of villagers and tent dwellers and a right villainous crowd they were. Goodness knows how they lived as there was no sign of cultivation or flocks. They were filthy and in rags, and the children, of whom there were dozens, were stark-naked, their small brown bodies turned a dirty grey with dust and dirt and streaked with liquid filth.

Hunger forced me to beg of the villagers for bread, or anything eatable, but I got nothing but jeers for my pains. The women—perhaps females would better describe them—delighted to draw their filthy claws across their throats and cackle at the significant gesture. Offers of clothing from several of our party, in exchange for food, induced some of them to fetch *chupattis* from their hovels. In the bargaining that followed those human jackals proved more extortionate than Shylock. One man of the Norfolk Regiment was offered one mouldy *chupatti* for his blanket, and so great was his hunger that he eventually parted with it for four. I had nothing to dispose of so I had to be content to help the others in the hopes that they would reward me with a mouthful of bread.

At last the Onbashi and his men returned, arm in arm with several Arabs, who had no doubt been their hosts, and we were herded together as closely as possible and told not to move again that night under pain of dire punishment. It was no hardship to be packed together as the nights were chilly and I, for one, was glad of the extra warmth due to the closeness of my comrades. But the order forbidding us to move was a different matter. Once during the night we were awakened by the screams of someone whose looseness of bowels forced him to get up and leave the party. He was beaten back to his place with a rifle-butt, the cause of his screams. No one else attempted to move, though many ought to have done, and morning brought scenes that cannot be described. One sepoy was dead and two others were so bad that they could not rise from where they lay.

They were carried to a filthy, roofless hut in the village and left to their fate. The dead man was stripped of his clothing and his body thrown into the river by his own friends. It was the only thing they could do as the Onbashi lost no time in getting us on the move again, using his rifle-butt to urge on those who were tardy from sickness.

Again we suffered the tortures of the damned as we limped along mile after mile over that dead land. The Russians, who had stuck things pretty well so far, now began to show signs that they too were feeling the effects of the unholy treatment we were getting. One or two of them were in the last stages of exhaustion before the end of the march and had to be practically carried by their comrades. Three of the English party had to be assisted also, and by companions who were themselves in need of assistance.

During mid-afternoon we came to a village and were met by two ragged soldiers who led us to an open space in the middle of a cluster of mud huts. Here, in the shade of a wall, sat an aged Turkish officer, a Mulazim Thani (Second Lieutenant), and I learned that he was in charge of the ration depot in the village. He got to his feet and upbraided the Onbashi for arriving during the heat of the afternoon! Then he carefully counted us before giving orders that we were to be taken to the outskirts of the village.

I thought fit to butt in at this stage of the proceedings and to tell the Mulazim that we had had nothing to eat for two days and were practically starving. He asked me why they had not given us rations at Tekrit. I explained that we had left Tekrit the day previously and had drawn one day's ration of flour the day before that. Further, that we had stopped overnight at a village where there had been no ration store, which meant no food for us. The old Turk asked the Onbashi if what I had said was true and when he heard that it was he smacked the Onbashi's face a dozen times and then let flow a stream of foul abuse and invective, interspersed with his reasons for the outburst.

From what I could gather it appeared that the Onbashi ought not to have stopped at the last place, as it was considered to be only one march from Tekrit to the place we were now at. Fearing reprisals when we should leave this place on the morrow, I pleaded the Onbashi's cause and said that the party contained so many sick men that it would have been impossible for us to have marched so far in one day. For this I too got my face smacked! I was rather glad I did, in a way, as the Onbashi would be less likely to vent his spite on me. Grumbling and wheezing the old Turk hobbled off to his ration store, telling the Onbashi to make haste and get someone to draw flour for us.

This was one of the places where we got under weight and we were a sorry company when, later that night, we lay down to sleep with our hunger only slightly appeased. A small half-cooked *chupatti* of gritty wholemeal did little to satisfy men who had been nearly three days without food.

To our great surprise we were awakened the next morning early and told to draw rations again. The old man must have had a good night's sleep for he was much more human, though he was just as stingy with his flour! I asked him whether we could have donkeys to carry the men who were very ill. He replied that there were no such animals in the village, but that we could leave the sick behind and they would be sent on when they were better. When I told him of the two sepoys that we had left behind at the last place, he promised to have them brought in and looked after with the others.

We left two Englishmen and one sepoy here and we ought to have left at least one Russian, but his friends would not hear of it, saying that if he was to die they preferred to see it happen rather than leave him to the mercy of the Arabs. That was fifteen gone from the party in a very few days.

We were given a short time in which to cook our flour before we were driven forth again. Fortunately there was plenty of thorny bracken about, otherwise we should not have had time to have both collected fuel and cooked our *chupattis*. As it was we had to be content to have them half-raw.

It was still fairly early when at last we moved off and the going was not too bad, at least for we that were well enough. We passed over cultivated ground that occurred among long stretches of ground strewn with stones as big as cricket balls.

That day was a repetition of the previous day so far as the discomforts of the march went, and it was not long before the column had straggled out from horizon to horizon. The Onbashi had apparently received orders from the Mulazim that one day's march had to be completed in one and not two days in future, for the halts were few and far between and of short duration.

I was in much better shape and my heels were not so sore, neither did I suffer the want of water quite so much, though it was still as hot as Hades. I kept alongside the flea-bitten mount of the Onbashi for the greater part of the day, and passed the time enquiring about Kirkuk and how long it would take us to get there, etc. He told me that we should reach the river that night, and from there the road would be much easier, all the way to Kirkuk. I had never heard of Kirkuk and hadn't the slightest idea whereabouts in Mesopotamia it lay. I guessed that it must be on the Tigris, somewhere near Mosul, after I had been told that we should be near the river from that night until we reached there. I was wrong, of course.

At last we came in sight of our next stopping-place, and at sunset limped into the village of Bisereria, a village on the banks of the Lesser Zab—the river I had wrongly guessed to be the Tigris. To reach it we had to ford the river, which flowed fairly strongly and was split into several channels. The water was cool and refreshing, and we lowered the river by many gallons as we stood up to our waists and drank of it.

Bisereria was a fair-sized village and had a dilapidated caravanserai on the outskirts. This had been taken over by the military and housed a squad of Arab soldiers and one officer. Here we drew our usual rations of flour and salt, plus about one pint of olive oil between the whole party. The small quantity of the latter that was each man's share was a welcome addition to our diet, and we spread it over our *chupattis* as though it were butter.

As usual we were stared at and jeered at by the villagers, though at this place they were not too bad. More articles of kit changed hands and the Mohammedans of the party attempted to ingratiate themselves by repeating "Islami, Islami" to all and sundry. They got no more by thus demeaning themselves, but they did not cease in their efforts.

We had several Ghurkas with us and these staunch little warriors were reviled more than we English were, particularly when they disclosed the wisp of hair, left long from birth onwards, on the top of their heads. The Sikhs, too, with their long hair done up in a knot on top of their heads, came in for a special share of ridicule and abuse from the Arab scum that used to pester us.

At Bisereria I was fortunate enough to get two eggs, given to me by an old grey-beard with whom I sat and chatted. He showed me how to cook them by dropping them into the hot embers of a fire and leaving them until the shell "popped," when they were found to be "soft" cooked. On subsequent occasions when I received eggs I made them last longer by leaving them raw and dipping bits of *chupatti* into them.

The following morning I was able to beg a drink of *libn* from a woman of the village and I felt very thankful that I was able to speak their language. I undoubtedly owe my life to the fact that I was able to glean sufficient knowledge of the language of the various peoples among whom I stayed to serve me, for during the whole of my captivity it was this ability that enabled me to get food where others had starved—apart from other advantages.

Several more sick were found to be too ill to continue when we were ready to move off again, and one of these was the Russian who had been very ill the day before. How he had managed to survive the gruelling march of the previous day is a mystery, as he was practically a dead man.

The Onbashi informed the officer in charge of the ration depot that he would have to leave the sick behind. He got his face smacked for his pains. The Arab Chaoush in charge of the squad of soldiers raved and swore and waved his arms about as he accompanied the Onbashi to collect the sick men. I gathered from his tirade that it was a waste of good rations to have to feed sick men when they would ultimately die! The outlook was very gloomy for the poor men we were compelled to abandon to such a creature's care. He was still arguing when the officer re-appeared, followed by a villager driving five diminutive donkeys. These, I was told, would carry the sick to Kirkuk. The Chaoush became all smiles and I was very thankful that the sick were not to be left after all.

The donkeys were equipped with neither bridle nor saddle, nor covering of any kind to their backs. The sick men must have endured agonies what short time they rode those hatchet-backed creatures. The owner, a foul-looking Arab, and two boys took charge of them once we got on the road, and they delighted in goading them into a jog-trot in order to see the looks of agony on the faces of the sick riders.

For an hour we kept to the river and then we bore off in a more easterly direction, across a dreary waste. Before we left the river a halt was called for the purpose of filling up water-bottles. The owner of the donkeys took this opportunity to muster his beasts and chase them back over the horizon. The Onbashi would do nothing about it and we had perforce to leave the sick on the river bank. I have always considered that the officer at the ration depot had deliberately connived at that scheme to get rid of the sick. It was worse than murder.

The country tended to become more rough and hilly, and long before the end of the day the escort was lashing the stragglers into a quicker pace. In vain I protested to the Onbashi that no useful purpose could be served in setting a pace that was beyond the strength of the majority. When I threatened to report him for allowing the *askars* to beat the sick he said he would shoot me if I didn't hold my tongue!

Nightfall found us still on the "blue" with no village in sight, so we had to camp where we were. Complaints went up on all sides that there was no water and no likelihood of rations so off I went for the Onbashi. I was getting rather fed up with my job as Terjiman as it entailed too much arguing against the stupidity of that ignorant and callous man. However, he said that if we liked we could continue to march until we came to water, but the sick would have to keep up or be left behind. The alternative—no water— was too awful to contemplate so after an interval to give the sick a rest we recommenced the march.

How many we lost that night I do not know. I had begun to lose count of numbers, days, time, or anything else.

Scores of times during that nightmare march in the darkness, after being on the road since daybreak, I stumbled over boulders as I staggered on literally asleep. It was terrible. All that could be heard was the shuffle of feet and an occasional clank of a mess-tin against a rock, or a burst of shrill, wailing song from one of the Arab *askars*.

Daylight came but still no water, and it was imperative now that we kept on until we did reach it. I put one foot before the other like an automaton. My lips were hard and dry and my tongue like a piece of leather. The condition of the sick can be more easily imagined than described. When the sun rose higher and its terrific heat beat down on us the agonies of the march were increased tenfold. Even the escort had slumped in their saddles and become silent as they led the reeling, stumbling column onwards.

About mid-afternoon we sighted our goal—Kirkuk. Long before we reached the town hundreds of people came streaming out to meet us, and they raced along our straggling column, laughing and jeering at our sorry plight.

We were halted on the outskirts by a Turkish Bimbashi (Major) and counted by a posse of Gendarmes. The count told less than a hundred men! We had marched over fifty miles without food and with only such water as could be carried at the start.

I was too exhausted to attempt any parley with the Bimbashi, who in any case looked decidedly unapproachable.

Donkeys arrived bearing, pannier-wise, large baked-clay water-jars which were immediately stormed by our party. One jar was broken in the scrimmage and the Bimbashi came among us lashing about him with his whip.

Meanwhile, a flat-bottomed *arabana* (cart) had arrived with a load of flat, black loaves. These were distributed at the rate of one per man. It was little enough, but at least we were saved the fatigue of hunting for fuel to cook our usual *chupatti*, a task which none of us could have accomplished that night.

As we sat and devoured our bread like animals the Bimbashi came swaggering among us, slapping his heavy knee boots with his whip and spitting with disgust whenever

MOSUL

[*See p. 78*

MOSUL BARRACKS

[*See p. 79*

TYPICAL OF THE
KURDS AT
GHIR GHIRO

[*See p.* 366

THE OLD GUNS
AT THE ENTRANCE
TO THE BARRACKS,
MOSUL

[*See p.* 84

he passed one of our number who presented a more than usual revolting appearance.

Many were badly blistered by the sun on the naked parts of their bodies, some had blisters that had broken and were festering, others had raw and bleeding feet, whilst all were covered with dust and utterly exhausted.

Fortunately, I had peeled instead of blistering and was now tanned almost black. Having no razor I had not shaved since Samarah and my hair had not been cut for weeks, so that I was becoming more like our escort every day!

The Bimbashi came up to the small party of Russians and commanded the Sergeant among them to stand up. Then he held a few minutes' conversation in what must have been Russian, as the Sergeant became very voluble. It ended by the Bimbashi spitting into the face of the Sergeant and knocking him down among his companions. He had no liking for Russians apparently.

At last we were left in peace and I fell into a deep sleep, from which I was awakened at dawn the next morning by the shouting of the familiar but unpopular cry of "Yellah, yellah." Stiff with cold and fatigue I got to my feet to see what was happening. The bread cart had arrived and another loaf apiece was being given out as the party formed up ready to march. Several were too ill to rise and groaned pitifully as a fresh escort of Arabs went among them with whips.

Two terribly emaciated Englishmen and five sepoys were brought from the town to join our party. From these I learned that they had been in a parody of a hospital at Kirkuk for months, and were of a party of prisoners that had been captured before the capitulation of Kut-el-Amara. They were the only survivors of the fiendish treatment they had received in the hospital and, hearing of the arrival of our party, had begged to be allowed to join us.

Until then we had no idea that we were to proceed farther

as the Onbashi had told us that we were to remain at
Kirkuk.

I edged my way along the lines of prisoners standing
ready to move off, until I reached a Chaoush who was idly
watching the proceedings. In answer to my query as to our
destination he said that we were going to Mosul. I asked
him how long it would take us to get there and he said,
"Yormeyn" (two days), and waggled two dirty fingers under
my nose, in case I failed to understand him.

Two days! It seemed more like two years before we did
eventually get there and it was as well that we did not know
what lay before us.

Once we got on the move I saw that the ruffianly crew
who had attempted to whip the sick to their feet at Kirkuk
were to be our escort and that the Onbashi had been replaced by a wall-eyed Chaoush of bestial appearance who
wore, in addition to the rifle he carried, a revolver and
a curved dagger.

All that long day the air resounded with "Yellah, haidi,
goom, yellah, yellah," and the swish! thwack! of blows being
dealt, followed by screams of the recipients. No captives
of old could have been treated more cruelly. I thought of
the pictures I had seen as a schoolboy of the captives and
slaves of the old-time Eastern kings and conquerors, and
it was easy to imagine myself one of them. The life we had
led under the British flag seemed like a fantasy of a long
past day and our future we could not imagine.

It was two days before we came again to the Tigris, two
days marching on one small loaf of bread. We had to wade
and swim the river to reach the other side and our next
stopping-place, Shergat.

We were to occupy a dilapidated caravanserai, now a
ration depot on the road from Mosul to Samarah. This
building was on the mound that is the site of Asshur,
ancient capital of the Assyrian Empire. Had those mighty

rulers of Assyria treated their captives as the Turks treated us, then it is doubtful whether their empire would have been as vast or whether their huge architectural and engineering enterprises would have come to aught. The tremendous drain on man-power would have been too great and the land would have been empty within a decade. It might be argued that the natives of the country would have stood the same hardships better and for a longer period than we did. I don't believe that would have been the case. I have seen both Turks and Arabs—and for that matter, Kurds, too—die in hundreds under conditions better than we had, and it must be borne in mind that we had withstood a siege of five months immediately prior to our capture.

We were to stay at Shergat for two days and for that I was very thankful. As soon as we got into the caravanserai we received a loaf of hard, black bread, and a few drops of olive oil. The sick were put into a room apart, and what treatment they got, if any, it was impossible to discover.

A Yuzbashi (Captain) was the officer in charge and he was a fairly amiable sort of chap. He even permitted us to bathe in the river the day after our arrival, though very few of us took advantage of the opportunity. Not many were in that state when bathing or swimming would have been a pleasure, and the majority lacked the energy to move from where they lay under the verandahs or in the cubicles.

On the second day out from Kirkuk I had been given a pair of boots by a Havildar of a Mahratta Regiment, taken from the feet of one of his men who had died on the road. They were without laces and much too large for me, but they served me for many a mile, though they were the cause of a spell of trouble for me at Shergat. I was leaping down the rocks to reach the water, on the evening of the second day, and one of these boots slipped half off my left foot just as I landed, causing me to sprain my ankle. Though I sat with my foot in the cool water for two hours or more my ankle continued to swell until it was more than double its normal size, and I was greatly afraid that I might be left behind.

Despite the pain of my sprained ankle, I managed to limp around and look at the excavations at the back of the caravanserai, dug by German archeologists.

By evening of the second day we were ready to take the road again. About thirty donkeys had been commandeered by the Yuzbashi to take the sick into Mosul. Quite a few of the sick had to be tied on and supported by their comrades. Because of my sprained ankle I was given a mount, a tiny, half-starved little beast without headgear or back covering.

A new escort had arrived to take us on to Mosul and they looked no better than the old. As usual they were all Arabs and mounted.

When we were given the signal to march we left the gates of the caravanserai in a disorderly mass, due in the main to the antics of the uncontrollable donkeys. I clung to the ears of my mount as it went careering down the mound that was Asshur, my feet trailing and my body almost jolted to pieces.

Awaiting us on the road below was the new Chaoush, who, when my donkey trotted up to him, ordered me to get back to the remainder. In vain I tore at the little brute's ears in an endeavour to bring it to a halt. With a foul curse the jackal of a Chaoush lashed me across the face with the loose end of a rope that served him for reins. I was brought to a halt quickly enough, even though the donkey careered gaily on! After much shouting and shrilling by the Arab donkeymen it was caught and I remounted. I was placed in the middle of the party so that I should not gallop all the way to Mosul on my own!

Away we went again, this time in darkness, up hill and down, mile after mile. After several hours of agony, astride my donkey, I came to the conclusion that I should find it less painful to limp along, so I handed it over to someone who was finding the march too much for him. The next few miles after that was painful going, but before morning my ankle was almost normal, strange to say, and I had little bother with it after that.

We continued to push on after daybreak as we had not yet reached the next and last ration depot before Mosul. The road lay between hills from which oozed bitumen and a thick viscous liquid that we guessed to be oil of sorts. Later we came to where a few old boilers were used to make a sort of crude oil out of an odorous mess that lay in pools on the surface of the ground. Several sulphurous streams trickled on their way to the Tigris, and we bathed our sore and aching feet in them on the offchance that it would do them good.

All day long we shuffled along under the relentless sun, goaded onwards by the everlasting "Yellah" and the whips of the escort. I have no very clear recollection of that day, beyond a dogged determination to keep going until we reached water. After that, I thought, it would not matter much what happened. It appeared to me then, as on subsequent occasions, that it would be a great pity if I had to die thirsty. I felt that I could die in comfort if I had one long drink of water first! Of course, after I had had a drink I no longer wanted to die or even felt like dying.

The march for that day came to an end when we reached Hammam Ali (The Bath of Ali), a village which, we were told, was a spa for the people of Mosul who came there to take the waters and to bathe in the hot sulphur springs. Before we were herded into a cattle compound, filthy with the animal droppings of centuries, I saw two domed buildings in the village and concluded that they housed the bath of Ali and his pals from Mosul.

Flour was issued to us as rations and we found a use for

some of the filth on the ground by using it as fuel for our fires. Water was obtained from a noisome well near by, where it was brought to the surface by an endless chain of old tins, kept in motion by a merry-go-round affair drawn by a bony, blindfolded horse. The water splashed out into an irrigation channel that soon became a morass as we crowded over and in it to assuage our raging thirsts. The poor old horse cocked its ears at the unaccustomed babble of voices near it, but it never ceased to go round and round, pulling the shaft that worked the contraption.

I wondered at the time whether we too were destined to go shuffling on and on, pacing a road that was endless.

Early next morning we commenced the last journey before Mosul. No sick were permitted to remain behind and we had to assist those that were too ill to walk alone.

As we staggered along those twelve or fourteen miles to Mosul nearly everyone of our sadly depleted party received blows from the whips of our escort. This was because we were supporting our sick and were therefore unable to keep up to the pace of the mounted Arabs, who no doubt were longing for the odorous shade of the bazaars of Mosul and wanted to reach there before the sun became too uncomfortable. We, too, wanted to reach there before it became very hot, though we didn't aspire to the stench of some tawdry bazaar. Our fate would, at best, be some verminous mud hut or filthy caravanserai.

Mosul simply broke into our vision, as we topped one of the many rises that had promised to give us a vista of the "promised land," but only revealed still another dip and rise. I shall never forget my amazement as I gazed on this, to us, almost mythical city. Below us, a wide, sweeping plain, green with herbage and backed with a fringe of trees, led up to the city and was a grand sight for our tired eyes, eyes that had not seen such green for many weeks. The fairy minarets and coloured domes of the mosques glittered in the sunshine, and the whole scene was like a verdant and jewelled island in a dun-coloured sea. It was a great pity that closer contact speedily brought disillusion, as is the case with nearly all Eastern cities.

Still being urged and goaded on by the escort, we crossed the plain and entered the quadrangle of a huge, cumbrous-looking barrack building. Scores of ragged soldiers were at the gate to watch us pass through. The quadrangle was enclosed on all sides by what looked suspiciously like cells, in two stories. A verandah was formed on the ground floor by the narrow balcony of the floor above which encircled the whole building. At the opposite end from where we had entered was a short flight of stone steps leading to the upper floor and concealing from our view another and—comparatively—more imposing entrance.

We were formed into two ranks to await the coming of the Commandant. As fast as the sick men dropped to the ground they were kicked to their feet again, so that before the Commandant arrived we were all hanging on to each other to give support to the sick. As we stood thus, a party of ill-clad women crossed the square on their way out from one of the side rooms. These, I learned later, were Armenian exiles who had survived the atrocities of the march from Mardin, Sivas, Ourfa, and other ravaged towns. They came daily to plead for sustenance from the Commandant, who, in exchange, made them perform the most menial tasks that could be found about the barracks.

The Commandant duly arrived, a great, hulking, swash-buckler in heavy knee-boots, green and red uniform, and green astrakhan fez. He carried the inevitable "rawhide" whip, which no self-respecting Turkish officer seemed to be without. Scowlingly he passed in front of us, keeping a good ten yards' distance so as not to be contaminated by such carrion as we. After a few minutes' conversation with the Chaoush of our escort—who stood at the salute the whole time—he strode back in the direction from which he had come.

We were told to occupy the space under one of the verandahs and there we squatted to await the next move. For an hour or more we waited, but there was no sign of food or water so I asked the Chaoush, who was still with us, where we could obtain water. He was in a bad temper, because he had not been relieved of his job presumably, and struck at me with his whip. I dodged the blow and hurriedly returned to my place. My friend, Sergeant R., had had a bout of malaria the previous night and now lay on the stone-flagged floor of the verandah moaning for water. A good many others were crying out for water too, and I was on the point of asking some of the soldiers near to get us some when water arrived for us. It was on the backs of a dozen donkeys and contained in dirty kerosene oil tins, fit enough, however, to hold the filthy stuff in them. Still, it was wet, even if it did stink to high heaven, and we were glad enough to get it.

Another hour passed before a party of Arab prisoners arrived bearing sacks of the now familiar black bread. We were ravenously devouring this and did not notice the going of our Chaoush and his escort. No sooner had we eaten than we dropped off to sleep where we were.

I was rudely awakened by a prod from the butt of a rifle and sat up, to be asked if I were the Terjiman. Wondering what was wanted I said "Yes," and, to the order of the soldier who had asked the question, followed him up the stone steps and into an office. Inside sat a dapper Yuzbashi who motioned me to be seated, which I did—on the floor! Then he asked in Arabic, "Where did you learn Arabic?" I told him and was then asked "Why?"

Why, indeed! That struck me as a most peculiar question and I wondered what he was getting at. I made some sort of explanation, though I found it extraordinarily difficult to explain just why. Why does one learn a language? A simple answer was no good to a Turk, who always thought that there was an ulterior motive in every word and action.

"What other languages do you know?" I was next asked.

I told the Yuzbashi that I knew a fair amount of Hindustani and he again asked why! I countered this by asking him if he were a Turk and when he said that he was I said that if he had found it necessary to learn Arabic in order to deal with Arabs, then it was just as necessary for me to learn Hindustani, as I had had to deal with Indians before the war and Arabs since.

"Can you read and write?" was the next question.

"Yes," I replied.

"Then why are you not an officer?" he demanded to know in a loud voice.

I was astounded both at the question and at the man's threatening attitude. As to a child, I explained that every British soldier could read and write, and that attendance at school was compulsory for every child in England.

At this point the Yuzbashi was joined by a second officer, a Mulazim Awl (Lieutenant), and a spirited conversation ensued between them. I gathered that my statement was disputed and, sure enough, I was given a pen and ink and told to write something.

I did so and was rewarded with "Afferim!" Turkish for "Bravo!"

Sitting down on the floor again I wondered what was the real reason for my being called to this office and peculiar interview. The Yuzbashi seemed amiable enough now and even gave me a cigarette.

I ventured to ask a few questions on my own account, such as whether Mosul was our final destination, when should we be given clothes and better rations, what work should we have to do, etc.

The only information I could get was that we might

Other Ranks of Kut   F

remain at Mosul for two or three days and then be sent
to the railhead at Ras-el-Ain, where we should be put to
work on the construction of the railway track. Alternatively,
we might be sent further into Turkey to other working
camps. It was most unlikely that we should be kept for any
length of time at Mosul.

For an hour I sat on the floor of that office talking to those
two officers. I was given a kind of short-bread, some *hulwa*
(sweetmeat), and a bowl of *libn*, and smoked their cigarettes
continuously.

It was the first time that I had been treated so kindly
since I had been a captive and I began to have hopes of
a better time. False hopes!

Among other things, I learned that civil prisoners were
confined in this building as well as it being a barracks for
soldiers. Also that a British officer was confined to his room
on the upper floor. I asked permission to visit him, but was
told that they had charge only of the soldiers and civil
prisoners and not of prisoners of war, and only the Commandant could give me that permission.

Though I tried on several occasions during our stay at
Mosul to visit the officer I was unsuccessful. I was unable
to discover his identity or even the room in which he was
confined, and all my requests for information were refused
in a manner that was decidedly threatening.

Before I left the Yuzbashi I asked him whether he thought
it was any use my asking the Commandant for clothing for
those of us who were almost naked. I pointed to my own
outfit and said that it was impossible for me to continue
much farther unless I got something. My shirt, which had
supplied rags for my feet, been head covering during the
day and a pillow at night, was literally falling to pieces. The
only other article of attire I possessed—my shorts—was
practically finished, and when clothing could be described
as "finished" in those days it was really bad.

The Yuzbashi said that he had nothing to give me, but no doubt we should be properly clothed when we came to the end of our journey and, in any case, it was useless to see the Commandant on the matter.

After telling those two officers how much I appreciated their kindness I rejoined my party. I did not see them again, neither was it my luck to meet many of their ilk during the time I was a prisoner of war.

The following day I was taken by a Chaoush to a small room near the main entrance and given a khaki shirt and an old pair of khaki drill slacks. The shirt looked remarkably like those our own officers were used to wearing, but I asked no questions. Both articles were much better than my own and I lost no time in putting them on, though I kept my rags in case I might need them.

The boots that I had received from the Havildar had rubbed blisters on my toes, owing to their being much too large for me, so I gave them to another barefooted Englishman whose feet were bigger than mine.

For five days we remained under the verandah of Mosul barracks, not knowing what was to happen to us. The sick were taken away and we were unable to learn what became of them. We were not ill-treated, but we were very much neglected.

During the mornings we received a loaf of bread and in the evenings we got a vegetable soup called *kurrawanna*. The vegetables used in the soup were always the same, tomatoes and bringals (egg-plant), and the grease element was supplied by olive oil. It was a vile watery mess, but we were thankful enough to get it as we had had nothing but black bread or coarse flour since leaving Samarah.

The sanitary arrangements in those barracks beggar description, so foul were they. I have never seen anything quite like them in the East, before or since, and we came to the conclusion that they had never been cleaned out since the days of Nineveh!

I was allowed rather more freedom than the remainder, by reason of my position as Terjiman Chaoush, and on two occasions I managed to get down to the river with the water-man and indulge in the luxury of a swim. It was then that I discovered why the water we got to drink was so filthy and smelt so badly. All the filth of Mosul found its way into the river and the current forced it in to the sides, so that when the populace filled up their water-pots they simply made a hole in the scum and debris and dipped in the pots!

I used frequently to chat to the sentries on the main gate and was very interested in two very old guns of the cannon-ball period that stood one on either side of the entrance. The Chaoush in charge of the barracks told me that the Turks had captured them from the Russians during some old war or other. I saw those guns twenty years later, when the sentries at the gate were British-trained 'Iraqi soldiers.

One day the Armenian women came in and one of them beckoned me to go to her. There was no *askar* in sight so I went, wondering what she might want of me. Under cover of her cloak she made the sign of the cross and handed to me a small bundle of *chupattis* and a handful of small coins. I was greatly touched by her great kindness for she looked as though she needed food and money as much as we did. She was obviously terrified of being seen talking to me and, before I could say much in thanks, hurried off to join her companions.

I shared out the *chupattis* as far as they would go and bought *libn* with the money, to give to those who were too ill to eat bread, but who were not ill enough—according to Turkish standards—to receive hospital treatment.

By one of those strange chances of fate I met the same good woman again, nearly twenty years later, in Baghdad, where she was living on a small pension she received as a retired linen-mistress of the household of King Feisul of 'Iraq. I have spent many hours with her and her two sons, discussing the bad old days when the Turks misruled the country. She came of a well-to-do family of Diabekr and had seen her husband, and most of the male members of her family, butchered before her eyes during the massacre of 1915. Driven into exile with her two baby boys, she had eventually been brought into Baghdad with many other Armenians by the British after the defeat of the Turkish forces.

Each day we watched the civil prisoners being marched to the latrines, their only exercise. They were loaded with chains and several had medieval iron balls shackled to their ankles. It was a picture I shall never forget; these scarce-human creatures being driven along under the lashes and kicks of their brutal guards, the chains and balls dragging on the ground. It was a picture taken from the Dark Ages.

On the evening of the fifth day we were joined by a party of Britishers and Indians from the Mosul hospital. Several of the Britishers had belonged to the force that had attempted to relieve us at Kut and they, as well as the others, were still far from being well. They told us that scores of our men had died in the hospital at Mosul, as much from the treatment they received as from their diseases. Arab orderlies —half-starved desert rats, pressed into such service because they were either too stupid or too cunning to learn the rudiments of military life—were never prevented from mal-treating the prisoner patients. The Mahommedans among them had had preferential treatment and had been kept apart from the British and Hindus. The Sikhs and Ghurkas had been particularly ill-treated and taunted by doctors and orderlies alike.

We listened in silence as these newcomers to our party recounted the tales of torture and misery of their experiences at Mosul. We had seen enough ourselves to give us a good idea as to the kind of treatment helpless prisoners in hospital would receive.

In the late afternoon of that day, we were taken through Mosul and over the half-pontoon half-stone bridge that spanned the Tigris. Arrived on the other side we were told that we should camp on the water-front until morning, when we should move off up country.

Before we dispersed, three or four natives of the Effendi class arrived, bringing with them red, boat-shaped slippers for those who were barefoot and a small bag of raisins for each of us. These, we were told, were sent to us by an English lady interned in Mosul! I have never succeeded in finding out who that Good Samaritan was, but I learned later that she did whatever she could for every party of prisoners that passed through Mosul; supplying boots to the barefoot until the supply ran out and then these red slippers, which were all she could procure. She deserves a medal as big as a plate!

The raisins supplied us with the first sweetness that we had tasted for many weeks and we slowly chewed them one at a time so as to make them last as long as possible.

We lay on the river-bank and discussed the probabilities of the future. So far as we knew we had to undergo a repetition of those terrible days and nights of marching, yet most of us were thankful to think that we should soon be on our way out of Mosul.

I was feeling quite fit and had learned quite a lot of useful Turkish words, words that came in very handy long before I reached Turkey proper.

We had been talking for about an hour when an incident occurred that might have ended in tragedy, and showed to us what type of men were to be our new escort. We were startled by shouts of "Aguf! aguf!" ("Stop! stop!") from the sentries as they rushed off in the direction of the bridge. A shot rang out and in the moonlight we saw a figure running along the bridge, closely followed by several *askars*. These latter soon caught the fugitive and we heard the sound of blows and the screams of pain that followed. The *askars* returned with their victim and I ran up to see who it was. To my amazement I saw that it was a Britisher they were holding. The *askars* threw him to the ground and commenced to rain blows upon him with their rifles. I called on the Chaoush to put an end to the brutality and to explain what it was all about. The Chaoush shouted an order and the *askars* yanked the unfortunate man to his feet and then forced him to kneel in front of the Chaoush. That ignorant brute then proceeded to load his rifle and said that he was going to shoot the man as an example to us all, in case anyone else might try to escape!

Ye gods! So that was what it was all about. I stepped in front of the Britisher—a "Scottie" of the Argyll and Sutherland Highlanders and of the party who had joined us from Mosul hospital—and asked him to explain to me why he had run off. Trembling with fear, and with tears streaming down his face, he told me that he was suffering from diarrhoea and had gone towards the bridge-end, in order to be away from the party, to relieve himself. As he rose to his feet to return he was overcome with giddiness and temporarily lost his sight. He made to return to the party but in his blindness walked away from us. When the *askars* had shouted he thought they were Marsh Arabs— a name given wrongly to those jackals that had trailed every party of prisoners in the hopes of catching the stragglers— and he had commenced to run. Inadvertently he had run on to the bridge and had there been caught.

Poor devil! He was just another victim of sickness and ill-treatment and had not the slightest intention of trying to escape.

I told his tale to the Chaoush and pleaded for his life. The Chaoush would not believe it and asked why, if he were not attempting to escape, he ran across the bridge. It was as hopeless to explain as it would be to try and make a monkey sing, but I did my best. In the end I had to guarantee, with my own life, that if he were let off he would not attempt to escape again.

My offer was pretty safe or I might not have made it!

The Chaoush hesitated and then put down his rifle and ordered an *askar* to get him a rope. This was brought and the poor old "Scottie" was trussed up like a fowl. He cried out in pain as the rope was brought from his ankles to his wrists and pulled tight behind his back. He was first kicked and then ordered not to move if he wished to live. I tried to cheer the poor chap up until I was driven away by the *askar* specially detailed to guard him.

All night he was left trussed up and no man can guess what agonies he endured. As a matter of fact I did not expect him to be alive the next morning, but he was.

At dawn we moved off on the next stage of our journey into the unknown.

CHAPTER FOUR

MORE HORRORS ON THE MARCH

VERY few of us had any knowledge of what country lay north of Mosul though most of us knew that Turkey in Asia Minor was north-west, yet none of us thought it peculiar that we should be marching on the wrong side of the river if Turkey was to be our destination. We were, by now, thoroughly used to the Turkish way of doing things, and had long since ceased to wonder at anything peculiar.

The ability to think independently was not a mental faculty encouraged among the rank and file of the pre-war army, and those who may have possessed that trait had very soon realized the futility of developing it once they became prisoners of war. So far as we were concerned, we were merely so many animals of a different species that were being driven around the country that the populace might see for themselves that the much-vaunted prowess of the Sultan's Imperial Army was not mere idle boasting. In other words we were being taken on show in order to raise the morale of the people.

We knew neither the day nor the date, and our outlook was bounded by the probable distance of the day's march, the ability to keep going, and the possibility of rations at the end of it.

The first day out from Mosul was neither long nor arduous and I, for one, felt a certain pleasure at being on the move again and away from the pestilential barracks of Mosul.

For a few miles we were within sight of the river Tigris until its course lay from the west, then it was hidden from us and we continued our dusty way north.

The poor "Scottie" had to march for the first few hours with his arms tied tightly behind him, and he was so ill from

his brutal treatment overnight that he had to be supported
during that time. It was only after repeated pleadings on my
part to the Chaoush of the escort that he was released, and
after that he began to recover somewhat. This unfortunate
man was a grandfather, and his one topic of conversation
was the tales he would tell to the "wee bairns," his grand-
children. With his flaming red hair and his rich Gaelic brogue
he was a true son of Scotland, and bore his hardships and
sufferings stoically. More's the pity he suffered in vain; he
was left behind at a place named Islahie, in the Amanus
mountains, and there died, more from neglect than anything
else.

After about sixteen miles had been covered we halted at
the village of Fil-Fil, where we received the usual dole of
flour. As usual, also, we became the centre of attraction for
the curious villagers, though they were not so abusive as
at other places where we had stopped. The Chaoush and
his *askars* had not worried us unduly, though they had
occasionally whipped up the stragglers.

We slept that night on the bank of a stream whose waters
at that season had become a mere trickle, and into which
the refuse of the village had been thrown so that it was
thoroughly polluted. There was no other water for us to
drink.

The nights were becoming decidedly cooler though there
appeared very little abatement of the intense heat of the day.
On that and subsequent nights I became saturated with
dew as I had no covering other than the rags I wore. I
actually became used to it, and would sleep as though I were
in a comfortable bed! Fatigue had, no doubt, a good deal to
do with that. However, as soon as dawn came I was always
awake and anxious to get on the move again in order to get
warm.

The second day out was very much as the first, mile after
mile of shuffling over a dun-coloured waste. Sometimes we

passed over stony tracts that were cut by gullies that shewed signs of having recently held water, but for the most part the way was flat and dusty and at all times it was unbearably hot.

An incident occurred during the afternoon that proved our escort to be of the same vile clan as the others we had had.

The column had gradually become extended, due to the inability of the stragglers to keep up to the pace set by the mounted escort, and reached from horizon to horizon. Two or three Indians and myself were leading whilst the nearest *askar* was some three hundred yards behind us. Along the road came an old Arab, driving before him a donkey laden with water-melons. We who were in the lead stopped him and asked the price of his melons. They were very cheap and one of the Indians—a Sikh—had just bought one when the nearest *askar* came galloping up, shouting to us not to buy any. Knocking the old Arab roughly to one side he seized the straw panniers from off the donkey and tipped the melons onto the ground. Throwing the panniers back on to the donkey he ordered the Arab to get on his way, and, as the old man demurred, advanced threateningly upon him. Mounting his donkey the old man trotted back in the direction from whence he had come. The *askar* next ordered the Sikh to hand over the melon he had bought, adding that he would sell the fruit at the proper price! Having paid the Arab the Sikh not unnaturally protested, and would not comply with the order. Without the slightest hesitation the *askar* swung his rifle and brought the butt crashing down upon the Sikh's head. The small piece of rag that he had tied round the knot of his long hair was insufficient to protect his head from such a smashing blow, and he went down like a felled ox with blood pouring out of a wound in his head. We who had witnessed this brief drama stood appalled at the stark brutality of it, used as we were to scenes of violence. There was not the slightest excuse to warrant such an act, unless the thwarted greed of the *askar* could be said to warrant it.

By this time the majority of the column had collected, and the Indians had gathered around the Chaoush, loudly protesting against the *askar*. For the first time since we had left Samarah I saw signs of collective action against our escort. Thoughts of what to do, in the event of the Indians making an attack, raced through my mind. The Chaoush realized the danger and shouted to his *askars* to load their rifles, loading his own as he did so. Then he drove the protesting Indians from him by jabbing them in their middles with the muzzle of his rifle, his finger in the trigger-guard. The great moment had passed and, truth to tell, I was relieved. No one would buy the water-melons, and what the escort could not carry they smashed up with their rifles and ground the fragments into the dust with their heels. With shouts of "Yellah, yellah," we were made to march again and the Sikh was left where he had fallen. Several other Sikhs had knelt round the dead man during the hubbub in an attitude of prayer, and had removed from the body a talisman of some sort that was on the neck.

As I plodded along in the afternoon heat, after this incident, I ruminated on the fate that had brought us to such a pass.

We passed one or two small villages before nightfall, but we were not permitted to halt at them, instead we were being urged to make greater speed, and the whips became more active. Night came and we were still marching, hungry and very dispirited at the event of the afternoon. Before we finally reached the stopping-place for the night we must have covered well over thirty miles, a great feat of endurance for a party of sick, lame, and utterly weary men.

There was a great deal of shouting and many dogs were barking as we arrived at what appeared to be a village on a hill, the night being too dark to distinguish anything clearly. We were made to lie down outside the village, and told that we should get rations the next morning! Had we not passed a small stream a couple of miles back we should have been crazy with thirst as no water was given to us, and no one was permitted to go in search of any. Fortunately, our bodily exhaustion was greater than our hunger, and we soon fell asleep.

Several times during the night I was awakened by the cries of men who were being robbed, and I could do nothing but curl up and go to sleep again, knowing that I at least was safe, as I had nothing to lose! I was told the following morning that villagers had circled around the party all night long, no doubt watching for an opportunity to rob some unfortunate man who was fast asleep.

It was long after dawn when I was awakened to supervise the drawing and issue of rations, and the scene that met my eyes when I looked around was a great change from any I had seen formerly. The village sprawled, for the most part, at the foot of a sugar-loaf mound, one of several that could be seen at distant intervals in the landscape. In the background to the north ran a range of mountains, almost due east and west, and stretching as far as the eye could see. The air was clearer, though it was still as hot as farther south, and any slight breeze that blew caused a rush of hot air like that one experiences when an oven door is opened. However, the change of scenery was very welcome, and we all hoped that we should soon march out of the dreary wastes of Mesopotamia.

The name of the village was Simel, and the villagers were of a type which we had not met before. They wore conical, rimless felt hats, or coloured handkerchiefs wrapped turban-wise round their heads, with the fringes hanging over their faces, short-sleeved felt jackets over white shirts with sleeves so long that the ends were wrapped in an ungainly bundle round their wrists, and baggy, sailor-like embroidered trousers. These latter were held in place with huge knotted cummerbunds that served as repositories for daggers and small arms. Moccasins worn over gaily coloured stockings completed their outfits.

I listened to their talk and found that it was in a language I had never heard before. The Chaoush told me, after I had asked him, that these strange men were Kurds, and that we were now nearing their country. They seemed a very light-hearted crowd as they were continually laughing at something or other, and I was intensely interested in them.

After we had drawn rations we were told that we had another long march before us, and could either start that day or wait until the next morning, but if we stayed we should get no more rations where we were! We elected to stay until the next morning in order to give the sick a chance to recover from the gruelling march of the day previously, though it meant two days between meals.

Our escort always lived on the country, getting their meals and enough for the road from the villages at which we stopped, and did not care whether we stayed or not. They were mounted anyway, and would not feel the fatigue very much however long the march.

During the morning I went "on the scrounge" and fell in with a very amiable Kurdish family. I saw a woman making bread in the courtyard of a house so I ventured in and begged some of her. An elderly Kurd was sitting in the shade playing with two or three children and, when I salaamed him, he invited me to sit down beside him. The children were all eyes and chattered away, obviously asking questions about me. The Kurd could speak Arabic and I was soon busy answering questions. The woman came over to us and she was particularly interested in the designs tattooed on my arms. I explained how it was done in our country and she shewed me the crude blobs and lines on her arms. The old man gave me cigarettes to smoke and I had a meal of newly baked *chupattis* and water-melon. I discovered that quite a few words of Kurdish were akin to Urdu, and I soon picked up the names of various things. The woman impressed me by her free-and-easy manner and her ready laughter; she appeared to act as though she had as much authority as the man, a trait quite different from any we had met with among Arab women. After the meal the old man seemed inclined to sleep so I thought it advisable to leave them. They gave me two large *chupattis* and a generous slice of melon to take away with me; these I gave to Sergeant R., whom I had told that I was going after anything I could get.

Nightfall brought the curious sightseers around us again, as we sat at little fires we had made of dung and bracken. My Kurdish friend of the morning came along, bringing several cronies with him, and I answered many questions as I sat and smoked the cigarettes they gave me. Before they left for the night the old man gave me four roasted eggs, which I shared with my pal. Those eggs were the last meal we were to get for the next thirty hours.

In the chill of the early dawn and to the barking of the village dogs we left Simel on our way to Sakho, our next stopping-place. We managed to cover a good many miles before the sun became uncomfortably hot. Travelling in a north-westerly direction we gradually approached the mountains, which seemed about three thousand feet high at this point. The Chaoush said that we had to cross them before we reached Sakho, and during the early afternoon we ascended into the pass, through which an attempt had been made at road-building—something new in our experience. Although the ascent was not particularly steep it proved too much for many of our number coming, as it did, on the top of a long march. These poor fellows were severely beaten as they lay down in utter exhaustion.

At one point in the pass we passed a vineyard, a cultivated patch on the hillside with the vines standing up like bushes. The fruit was ripe and a party of Kurdish women were busy gathering it in—large bunches of luscious black grapes.

Several of us were lucky enough to get a bunch from those good women and, had the escort not hurried us onward with curses and blows, I fancy that all of us would have been given our fill. Even the women came in for their share of curses as a reward for their charity.

At last we reached the summit of the pass and commenced the downward journey that was to end shortly after at Sakho, on the river Kharbur.

We passed to the south of the small town and camped on the left bank of the river. A squad of soldiers relieved our escort, and we had to wait until the following morning before our wants were attended to. At least we had plenty to drink, even if the water of the river was polluted with the offal and filth from the town.

Donkeys laden with sacks of bread arrived the next morning, and it did not take us long to dispose of the black loaf we each received. The donkeys were utilized to carry the sick back into Sakho. Two men were placed on each donkey and, clinging desperately together, they left us, to what end no one could say, though most of us could guess.

Once more we got on the way, tramping along a dusty track that followed the winding course of the Kharbur. At a point just below a confluence of the Kharbur and one of its tributaries, we forded the river. It was a difficult crossing as there were many rocks in the river which caused the waters to swirl on to us at a fair pace, and it was rough going over the stones that formed the bed of the river. The river was not very deep, but even so several of our number were swept off their feet before they got across. Fortunately it was during the day so that wet clothes were not a great discomfort and the sun soon dried them.

After crossing the river we left it and once more headed north-west and, in the late afternoon, came to a fair-sized village where we halted for the night.

The same rations and the same gaping crowd of villagers

as usual were our lot. I was too tired even for foraging and, after cooking and eating my one *chupatti*, I curled up and went to sleep.

Morning found us cold and stiff and anxious to be on our way again. I was in excellent condition myself, but I was very sick of the continual marching, the continual gnawing of hunger at my vitals, and the long hours under a pitiless sun, usually without water to quench my raging thirst. Hardened as I had become I could not possibly keep it up indefinitely, and I was haunted by the fear that I too might succumb to some illness that would earn for me brutal beatings that were the portion of the sick prisoners on the march.

The Chaoush told me that we were making for the town of Jezerieh-ibn-Oman, where we should probably be put to work of some kind. He was very enthusiastic about the place and painted a word picture of it in very glowing colours. He told me also of the many Armenians that had been killed there, saying that the horse he rode had belonged to one of them, one whom he himself had dispatched, signifying the method of dispatch by drawing a dirty finger across his throat!

During the afternoon we reached the Tigris and continued near it until we eventually reached our destination. We passed several villages that were empty but shewed signs of recent occupation. These, we were told, were once the homes of some unfortunate Armenians.

On the outskirts of Jezerieh we halted to await means of transport over the river. This proved to be a *killick*, a raft made of poles with floats of scores of inflated goatskins. When we had all been ferried across we were taken to a sheep-pen that had been built into a hillside and roofed over with stone covered with turf. The entrance was low and narrow and the inside as dark as night. The floor was inches deep with sheep droppings and the stench was simply vile. Into this stinking place we were packed like sardines, and stayed there for over

Other Ranks of Kut　　　　　G

an hour, until our escort was relieved by soldiers from the town.

After being counted three or four times we were given a ration of flour from a stock the soldiers had brought with them, and then commenced a search for fuel. The soldiers were quite a decent lot, but they would not let us stray too far in our search, with the result that we had to be content with half-raw *chupattis*. The soldiers were even sympathetic, but they were unable to help us in the matter.

We were not put into the sheep-pen again so we slept just outside. The following morning I took a ration party into Jezerieh to draw our flour and salt as usual. Instead of taking it back to the party we carried it to a baker's shop in the heart of the town. The Onbashi who had accompanied us left me at the baker's to see that the whole of it was made into bread, and took the remainder of my party back.

That was a great stroke of luck for me. The baker, a huge bearded Arab, was a grand fellow. He allowed me to eat my fill of bread from his stock, and even brought me a large handkerchief full of grapes! It was the one bright episode of the whole ghastly march, and I have the liveliest recollections of the time I spent in the baker's shop at Jezerieh.

Shortly after the bread was drawn the Onbashi returned with a party to collect it, and I returned with him. Just before I left the shop the kindly baker pushed a hot loaf into my shirt front and cautioned me not to mention anything about it to the Onbashi or he might not give me my ration loaf. I was careful enough over that, as can be guessed, and my pal, Sergeant R., got the benefit of the extra bread.

For the first time for many long weeks I slept that night with a full stomach.

When I went to draw rations the next day, the Effendi who issued the flour called me into a store where a great pile of wheat lay on the floor. Inside he made the sign of the cross and, putting his fingers to his lips to signify that he was about to tell me a secret, said, "Armeni" (Armenian). Then he groped among the wheat and produced a broken brass crucifix, part of an altar ornament; this he gave to me, telling me at the same time to keep it hidden. I put it into my shirt front—the only place of concealment I had—as I had no wish to offend the man by refusing to take it, although I had no use for such an article. He next took me to another room where I was shewn a heap of torn vestments and broken church ornaments and religious pictures. These, he told me, were taken from the Armenian church in the town, after the Armenians who had taken sanctuary there had been massacred. He said that he had saved his own life by professing to turn Mohammedan, though actually he loathed them; to show how much he spat violently on the floor.

Hearing footsteps outside he commenced to shout "Yellah yellah," and pushed me along into the room that contained the flour, and where the remainder of my ration party were waiting for me. By the smug looks on their faces I guessed that they had not wasted the time they had been left in the flour store!

The Armenian continued to shout and bully, but he grinned at us so that we should understand that his shouting was only meant to be heard by the waiting Onbashi and soldiers outside.

Again I went to the bakery and the good baker and his assistant welcomed me boisterously. After a good feed I wandered out into the bazaar, where I met and made friends with two Turkish Chaoushlar (Sergeants). They bought me glasses of tea and a pile of grapes, and after I had disposed of those I sat and chatted to them on all sorts of subjects, smoking their cigarettes meanwhile. A little circle of idle listeners collected, and all of them were very pleasant to me and commiserated me on being a prisoner. Had we had the good fortune to have been kept at Jezerieh I think we should have had, at least for some months, a lenient time, as no one seemed to bear us animosity.

When I was ready to leave with the bread I received, in addition to an extra loaf, a lump of honey. True, it was all mixed up with bits of honeycomb and a few dead bees, but it was delicious to me all the same!

Early the following morning we were roused by our old escort and were marched to the river, which we recrossed.

The sick had been taken away to a small *serai* the first day after we arrived, so that we had little to worry us as, greatly refreshed after two days' rest, we headed north once more.

We had not covered many miles before the road became very rough and we got into hilly country with a high range of mountains facing us. Higher and higher we climbed until at times we were travelling on a bridle path. On one of these occasions we came to where the hillside was festooned with wild grape vines, loaded with ripe fruit. The Chaoush halted us and made us all sit down whilst the *askars* collected a large quantity of them. Then, to our utter amazement, they offered them to us *for sale*! This was even worse than their attempt to sell us the stolen melons, and words failed us with which adequately to express our loathing of those foul men. Failing to find any buyers among us they offered to exchange the grapes for articles of clothing or blankets. Again they failed and in their rage they lashed us to our feet and drove us onward.

Late that afternoon we came through a pass and into a long sweeping valley, running east to west. At the foot of the pass we turned left and in a short time came to a stone-built village, something new in architecture for us. Close to the village was a small rock plateau, and on this we were to camp. The villagers were Kurds and they lost no time in crowding round us, laughing and joking among themselves. The Kurdish women came along, too, and mixed freely with the men unveiled. That was a new departure from the Arab women of the southern villages. All at once the women noticed the Russians we had with us, and then a great shouting and jeering went up. The villagers became threatening and, pointing at the unfortunate Russians, kept drawing their fingers significantly across their throats. I was at a loss to account for this sudden change of attitude on their part and wondered why they took such great offence at the sight of Russians particularly.

The Chaoush and his *askars* moved about among the thoroughly enraged villagers, talking to them earnestly and gesticulating fiercely until they became calmer.

There were no official rations for us but the Kurds gave us all, with the exception of the Russians, plenty of fruit and a couple of *chupattis* each.

Later that night I chatted to one of the Kurds who could speak Arabic and learned the reason for the demonstration against the Russians. It appeared that when the Russian army defeated the Turks before Erzerum and entered the town, they had committed unspeakable atrocities on the inhabitants, many of whom were Kurds. Also in the fighting around Van and Erivan the Russians had been exceptionally cruel and bestial toward the Kurdish peasantry. I had no means of judging the truth of this at that time, but later on I mixed with hundreds of Kurdish refugees and they all told the same story, and I have learned since of the atrocities they committed on the Kurdish inhabitants of Rowanduz, a town not a great many miles from the Persian frontier.

The attitude of the Kurds towards the English members of our party was very friendly, and they condoled with us in being captives of the Turks, for whom, apparently, they had no liking. During my campaigning in Mesopotamia I had heard from various sources quite a lot about the cruelty of the Kurds, and perhaps they had earned an evil reputation, but I saw no evidence of it then or subsequently; in fact, my experience was the reverse.

I spent that night in a small cave, lying on a bed of dried sheep droppings, where it was considerably warmer than outside.

Crossing the valley next morning we ascended into the mountains on the opposite side. Climbing the bridle paths, hour after hour, soon caused a good many of the party to lag behind, and the escort got busy with their whips again, but they were unable to keep the column from becoming greatly extended. The Chaoush called frequent halts in order to get the party together, and he seemed to have an idea that the stragglers might attempt to escape into the hills. He gave orders to the *askars* that no one was to be allowed to stop for any purpose whatever, except he himself gave the order to halt. What that meant to those who were suffering from diarrhoea and similar complaints can be better imagined than described. Those sufferers were brutally maltreated, and had to be helped along by those of us who were less unfortunate, and some of the helpers were beaten if they did not move quickly enough to suit the escort.

The day came to an end when we reached an elevated plateau on which was the town of Sairt. Here we were met by a Turkish Bimbashi (Major) and a squad of Turkish soldiers, who led us to a barrack-like building and told us to rest in the quadrangle. Bread and water was brought immediately, and the sick were taken elsewhere.

As we sat and ate our bread the Bimbashi held an excited conversation with the Chaoush, but I was too far from them to hear what was being said. Eventually the officer strolled among us, looking extremely sympathetic and frequently saying, "Allah! Allah!" ("God! God!"), which words conveyed to me—with the expression with which they were spoken—"My God! what a sight!" He chatted for a time with the Russians, who by now were looking very much the worse for wear, and when he left them I got into his way in order to speak to him. I saluted and then asked permission to speak, which he readily granted. I said I was the Terjiman Chaoush of the party and would like him to give me some information as to our ultimate destination so that I could inform the others. I told him that our party numbered less than half of the original, including those who had joined us at Kirkuk and Mosul, and we were beginning to think that the policy of the Turkish Government was to have us marched around until we were all dead.

For a few moments he hesitated, and I had a horrible feeling that perhaps I had hit upon the truth. Then he said that he had not the faintest idea why we had been sent to Sairt as he had neither work nor food to give us for more than a day or two. The Chaoush had told him that his orders were to take us to Sairt, but what was to happen after that he had not been told. I complained bitterly about the brutality of the Chaoush and escort and asked that they might be punished. He sympathized, but beyond saying that we should see them no more gave no promise that he would bring them to account. I was not in a position to argue on the point, so I pointed out the condition of our clothing and asked whether we should ever get any or were we to continue until we were completely naked. He replied that he was unable to supply us, and that all he could do for us was to let us rest for a day or two and then send us elsewhere. I saluted and thanked him, and returned to my place.

When he had gone I told the party the gist of the conversation, and they were very despondent when they heard it. The Indians held long conversations on the matter, and I am convinced that more than one of them left us that night, for no guards were mounted over us.

I have often wondered whether the Bimbashi had arranged that opportunity for any who wished to escape. He did not count us on arrival or when we left, and at no time were we restricted as to our movements.

Although I huddled close to my friend the Sergeant, and

shared his sack blanket, I got very little sleep that night, for I shivered with the cold.

Early the next morning the Bimbashi sent for me and, after giving me a cigarette, told me that he had decided to send us on to a place called Nisibin. He drew a delightful picture of the charms of Nisibin, but I am afraid that I was not at all impressed by it, having heard the same sort of thing before. He explained that he had not sufficient rations to keep us until he heard from his superiors; in fact, he had only enough flour to spare that would make two more loaves each for us. He advised me that, as it would take us three days to get to Nisibin and there being no other ration depot on the road, it would be much better for us to leave that day. He made it quite clear that we could rest there another day if we wished, but that two more loaves apiece was the limit of rations we could get.

I said that I would ask the rest of the party what they would like to do, so he accompanied me to them. After I had explained the situation there was a good deal of grumbling, and a few were inclined not to believe what the Bimbashi had told me, especially with regard to his inability to feed us indefinitely. However, as the majority were in favour of leaving that day, provided the sick could remain, I told the Bimbashi that we had decided to leave as soon as he could give us the bread. He promised to look after the sick until they were able to leave, and left us to get the bread baked.

Before noon we were on our way, the Bimbashi having shaken hands with me and wished us all "Good luck." He had provided an escort of an Onbashi and four *askars*, all of whom seemed decent enough. They were Turks, and quite unlike any other escort we had had. There was neither bullying nor whipping, though the Onbashi said that it would be better for us to make as sharp a pace as possible, as Nisibin was a long way off, and we must get there in three days.

The going was very rough for the most part, and at one point we recrossed the Tigris by a very ancient and ramshackle bridge. We continued to march until midnight, and then lay down and slept until morning, when we started off again to continue steadily all day. There were very few halts and nearly everyone was able to keep going without assistance.

Towards night of the second day we reached a place called Midjat, where the escort halted us whilst they went in search of food for themselves, and we ate what was left of our bread. I have not mentioned that this particular escort was the first that had been unmounted, so that their pace was easier to keep than any previously.

Again we continued to march well into the night. At one point we passed over an area that was strewn with large black boulders, and it was laborious work twisting and turning along the narrow bridle path that led over this patch. The moon shone brilliantly, and it seemed when we were passing through those boulders that we were in a huge cemetery. We slept that night just where we halted.

The morning of the third day found us very tired and hungry, and we were not so anxious to start quite so early, but the Onbashi said that if we kept going as we had done we should reach Nisibin that night. So once more we got on the way.

By sunset we had left the hills and were following a track that led in a westerly direction over gently undulating ground. Here it was considerably easier, and we were able to march five and six abreast. Darkness fell and we plodded on in silence, thoroughly tired but determined to keep going until we reached Nisibin. For the first time since we had left Samarah the column resolved itself into formation by nationalities; the British leading, followed by the Russians, and then the Indians. The Onbashi chided me for being so silent (I had chatted to him most of the way up to that night) and told me to cheer up as Nisibin was quite close, and we

should be there within an hour or so; so, for the first time
also, I began to sing to help us on the way, and in a very
short time nearly all we Britishers were singing the old, old
soldier choruses. It was wonderful how much that helped us
to swing along that dusty track. After a time the singing
tailed off, and again we plodded on in silence.

The Onbashi said, "Why don't you sing, Terjiman?"

I replied that I was too hungry.

"Take this then, it is all that I have," and he gave me half
a *chupatti*. It was hard and dry, but it was grand eating to me.

Again I started the choruses and for a time we continued
to sing. When we fell silent the Russians started and, though
their songs sounded plaintive, they were infinitely beautiful,
and the harmonizing was wonderful. When they stopped we
gave them a cheer and asked them to continue, which they
did for another quarter of an hour. The Onbashi tried in
vain to get the Indians to sing also.

Suddenly someone shouted, "A light!" and sure enough
there was a faint light which seemed a long way off. We
became quite excited as we had begun to look on Nisibin as
a sort of Mecca. Heightened spirits flogged our aching limbs
to a smarter pace, and at long last we reached the Jag-Jag
river and the eastern boundary of the village.

No Roman legionary was happier to reach Nisibin—the
ancient Nisibis—than I was, though it was not until the
following morning that we received food. We slept on the
left bank of the Jag-Jag river that night—or what was left of
the night.

At daybreak a party of soldiers brought an issue of *chupattis*
to us, and shortly afterwards we were visited by a Turkish
Colonel, the Kaimakhan of Nisibin. He walked among us for
a few minutes, taking care not to touch anyone, and then,
after chatting to the Onbashi, strode off from whence he
came, the officers who had accompanied him strutting along
in his wake.

The Onbashi said that we were to remain two days where we were before going on to Ras-el-Ain, at which place we should entrain for Stamboul; meanwhile I must collect the sick during the afternoon and take them to the hospital in the town. He added that he and his *askars* were to return immediately to Sairt.

We were genuinely sorry to see the last of the Onbashi and his *askars* for they were all very decent fellows, and had been the only ones so far to show us any consideration on the march. Most of us shook hands with them before they left.

During the morning we were greatly surprised to receive a ration of flour, as we had already had *chupattis*, and we immediately started a hunt for fuel. It was very pleasant on the river-bank though there was not a vestige of shade. The soldiers prevented the curious from coming near us and they themselves were not unduly officious.

In the afternoon I collected the sick together, some nine or ten of them, one of whom was an Englishman who had gone into a coma, and took them into Nisibin on the way to the hospital. As we crossed the stone bridge over the river I was stopped by a huge negro, resplendent in the uniform of a German Sergeant-Major, and wearing a sun-helmet on the front of which was a heavy-looking brass eagle; a brass chain for the chin kept the magnificent head-gear in place.

In broken English the negro said that his officer wanted us and pointed to a mulberry-tree on the river bank, beneath the shade of which was a party of Germans, whilst close by stood a motor-lorry.

My little party limped painfully up to the Germans, two of us half carrying, half dragging the Englishman, who was past knowing or caring what was happening. We laid him in the shade and I saluted a German officer who sat in a deck-chair watching us. He acknowledged my salute and, through the English of the negro, asked me where we had been taken prisoner, etc. When I had told him, adding something of the treatment we had received, he expressed his sorrow at seeing Englishmen in such a state, and then gave us a few apricots and plums and a bread-ring each. He poured out a glass of lemonade and told me to give it to the man we had placed on the grass. I had to force it between the sick man's teeth and most of it was slobbered away. When I told the officer that I was taking the party to hospital he gave me two eggs which he said were to be given to the very sick man before I left him; then he motioned me to be off. I thanked him on behalf of my comrades and once more saluted, and then moved off to find the hospital.

The hospital was at the top of the town, and to reach it I had to pass through the bazaar, which was really the main road. It was very tantalizing to see the piles of fruit and foodstuffs, and the smell of it was enough to give us a feeling of nausea.

No one had escorted us and I had repeatedly to enquire the way until a gendarme took us in tow.

Arrived at the hospital we crossed a dusty yard in order to reach a small annexe where I was to leave the sick. The Arab orderly who took them over was a more than usually unprepossessing brute, and I was very thankful that I was not one of the sick and had to rely on such as he to look after me. Recrossing the yard I noticed a row of bodies lying in the sun near a mud wall. They were stark-naked and I noticed that one of them was heavily tattooed. I crossed over to them and saw that what I had suspected was true—they were dead Englishmen, at least three out of the seven were; the others may have been. It was difficult to tell as all their heads had been shaved quite bald, and all were deeply sun-tanned. Thinking that I recognized the tattooed body, I bent over it to look more closely and saw a faint twitching of the lips. I ran back to the annexe and told the orderly

THE RIVER KHARBUR AT ZAHKO

[See p. 96

THE DREARY WASTES OF MESOPOTAMIA

[See p. 38

THE BAZAAR, NISIBIN

[See p. 108

that one of the men outside was alive. He swore and spat at me and told me to clear out, but I threatened to tell the Kaimakhan if he did not have the man brought inside and looked after. At that he picked up a water-bottle and asked me to show him the man. Suspecting nothing I did so, and the Arab walked round to his head, and, forcing open his mouth, inserted the neck of the bottle inside. A few bubbles, a convulsive twist, and the poor fellow was dead, deliberately choked to death! It was horrible and I stood gaping until the orderly pushed me away and said, "Hussa moot, roo, roo" ("Now he's dead, go, go").

I could do nothing so I made my way back to the party, where I related what I had seen.

The rest of the day Sergeant R. and I spent in collecting fuel for the morrow's cooking. It was as well that we did so, as, in addition to the usual ration of flour, we received a small piece of mutton each. That was luxury indeed, and how we enjoyed it can be imagined when it is remembered for how long our diet had consisted of bread and salt.

I have never, since those days, blamed the Children of Israel for complaining of their daily ration of manna!

During the afternoon I was told that any other men who were too sick to march had to be taken to hospital, as we were to proceed at nightfall. Needless to say, after what I had seen and reported, there was none willing to report sick, though several were unfit to march, particularly the "Scottie."

At sunset we commenced the last lap of that terrific trek into captivity. We had left behind us a trail of dead and dying, as we traversed a road that had seen hundreds of our comrades sicken and die before us.

The first night out was uneventful, and we stopped for the day at a place called Serchikhan, where we got the usual ration of flour and salt.

During the second night we had a little excitement. About midnight the Onbashi of the escort suddenly halted us and told me to tell everyone to lie down flat. We did so, whilst the escort lay in the midst of us and loaded their rifles. I asked the Onbashi what was wrong, and he replied, "Shuf, Bedouwi!" ("Look, Bedouin!"). I strained my eyes in the direction he indicated and saw, dimly silhouetted against the starry sky, several horsemen. I admired the keen observation of the Onbashi, for I am sure that none of us had seen anything previously. After a few moments, as we lay wondering what would happen, a shot rang out and a bullet whined harmlessly over us. Our escort blazed away in the direction of the flash, firing one after the other and about five rounds apiece. There were no answering shots, and the horsemen disappeared, so after a few minutes' wait we got up and continued the march. Nothing else untoward happened and shortly after sun-up we arrived at a small, fort-like ration depot, garrisoned by twenty-odd men, where we were to stop for the day. Far away to the north we could see a range of mountains, and that sight was the only relief to the eye for miles. We were on a vast desolate plain, and I didn't covet the job of guarding that ration post.

We drew our flour and cooked our *chupattis* before we moved off again to a place several miles farther on beyond our present horizon, where was a tiny stream edged by a few lanky poplars on the outskirts of a mud-built village. It was far more pleasant and restful here than it would have been at the ration depot, and it was very soothing to be able to bathe our feet in the stream. Sergeant R. and I spent an hour or two searching for fresh-water crabs, and caught a dozen or more tiny ones. These we cooked and ate with watercress in lieu of bread!

The Onbashi decided that there was no further need to march at night and informed us that we could stay where we were until the following morning. I asked him what we should do for food, and he replied that we had no need to worry as, if we started early, we should get to the next place before night. It was not a case of worrying with us, but a case of starving. The meagre ration that we were getting was only sufficient to keep us alive, and it was a serious matter to miss a day, or even half a day. However, there was nothing we could do about it so we remained where we were until dawn, getting soddened with dew in the night by being so close to the stream.

The Onbashi had misjudged the distance for once, and by mid-day we had arrived at the next ration depot.

We had still two more days of marching, and I wondered how many would drop out of our party before they were ended. The majority were almost at the end of their tether, and I, too, was feeling the strain pretty badly, so much so that I have very little recollection of the next two days, beyond the endless plodding over a featureless plain under a grilling sun.

We arrived at Ras-el-Ain five days after leaving Nisibin, and were met by a ruffianly crew who beat the stragglers into some sort of formation so that we could be counted. More than one poor fellow dropped in his tracks only to be yanked to his feet and spat upon. Standing swaying like drunken men we were counted over and over again before we were marched to a low mud building near a river, where we were able to drink and rest. For rations we were given one foul black loaf between two men.

The next morning we had to carry water and firewood to where two huge cauldrons were set up. I was on the water-carrying gang and had to carry two heavy buckets a distance of four or five hundred yards. The *askar* in charge of us would not permit us to rest on the way, but playfully jabbed with his bayonet those that put down their buckets for a second. My arms were nearly pulled out of their sockets before those insatiable cauldrons were filled, and I received more than one jab from the bayonet. The bitterest part of the job was the knowledge that whatever was to be cooked none of us would receive a share. Nor did we, a sour gritty black loaf being our portion for that day.

After the bread had been issued the Hindus and Sikhs were taken away to join others of their race who were working at Ras-el-Ain, which was now the railhead of the Constantinople to Baghdad railway.

Left more or less to our own devices, several of us walked over to where the prisoners of war were camping. Nearly all of them were of the Kut garrison, and all were Indians of various races and religions other than Mohammedans. Their condition was truly pitiful. They resembled animated skeletons hung about with filthy rags. No tents or other shelter had been provided, and they were living in holes in the ground, like pariah dogs. To the fanatical Moslem Turk anything was too good for *giours* (infidels), and those unfortunate Indians were being treated far worse than even the Arab treats his animals. Scores of them were too sick to move from their holes, and I saw many who were obviously dying, yet I was told that they received no medical attention whatever. I chatted to a few of those men, and as we talked the tears streamed down their faces. These were loyal soldiers of the British Empire, and it was awful to think that this was the end of their service of devotion. They told me that if anyone was too sick to draw his rations himself he had to go without, and the normal ration was so small that it scarce sufficed to keep alive those that were working, so that they had none to spare for the sick. Despite that they *did* share their rations, with the result that they all suffered together.

We English of the party were very glad that we had not to stay at Ras-el-Ain, and hoped that conditions where we were to stay would be much better. We had still a lot to learn.

It was not until the third morning after our arrival that we were taken to the railway and entrained. We were packed into goods vans until it was impossible to get another man in and then the doors were shut and locked, leaving us in the

darkness of the interior. British and Indian—the Mohammedans of the party—were mixed together, and a percentage
of each van load suffered from stomach troubles.

We felt the train move out, and then began a nightmare
journey, a journey that made me long to get out and be on
the march again. Rattle clank, rattle clank, hour after hour
the train rumbled on whilst we stewed in an indescribable
stench; the polluted atmosphere of emanations arising from
our sick and unwashed bodies.

In vain we tried to ease our cramped limbs. On one
occasion I moved an arm and, in doing so, touched a haver-
sack belonging to someone. I immediately received a blow
in the face, a blow that had no force because there was no
room—fortunately for me—for the striker to use his weight.

"Who the blazes was that?" I asked angrily.

"Oh, it's ye, is ut?" answered a voice in a broad Scots
brogue.

"I thought it was some deil after ma bit gear," the voice
explained. I recognized the voice as belonging to an N.C.O.
of the Argyll and Sutherland Highlanders, one of the men
who had joined us at Mosul, and of a party that had been
captured during the attempt to relieve Kut. It was easy to
understand his action as kit meant something that one could
sell in an emergency in order to buy food, and the finer ethics
of comradeship did not apply to us all in those days. Dire
necessity was often an incentive to a man to take what he
could get, no matter to whom it belonged.

The shaking and jolting, combined with our inability to
remain standing for hours, caused us to slither into one heap,
limbs overlapping limbs, and in some cases limbs over
heads. It was simply ghastly!

At long last we felt the train slow up and jolt to a standstill.
There was much shouting and banging, and then the door
of our van was opened and we were told that any who wanted
could get out for sanitary purposes. Out we tumbled and

Other Ranks of Kut   H

found that it was late afternoon and that we had stopped outside a fort-like station. Guards with rifles at the "ready" lined the train, and refused to let anyone budge from the railroad. The ensuing scene was disgusting and degrading to both English and Indians alike.

Many of the sick collapsed on the track and had to be hoisted back into the vans, and a good many were now sick who had been comparatively well before they had been locked into those horrible goods vans.

In a very few minutes we were all hustled back and the doors clanged to behind us again. The train moved off, and by the time it stopped again—some two hours later—we had once more been jolted into a writhing heap. This time we were not let out and, after a time, concluded rightly that we had halted for the night.

I pass over the misery of that night, it can be only too well imagined.

At daylight the doors were unlocked, and we were allowed out for the same reason as before. The station at which the train had stopped was exactly similar to the other, merely a cube of concrete containing windows and doors, a most unlovely building. We seemed to be in a mountainous district but, beyond that, we had no idea whatsoever where in Turkey we might be. Before we were once more herded into the train we each received a sour black loaf.

Another day of durance vile until, at sunset, we had another breath of fresh air. The wonder was that all of us were not seriously ill by this time. Two dead men were removed from the van I was travelling in. When they had died no one knew, and it was not until we had all got out of the van that we had any idea that anyone had died.

We spent that night in the vans, and after a few hours' travelling in the morning the ghastly journey came to an end. Tumbling out of our temporary prisons a glorious vision of green-covered mountains and a grassy vale met our eyes, eyes that had become bloodshot and bleary by long hours spent in an abominable atmosphere and darkness. We were at Islahie, the terminus of the railway on the south side of the Amanus mountains.

It was wonderful to lie on the grass and rest our eyes on the dark green of the pine-clad mountainside.

We were left in peace for a couple of hours whilst the train was loaded with stores by a company of Turkish soldiers, who later entrained and left us. Then we drew bread and salt, our rations for the day.

It was here that the increasing truculence of the Mohammedans of our party brought an end to the patience of the sorely tried Britishers. Some trivial incident concerning the drawing of rations caused loud and belligerent cries from the Indians against the English, and in a few minutes a free fight was in progress, which brought the guards running from a wooden shack near the line. The mêlée was brought to an end before much damage was done, but the English were blamed for the affair.

It was here also that the Scot who had joined us at Mosul, and had received such brutal treatment there, left us to go into hospital where he was eventually to die. Several others were too sick to continue and they too went into hospital, leaving a very small party indeed to finish the march.

Shortly after midday we were "yellahed" into a column and started to march into the foothills of the mountains. A new escort accompanied us, and they told me that we should soon be among our comrades who had come along weeks before.

Within half an hour of our start we came unexpectedly upon a party of six Englishmen who were quarrying rock for road repair work. Two of them were acquaintances of mine and in the few brief minutes that we were able to exchange news I gathered that the majority of the Kut prisoners were at a place of evil repute named Bagtchi and were having a very thin time. My joy at being on the march again, after the awful train journey, was dispelled at that piece of news, and the few details those men were able to tell me of the horrors of the labour camp they were at. Apparently our life as prisoners was to be one continual round of ghastliness and death.

We left them and came to a fairly well-made road that turned and twisted its way up the mountain-side. Darkness came, but we continued to pad along, puffing and blowing as the ascent became steeper. Occasionally, parties of soldiers passed us going in the opposite direction, followed by crazy *arabahs* that raised clouds of dust that covered us with a white film and half choked us. Somewhere near the summit of this 5,000 feet high pass we reached a roadside spring, where we halted to quench our thirst. That was the first water we had encountered since we commenced, and we were sorely in need of it.

After that the going was much easier and we were able to notice our surroundings in the light of the moon. Here and there could be dimly seen houses, perched high up on the mountain-sides, and at one point we passed through a village, a village that was as silent and as still as the dead.

Our escort allowed us an hour or two to sleep before dawn, and then we continued along a road that climbed and dipped, twisted and turned its tortuous way among the overhanging peaks. High above us we saw the remnants of ancient castles, perched dizzily on the rocky peaks—all that was left in these parts of the Byzantine empire. Far below us, on our left, we could hear the noisy waters of some mountain stream crashing its way along a boulder-strewn bed. It was a tantalizing sound as we were once more gasping with thirst, and there appeared to be very little chance of quenching it as we came across no other spring that day.

At one point we could see, far away to our right, a defile, at the end of which was a dark patch which our escort said was a tunnel mouth, and the place where the prisoners were working. Near by we could see a number of tents and huts and we wondered whether we could see in them the end of our journey.

The descent assumed a sharper angle and we saw below us the railway and a cluster of buildings. We reached the valley and were at last able to quench our thirst at the stream that had noisily promised us that pleasure for many an hour.

A small party of soldiers met us here and held a confab with our escort, the result of which caused us some surprise. The Indians—now all Mohammedans—and the Russians were taken away from the party and marched off towards the mountains in the east, whilst the remainder—all English— continued on to the railway and the buildings we had seen earlier that morning.

So we arrived at Mamourie; ten Englishmen out of a party of one hundred and fifty Britishers, Russians, and Indians, to leave Samarah. Some had died by the wayside, others had been killed on the road, some had been taken away from us, and many had been too ill to continue.

CHAPTER FIVE

A BID FOR FREEDOM

TEN utterly weary Englishmen dumped their odds and ends outside the railway station of Mamourie and sat to await the next move of an unkind Fate. Ten men who had marched nearly eight hundred miles; across the wastes of Mesopotamia, on into the rugged hill country of Kurdistan, along the desert marches of Syria, to finish on the fringe of the plains of ancient Cilicia.

I gazed wearily at the scene. There was a conglomeration of huts, outbuildings, tents, and fruit stalls, etc., but no sign of a town or village. A large brick building near the railroad track I rightly concluded to be an engine shed. There was nothing to inspire me or to raise my drooping spirits.

I turned to look at my companions. We were a sorry-looking crowd, dressed in the ragged remnants of what had once been Indian drill uniform, and odds and ends of rags picked up *en route*. Bearded and with long uncombed hair, sun-blackened and fearfully emaciated, we looked anything but what we were, soldiers of His Britannic Majesty's Imperial Army, albeit prisoners of war.

Our escort—reduced to one decrepit Turkish soldier—had left us, after telling me that no one was to move from where we were until his return.

I amused myself in turning over all that I possessed. Little enough in all conscience, but all very valuable to me. An old sack containing a battered and rusty tin, a broken crucifix, and several old bits of rag, which I used to cover my bare feet when the going had been more than usually rough, completed my inventory of possessions.

Again I gazed at the scene, and wondered whether the

askar had gone to get us rations or had merely gone to get food for himself.

We sat on and on, but still there was no sign of our escort returning, so, desperately hungry, I determined to try and interview the Commandant of the place. It did not take me long to find his quarters, for they were conspicuous by reason of the Turkish emblem of misrule—the Crescent and Star—that flew over them.

On approaching the door my way was barred by a sentry, a dirty-looking ruffian who, if only because of his dress, deserves some mention. His uniform—save the name—consisted of a pair of very baggy trousers and shapeless coat made of sack-like material, dyed green. Most of this outfit was covered with multi-coloured patches, sewn on with coloured worsted with stitches of half an inch in length. His coat was buttonless and revealed the fact that he wore no shirt. Supporting his voluminous trousers was a piece of machine-gun belt, into which was stuck half a dozen different makes and sizes of cartridges. On his feet were a pair of dilapidated slippers; a filthy rag, wound turban-wise around a shaven poll, completed his outfit.

He had been eating garlic and, after taking stock of him, I decided that he was altogether an unpleasant person, particularly when I caught a whiff of his odour.

Without waiting for an answer to his question as to what I wanted, he raised his rifle and told me to "yellah." I told him that I wanted to see the Commandant and, furthermore, that I *was* going to see him! Then followed a wordy argument in which I was variously called a dog, brother, ass, and infidel. I was alternatively abused and cajoled as I shewed no signs of going away. Becoming impatient at this delay I dodged by that "ragtime" soldier and dived into the Commandant's quarters.

Seated crossed-legged on a rickety stool in a filthy room was an elderly Bimbashi, feasting on bread and water-melon, and spitting the seeds on the floor.

"Greeting, Effendi," I said, as he looked up.

"So you want food, do you?" he queried, without returning my greetings.

Obviously he had overheard my argument with the sentry, who was now in the room endeavouring to explain how I came to get inside. His explanations were cut short by a curt "Iscut" ("Silence") from the Commandant.

The sight of food served only to increase my hunger, and I commenced telling my tale of woe, emphasizing that we had had nothing to eat for two days, and that our escort had apparently deserted us. The Commandant listened to me without a word, continuing to eat his fruit and spit out the seeds. When I concluded he said nothing to me but ordered the sentry to bring along the baker. The baker duly arrived and received instructions to issue two days' bread and salt to our party. I was dismissed by a wave of the Commandant's hand, and I returned to where I had left the others, greatly elated at my success.

We became almost hysterical when we received two large loaves apiece and, despite the coarseness of them, fed right royally. This particular bread was peculiar stuff, quite unlike anything that we had had hitherto, and was made of what seemed to me to be the flour of unhusked black rye and millet. The quality did not concern us very much, enough that we had something to eat, and the loaves weighed nearly three pounds apiece—though the size of them belied their weight!

Only those who have experienced the horrible pangs of semi-starvation can really appreciate the avidity with which we ate that gritty, glutinous, black bread. The baker sent us a large pannikin of water to help wash down the bread and to round off our meal.

Our opinion of the Commandant ranked high, but it was to undergo a sudden change, and that within a very short time.

We had made ourselves comfortable in anticipation of

remaining where we were for the night, and several were asleep, when the Commandant appeared, accompanied by four Arab *askars* who were equipped for the road.

"Goom, goom, blaghil," he cried, as he approached us. ("Get up, get up, quickly.")

I scrambled to my feet and, saluting, inquired his wishes.

"I am sending you to Bagtchi, at once," he informed me.

"But we are all sick, Effendi," I protested.

"What matters, if you remain here I shall have to feed you. Get the others up and get on the move quickly," was his rejoinder.

To get to Bagtchi from Mamourie would, I guessed, take us all night, and my heart sank as I thought of what we had been told to expect there. Blank despair was registered on the faces of my companions as I interpreted the orders of the Commandant, so I advised them to follow my lead and back me up in refusing to go.

I turned to the Commandant and again protested that most of us were too sick to march that night, but that we might be well enough to proceed in the morning. He would have none of it and insisted that we get going immediately. Then I told him that we refused to go, and I was promptly knocked sprawling among my companions. I continued to protest from where I lay until he threatened to shoot us if we did not get up, even going so far as to order the *askars* to load their rifles. Not in the least impressed by his threats I told him to carry on and shoot us as we were unable to march in any case! Cursing and swearing he kicked me in the stomach before calling off his *askars* and striding off in the direction of his hut.

We were still debating the position when the *askars* returned and, taking off their packs, prepared to spend the night beside us. Addressing myself to the least repulsive of them I inquired what his instructions were. He told me that the Commandant had decided to let us stay where we were until morning, when we should be taken to Bagtchi, without receiving any more bread at Mamourie. From what this *askar* told me after that I came to the conclusion that the escort would have been better pleased had they been allowed to have shot us off hand. That would have satisfied their lust for killing and have removed the necessity for marching to Bagtchi with us.

I engaged the *askar* in conversation for some time, a one-sided affair for the most part, as he was very fond of his own voice. He went to great lengths to impress upon me that the English were mad when they thought that they could defeat the Turks.

"Why!" he exclaimed, "how did they expect to win when we have such a wonderful thing as that in our country," and he pointed to the railway.

Imagine trying to explain the elaborate railroad systems of England to such a man.

The remainder of my party were well asleep when night fell, and it was not long before the sentries followed suit. I, too, was not long in following their example, so that I should be fresh enough for the day's march on the morrow.

It must have been after midnight when I suddenly awoke, from no apparent cause. My pal the Sergeant was lying on his stomach busily chewing bread. Seeing me move and awake he motioned me to be silent. Wondering what was in the wind I turned over on to my stomach and looked around me.

We were in a circle of light thrown by an arc-lamp in the station yard. Not a soul was to be seen, other than our own party and escort, and all was very silent. The *askars* were curled up under their overcoats and apparently fast asleep, whilst the rest of our party were definitely asleep.

The edge of the circle of light just reached to the scrub and bushes surrounding the station buildings; beyond was blackness.

Presently the Sergeant whispered, "What about making a bolt for it?"

I pondered that for a few minutes and then said, "Where should we go if we managed to get clear away, and how should we get food?" and half a dozen other questions that crowded to my mind.

He replied to them all by pointing out that no condition could possibly be worse than our present one, and that the question of food could be no harder to answer than the matter of food had been all the way up.

Not knowing what the future held for me I agreed that he was right, and that I was willing to take a chance.

We chatted in whispers for a little while, discussing the first problem—how to get away from where we were without being seen. I decided that the best plan was to get up quietly and walk boldly into the scrub. I said that if anyone saw us and asked us where we were going we could easily say that we were going to the latrines.

The Sergeant agreed with me and, without further delay, got to his feet and walked out of the light into the darkness of the scrub. No one moved or called out and I concluded that he had not been seen. Securing my sack around me I waited a few moments before, watching and listening, I got to my feet and followed him. As I passed one of the sentries my heart pounded my ribs, and I was deadly afraid that he might waken and see me. Trembling with apprehension I reached the cover of the bushes and waited for some signal from the Sergeant. A low hiss directed me to him, and we shook hands in silence before plunging off into the darkness.

During my conversation with the *askar* I had learned that the nearest town of any size was Adana, which lay some two days' march to the west, so it was in that direction that we went as we pushed our way through the bushes for the first half an hour. The Sergeant said that the next place to Adana was Tarsus, and after that the Mediterranean seaboard near Cyprus.

He certainly knew a good deal more of the geography of the country than I, for I had no idea where the exact spot of either town might be; in fact, I only connected Tarsus with an episode in the life of St. Paul.

After a brief discussion we decided that the sea might offer some means of escape from Turkey, so we pushed on in the general direction of Adana.

Another half an hour of pushing our way through bushes and brambles, and then suddenly we came on to the railway, and discovered to our great dismay that we were within five hundred yards of Mamourie. We had gone round in a semi-circle. Cursing our luck we made off at right-angles to the railway, scratching ourselves badly in our haste to get farther away from the station.

All through the remaining hours of darkness we continued on without a moment's rest. The memory of that first night of freedom will always remain with me. It was a perfect nightmare and, although I endured worse on subsequent occasions, no other night march affected me like it. We threw ourselves down at the slightest rustle of the bushes or long grass, and whenever a shadow darker than the normal surroundings came into view we made a big detour to avoid it, although it might only have been a rock or a bush. On one occasion we were confronted by a forest of "tiger" grass of great height and, not knowing where the ends of it might be, we pushed our way into it only to find our way barred by a stream. We had no idea how deep the stream was and we clung desperately together as we gingerly trod our way across it. Fortunately, it was not very deep, and we got across without much trouble. After an hour wandering about in that grass we came abruptly into the open and on to a rough track.

For a time we followed the track until the braying of an ass sent us scuttling back into cover again.

So we continued until we reached the foot of a low range of hills, where we began a search for a place where we could lay up for the day. Before long we came to a tiny stream with banks covered with long coarse grass, and there we decided to stop.

We had only such bread as each of us had saved from the two loaves we had received at Mamourie, so we thought it wiser to save that until nightfall, making do with a long drink from the stream. Curling up in the long grass we fell quickly into a deep sleep, completely tired out with our trekking and excitement. I awoke several times in the afternoon craving sustenance, and it was with the utmost difficulty that I was able to resist the temptation to eat what little bread I had.

The sun was sinking over the distant mountains as we sat by the stream and ate our frugal meal before once more taking to the road. We were very jubilant and optimistic for the future and, I am afraid, patted our own backs in appreciation of the manner in which we had eluded the Commandant of Mamourie. We had much to learn.

The fact that we had no food left after we had disposed of our bread did not worry us at all, neither did the prospects of getting any in the near future. I told the Sergeant that, even though it might be risky to beg in the villages, I had done so before with success and could do so again. One thing did worry us greatly and that was the health of the Sergeant. As I have stated before he was subject to periodical attacks of malaria, and to get an attack under our present condition would be fatal. The long march from Samarah had weakened his powers of resistance to the fever, and I was greatly afraid when he said that evening that he was not feeling any too good.

We waited until it was quite dark before we set off again as we were too close to Mamourie to risk travelling in the open in case anyone had been sent out to search for us.

Before it was quite dark we had noted a track running along

the foot of the hills, and when we did start we made a bee-
line for it and, having reached it, found the going very much
easier.

For a couple of hours all was well and we made steady
progress, then the Sergeant called a halt, saying that he felt
considerably worse. He had a slight touch of ague—the
preliminary to a bout of malaria—and a bad headache. We
sat and discussed the matter until he said that he would try
and keep on until daylight, when perhaps he could sleep it
off. So off we went again, with the Sergeant in the lead.
Occasionally he stumbled, and I guessed that he was having
a rough time of it, but I was powerless to help him. Eventually we came to a stream, and I found that he had lost the
ague but had developed a temperature. He drank pints of
water and slashed some over his head in an attempt to lower
his temperature. When he was somewhat refreshed we
started off again, very much against my wishes, as I considered that he would have benefited by resting near the
stream for the rest of the night.

The track led us on to a rough road, which we guessed
might be the road to Adana, and along this we trudged for
another two hours. It was ankle-deep in dust and we became
parched with thirst long before we came to the next water.
The Sergeant was staggering along like a drunken man, and
several times I urged him to give up, but to no purpose; he
was determined not to let me down, as he said.

There could only be one end and, at last, he collapsed into
the dust of the road. I dragged him off the road and on to
the grassland that bordered it. It was pitiful to hear him
moaning for water as I sat wondering what to do next.
Although I hated to leave him I felt that I must go in search
of water, so, covering him with my sack and his own, I set
off on my search. I described concentric circles in my search
but was unsuccessful, and daylight came with me still
searching.

. About half a mile away I could see, at the foot of the hills, a village, and I determined to go boldly over and try to get milk or assistance for the Sergeant. Whether we were retaken or not did not matter as the chances were even that he would get some sort of treatment, whilst now he was getting none.

As I drew near to the village I found that the surrounding land was under cultivation and there were large vineyards. Fig-trees and tall poplars grew around the village and a small mountain stream passed through it.

I reached the first house without encountering a soul and walked boldly into the little mud-walled compound. Sitting outside the doorway of the house were two women busily engaged in grinding corn. I addressed them in Arabic and asked for water, making descriptive gestures to make clear my meaning, in case they did not understand Arabic. Without a word one of them got to her feet and disappeared inside the house to return with a large wooden bowl of *libn*. Thanking her I gulped down a couple of pints of that wonderful drink, for I, too, was desperately in need of a drink. Seating myself on the ground about three yards away from the women I asked them if they understood Arabic, but they both said, "Nay sani," which was Kurdish for "Don't understand." I tried Hindustani and the few words of Kurdish that I knew until one of them said something to the other and then went upon the flat roof of the house and called out, "Ali-ee-ee!" in a piercing voice. I got to my feet nervously, wondering what sort of reception I should get from Ali, whoever he might be. He soon appeared, striding through the gateway of the compound, a tall, bearded Kurd. I stood still until the women had spoken to him, and then ventured a "Salaam Aleikum" ("Peace be on you").

"On you be peace," he answered, as he came towards me the better to look me over.

I was pleased to see that he was an elderly man as my experience had taught me that the young "bloods" of the

East were inclined to be hard and callous and hasty in coming to conclusions.

"Who are you?" he asked in Arabic.

"An escaped prisoner of war, English," I replied.

Without a word he strode over to the gate of the compound and shut it, and then motioned me to sit down before telling me to explain. Thinking of the Sergeant I rapidly and briefly told him why I had dared to come begging for help, pleading that he would help me do something for my pal who was lying away outside. Ali spoke to the women after I had finished, and then ensued much gabbling and gesticulating on part of the three of them. I waited impatiently, hoping against hope that they would help me with the Sergeant. At last Ali turned to me and said, "Take me to your friend."

Knowing that the Sergeant would be half crazy with thirst by now, I asked for something to drink to take with me. A gourd of *libn* was brought and off I went, with Ali close to my heels.

I had some difficulty in finding the Sergeant as he had crawled away from where I had left him, probably in search of water. When we did find him he was moaning feebly and delirious. I managed to pour some of the *libn* into his mouth whilst Ali sat watching me, occasionally muttering, "Allah! Allah!"

I asked the Kurd whether he would help me carry the Sergeant to a place where we should be near to water. He did not answer at once but appeared to be thinking, then he got to his feet and, picking up the Sergeant like a baby, strode off in the direction of the village, saying just one word, "Taal" ("Come").

Arrived back at the house Ali placed the Sergeant on a sheepskin that was spread in the shade of the wall, and told the women to bring water. When they had brought it he helped me to give the Sergeant a bath—or at least a sponge over—which seemed to ease him quite a lot. After that I got him to drink some more *libn* before I covered him up with our sacks and left him in peace.

I was desperately tired, as I had been up all the night marching and searching for water before I had gone to seek aid, and I was almost asleep as I sat thanking Ali for his great kindness. The old chap noticed this and told me to lay down and sleep if I wished as we should have plenty of time to talk later on. I lost no time in taking him at his word.

It was quite dark when next I awoke, considerably refreshed and very hungry, which latter could scarcely be wondered at seeing that I had had only a hunk of dry bread for the past two days, unless the *libn* could be counted as food.

Seated around a charcoal fire I saw half a dozen grey-bearded Kurds, earnestly debating some problem, and I wondered whether my friend and I were part of that problem.

I rose to my feet and approached them, giving the customary "Peace be on you" as I did so. The returning "On you be peace" seemed fairly unanimous so I sat down near to friend Ali, observing as I did so the women busy at some cooking pots over a nearby fire. Several children were with the women and gazed at me with wide-open eyes as I sat in the circle of men.

For several moments no one spoke as all the Kurds sat and scrutinized me closely, then one old chap asked, "Are you Osmanli?" (Turk).

"No, Ingleezi" (English), I replied.

Several grunts replied to this, and there was continued staring before the next question was asked.

"Why are you here, and in rags?" queried the first speaker.

Without more ado I told them as well and as briefly as I could how and why we had left the loving care of our hosts the Turks. I told them of the rough treatment we had received and the starvation rations that had been our portion.

Other Ranks of Kut   I

I pointed out that though we were of the despised *Nasara*
(Christians) we were people of the "book" and soldiers, and
our treatment was not in accordance with the teaching of the
prophet Mohammed. Whether it was or not I didn't know,
but I guessed that in all probability my audience were no
wiser! They listened to my tale without interruption, except
to occasionally interject "Allah!" or "Kaffir!" ("Infidel") at
various points of my story. When I had finished Ali interpreted for those Kurds who did not understand Arabic. As
he was talking the Sergeant moaned, so I got up and went over
to him and asked how he was feeling.

"Pretty rotten," he replied; then, "Where are we?"

As rapidly as possible I outlined the events of the day and
told him not to worry, as I thought that we should be treated
all right by the Kurds. I made signs to the women, who were
watching me, that the Sergeant wanted a drink, and they
quickly brought some *libn*. After he had taken a deep drink
the Sergeant told me to get back to the Kurds as he would
be all right, and I could tell him later what they had said.

I returned to the fire and Ali asked me how my sick pal
was getting on. I told him that he was much refreshed by his
sleep and the *libn* but was still very ill. The old chap asked
me when I thought of continuing our journey. This was a
poser and I thought for a few moments before I answered,
as much depended on what I said. Then I said: "If it is
the wish of Ali that we leave now, then we will go, though
only God knows how far my 'brother' will get in his
present condition. We thank you for your kindness to us
and shall leave with good thoughts in our hearts for the
Kurds."

To which Ali replied, "When you desire to go, go in
peace; until then you are my guests."

There were grunts of approval from those who had understood, and then the old chap pointed out that should we be
discovered by the Turks then Ali would be beaten and

thrown into prison and his house probably burned to the
ground.

I could readily understand that!

The old chap further informed me that all the young men
of the village had run away to the mountains to avoid being
taken for military service, so that Gendarmerie were
constantly patrolling the district on the look-out for them.

I began to feel uneasy, and hated to think that we might
be the cause of disaster to Ali and his women after their
goodness to us. I said as much to the old man, and asked
what I could do under the circumstances. He replied that
providing we left as soon as the Sergeant was fit they would
all assist in concealing our whereabouts from the Turks. I
thanked him as well as I could and solemnly shook hands
with them all.

That concluded the palaver and they rose to their feet
and picking up the brazier ascended to the roof of the house,
inviting me to follow them. A low mud wall surrounded the
roof-top, and in one corner was a water ewer and copper jug.
Here we all washed our hands and feet before sitting on a
large woollen rug that was spread over one portion of the
roof.

Very shortly the women arrived, bearing a huge copper
dish of *pilaff* (prepared wheat and mutton), a stack of *chupatti*s,
and a wooden bowl of *libn*. The food was placed before us
and we took up our positions round the common dish. At
this period I was not an adept at eating such a mess with my
fingers; notwithstanding, I think I did fairly well, and I
know that I did justice to the fare. Ali asked me whether the
Sergeant would be able to eat some of the *pilaff*, but I said
that some hot milk would do him greater good. He immediately shouted out something in Kurdish to the women—who
had gone below whilst we were eating—and the Sergeant told
me later that he had had as much hot milk as he could drink.

When we had finished eating the women removed what

we had left and we once more washed our hands before returning to sit on the rugs. For a time I was kept busy answering questions until, one by one, the old Kurds had all left us. Ali and I continued to chat for a little longer whilst the women brought up padded quilts and sheets of thick brown felt. I was given a quilt and a felt and told that I could sleep on the roof or down below with my friend. I preferred to remain on the roof, but I went down to the Sergeant first to see how he was getting on. He was well covered up, and said that he was very comfortable, and had no wish to go on to the roof. We discussed our good fortune before I returned to the roof and to bed.

The air was quite cold but wonderfully refreshing after the heat of the day, and I spent the best and most comfortable night that I had had for many months. I decided that I should be quite contented to spend the rest of my period as a prisoner of war with Ali Agha and his good women!

For nearly two weeks we stayed with the Kurds, each day being, more or less, a repetition of the first. On several occasions one or other of the old men came and warned us that the *askari* (soldiers) were about, and then we hid inside the house under a pile of bedding, in fear and trembling that we should be discovered. I used to do any little job that I could in an endeavour to repay Ali for his kindness. The women were greatly amused when I took a turn with the primitive churn. This consisted of a goatskin—turned inside out—slung between a tripod of poles. The milk was churned by jolting the skin to and fro; a monotonous and laborious task. As the butter formed it was squeezed out of the neck of the skin in balls the size of cricket balls, and I noticed that it contained quite a few hairs from the inside of the skin!

There were three children of the household; two small boys and a girl of ten, and these I used to amuse in various ways and became a great favourite. The women were greatly pleased at my attitude towards the children, and were ever ready to provide me with odd tit-bits of food. I grew quite fond of the members of that Kurdish family, and have ever since had a warm spot for the Kurds, their faults notwithstanding.

Meanwhile the Sergeant gradually recovered until, at last, he was able to take the evening meal with us on the roof. Most nights one or other or several of the old men joined us on the roof, and I got into friendly arguments about religion or some other subject.

The day came all too quickly when we considered that the Sergeant was able to take to the road once more. Another week would have done him a lot of good, but we decided that to stay any longer would be an imposition on our good friends. When we announced our intention of leaving, Ali protested that it was too soon! We had anticipated that he would adopt that attitude, and told him that we were determined not to embarrass his household a day longer than we could help. After a good deal of protesting on Ali's part, it was arranged that we leave after the evening meal the following night.

That last meal with the kindly Ali and his family and the other old Kurds—who had arrived to bid us farewell—will live long in my memory. I did not enjoy it near so much as I had the first, for I was not so very hungry as on that occasion, and I was thinking all the time of what lay in store for us once we had left the comparative security of Ali's house. At last it was over, and we commenced our leave-taking. Very little was said on either side among the men; the women were openly distressed and the children embraced us.

To my last "Fi imman Allah" ("Good-bye") there was returned a hearty "Allah wiuk" ("God be with you"), and a parcel of bread and a few knobs of very hard cheese was thrust into my hands.

It was with heavy hearts that we trudged the dusty road

to Adana that night, and for several hours we scarcely spoke, each busy with his own thoughts. The Sergeant was not feeling fit enough for a long march, and as soon as he became tired we looked for a suitable place to hide up for the day.

Several times during the first day out he complained of not feeling well, but expressed the opinion that the chill night air would no doubt brace him up. I was very worried, for if he fell ill again it was not to be expected that we should be so fortunate in finding friends. He had good reason to complain as he had suffered a pretty severe bout of malaria, and had no weapon but Nature to combat it, and his constitution had been seriously impaired by the rough treatment he had previously suffered.

We waited until dark before we set off again, keeping for the most part to the open road, though we occasionally scurried into cover when we heard—or thought we heard— someone coming. About midnight the Sergeant fell silent, and I guessed that he was not feeling well, as we usually chatted in whispers as we plodded on through the darkness.

I imagined that we should have been quite close to Adana, but beyond the fact that we were in a cultivated area there was no sign of any town.

All at once the Sergeant collapsed and I bent over him in great alarm. He said that he was dead beat and feeling very weak, so we decided to get off the road and remain there for the rest of the night and search for cover at dawn, by which time the Sergeant thought that he might be recovered. I half carried, half dragged him well off the road, and then we both lay down to await the dawn, but we both fell asleep.

CHAPTER SIX

RECAPTURED

I was awakened by the sun shining on to my face, and I sat up to see where we were. To my great alarm I found that the nearest cover was over three hundred yards away, and that we were in a most exposed position where we were. I roused the Sergeant and told him that we should have to get to cover as hastily as we could. We got to our feet, and were making for a patch of scrub that I had seen in the distance when I saw two mounted figures coming towards us, about half a mile distant. The Sergeant did his best to hasten but he was in worse shape than he had been during the night. A bullet whined its way over us, and I turned to see the horsemen galloping straight to us. We could do nothing but stop and hope that we might be able to bluff them. That hope soon died for the horsemen proved to be Gendarmes.

When they reached us they jumped from their horses and at once commenced to beat us with their whips, those same horrible whips that I have mentioned previously. Unseen by me an old Arab had come up behind us as we were being beaten, and he assisted the Gendarmes by hitting me full in the face with a knobkerrie, knocking me temporarily unconscious. My nose was completely smashed from the blow, and has been a disfigurement ever since, despite the attentions it received after I reached England.

When I became conscious again I shouted "Ingleezi, Ingleezi," so that there could be no mistaking us for absconding recruits or conscription-dodging Kurds.

The end had come to our spell of freedom with a vengeance and it was as well for our peace of mind that we could not foresee the future.

In answer to their questions I told the Gendarmes that we were escaped prisoners of war. There was nothing else to tell them. I, for one, had no wish to be taken as a deserter, and we were practically unrecognizable as Englishmen. That, no doubt, accounted for the beating we had had when the Gendarmes first came up. We were both wearing sheepskins across our shoulders—presents from Ali—and they had made us look more like natives than our beards and sunblackened complexions.

The Gendarmes were highly delighted when they discovered that they had captured would-be escapees, and proceeded to bind our arms securely behind us, cursing the English as they did so. When we were trussed up to their satisfaction and our extreme discomfort, they remounted and ordered us to march in the direction from whence they had come.

The Sergeant very soon staggered and fell and as one of them lashed him I protested that he was very ill and could not march. They quickly remedied this by tying us together, so that if he stumbled I should either prevent him from falling or go down myself. I was feeling very groggy from the effect of the blow I had received, and cannot imagine now how I managed to keep up as well as I did. The bestial policemen amused themselves by urging forward their horses until we were knocked down by the horses' heads butting us in the back. They would then sit and laugh at our antics as we attempted to regain our feet, bound together as we were.

Fortunately we had not far to go, as we counted far in those days, and we were soon at the outskirts of Adana. At a group of tents we were handed over to an armed sentry and our captors left us, to return shortly after accompanied by an officer, a Mulazim Thani (2nd Lieutenant). This brave young officer ordered six men, with fixed bayonets, to fall in beside us and escort us to the town prison.

To those who have not experienced the like, the picture now presented would be unbelievable. Here were we, two bound and helpless men, being escorted to prison by an officer leading, three soldiers with rifles and fixed bayonets on either side of us, and two armed and mounted policemen bringing up the rear! As we passed through the town quite a procession of curious natives was formed, and I have no doubt that they thought that we were most desperate characters. The Gendarmes enlarged on the story of their capture and the struggles they had had to secure us to the many of the crowd who questioned them.

In the centre of the town—as near as I could guess—we reached the town police courts and remand prison, where the answers I gave to the many questions we were asked were duly entered into a ledger. Then we were pushed into a filthy room which almost beggars description.

It measured some twenty feet by sixteen and seemed packed to suffocation before we entered. The stench that assailed our nostrils was appalling and breath-taking. The door was slammed to behind us and we stood still until our eyes became accustomed to the semi-darkness of the interior, then we took stock of our surroundings. It was as well that we had not advanced into the room for we should have fallen over the human dregs that covered the floor in every attitude. At the end of the room farthest away from the door was a tiny window about two feet square, around which were clustered several of the most bestial-looking men it had been our lot to have seen thus far, and we had seen not a few. They succeeded in effectively blocking the light and polluting what fresh air managed to find its way in. In vain we looked for a place where we could at least sit down. The only place not covered by a body was the place we were standing on, and there the floor was rotten and contained a hole from which emanated a ghastly odour of putrefying matter. There was nothing for us to do but cover the hole with our sacks and squat down where we were, and wait for what might happen next.

None of the inmates of this foul den spoke to us, though I heard someone query in Arabic, "Who are these?" to which no audible answer was given.

Before long the Sergeant slithered over on to someone's feet and stayed there, despite the kicking and grumbling of the owner! He was too far gone to worry any more and in a few minutes was sleeping the sleep of the utterly exhausted. I was greatly concerned for him as I knew that he could not possibly survive many days in that place.

Thinking to obtain some information from the group at the window—the only ones to show any signs of animation—I stepped gingerly over the bundles that were men on the floor and, on reaching the group, asked if any of them could speak Arabic. They all could, and when I asked what our prospects were of getting food laughed in my face and called me a donkey. When I told them who we were, in answer to their question, they reviled me and all my race, and told me to leave them as I was an unclean infidel!

Not a very encouraging welcome, so I made my way back to the door.

Apparently our conversation had been listened to by some of the men on the floor, for one of them called to me as I was about to sit down. Following the sound of the voice, for it was impossible to distinguish the huddled bundles on the floor one from the other, I found it to come from a wreck of a man who whispered "Armeni" ("Armenian"). In the jerky gasping voice of a very sick man he told me—in English—that he had been educated at an American college at Tarsus, and that he came of a wealthy family of Ourfa. This was the prelude to a terrible tale of brutal treatment that he had received at the hands of the Turks. Before he had finished I had grave misgivings as to our own fate. He told me further that nearly all the sick men on the floor were Armenians who had received similar rough treatment, and that a death occurred among them almost daily. I asked whether we were likely to get food, and was told that unless we had money and could pay for it, or had friends outside who could bring some to us, then we should assuredly starve. No doctor would visit us unless he were paid beforehand, and the sentry had to be bribed before he was sent for. No one was allowed outside except for sanitary purposes at sunset and dawn.

In answer to my query as to how long we might be kept there, I was told that the place we were in was supposed to be a remand prison, but some of the occupants had been in for months, and had not seen an official of any sort, neither had they been tried for any offence nor remanded. I learned that the Arabs at the window were the bullies of the place, and had been caught fighting with knives in the bazaar of Adana. They would permit no one to take their place at the window with the result that they were the only ones who could see what was happening outside or to get fresh air. I promised myself a little excitement if I were compelled to remain in that stinking room many days, for I intended to get a little of what fresh air was going.

Before I returned to my few inches of floor space I promised to chat to the Armenian again. The Sergeant turned uneasily as I sat down, and I asked him if he were all right.

"Not too bad," he replied, but I knew that he was not too good either. I told him what information I had been able to glean, and he said that as long as he was free from malaria he would be able to stick it out with me.

The hours passed and we grew ravenous with hunger and terribly thirsty. There was no water or receptacle for any so far as we could see.

Sunset brought a rattling of chains on the door, which was suddenly thrown open, and I was precipitated outside as I was leaning on it at the time. It was the time for those who wished to go outside for a few minutes. The Arab bullies from the window were the first out, followed more slowly by some of those who had lain all day huddled up on the floor. These latter were terribly sick men, if looks went for anything. They were a ghastly yellow, and with sunken eyes and protruding cheekbones; they shambled out like animated corpses.

Telling the Sergeant to follow me, I went back inside and, picking up my sack, I took up a position near the window, telling the Sergeant that in all probability there would be a rough house when the Arabs returned and if he did not feel up to it to take no part. He replied that he felt a little better after his sleep and that he would do his best to help me if there was to be any trouble.

Outside the sentries commenced to bawl the usual "yellah" and the prisoners began to troop back in, the bullies bringing up the rear. Finding that we had taken up a part of their position they ordered us to get out of the way and go back to the door. I told them that we should do no such thing unless the sentry ordered us to move, and that they were welcome to our place if they wished. Shouting threats and waving their arms about they worked themselves into a fine old fury, but we were not at all impressed. Tiring of that one of them tried to grab me. Putting all my weight into an uppercut I caught him full on the nose and sent him sprawling on top of the men on the floor. He got to his feet, with blood pouring from his nose, and, with the others, made a wild rush at us. We knew that unless we could maintain the position we had taken up, life would be impossible for us as long as we remained in that prison, so we hit out right and left, and did not pay too strict a regard for Queensberry rules! Had they managed to have grappled with us things might not have been too good; as it was we speedily found out that they were not used to fisticuffs, and we managed to get in a few well-placed blows. In a very short time the place was in an uproar, and the door was flung open to admit two sentries. These worthies took a hand by clubbing with their rifles anyone who stood in their path, as they stepped over and on

HERE HAVE BEEN RECOVERED
AND INTERRED
THE BODIES OF
BRITISH OFFICERS AND MEN
WHO AFTER THE FALL OF KUT
BEING PRISONERS IN THE HANDS OF THE TURKS
PERISHED DURING THE MARCH
FROM KUT
OR IN THE PRISON CAMPS
OF ANATOLIA

THESE ARE THEY WHO CAME
OUT OF GREAT TRIBULATION

THIS NOTICE BOARD WILL BE REPLACED BY A
PERMANENT COMMEMORATION STONE

THE "KUT PLOT" IN BAGHDAD CEMETERY

CTESIPHON ARCH

[*See p.* 25

THE AUTHOR AT THE DOORWAY OF THE HOUSE IN WHICH HE WAS
BILLETED DURING THE GREATER PART OF THE SIEGE OF KUT

the figures on the floor on their way to us. Order was quickly restored, and the sentries demanded an explanation. The bullies all spoke at once and at the top of their voices. The sentries cut them short and asked me what I had to say. I told them my version of the affair and, to my surprise, they took my part. The bullies were threatened with dire punishment should they attempt to interfere with us again, and were ordered to move their gear to some other place, which meant that they would have to take the rotten part of the floor which we had vacated. The English-speaking Armenian and one or two of his pals made a little room for them by joining us at the window, at our invitation. With tremendous relief we filled our lungs with fresh air as we gazed through the bars into the great quadrangle, and at the buildings surrounding it.

Darkness came and we received no food for that day. The Armenian gave us a drink of water from a bottle that he had filled up when he went outside, and he forgot his own troubles for a time as he commiserated us in ours.

We were too hungry to fall asleep again, and for hours we discussed our position. Anything might happen to us now, and no one of our own people would be any the wiser we thought, and wondered just what would happen to us.

At dawn the door was opened again and this time we went outside. We were able to wash at a tap just outside, and I felt decidedly better after I had washed off the blood that had caked on my face from my smashed nose. I asked the sentry when we were to get rations, and how long we were to be kept in prison, etc., to all of which he replied, "Ma aruf" ("Don't know"), until, becoming sick of my questions, he abruptly ordered me inside.

As we were re-entering the building a dead Armenian was being removed, and we wondered how long it would be before a similar fate overtook us.

During the morning food was handed in to most of the

inmates through the window by friends or relatives. The Armenian told us that only once or twice a week were they permitted to receive food, whilst the Turks and Arabs could get food as often as it was brought to them. All the scraps and water-melon rinds were thrown into the hole in the floor, which explained to us the reason for the horrible smell.

All that day we sat hoping against hope that we should get something to eat, but night came and again we went without. Our Armenian friend became very ill during the night, and I judged that it would not be long before he would be beyond the brutality of the Turks.

We were very faint from the lack of food when we went outside the next morning, and I begged the sentry to send an officer to us or to report our condition to his Chaoush. He pushed me away and said that he could do nothing.

We returned to our place at the window and stood watching the people passing in and out of the main gate, which was close to our prison. During the afternoon we saw an officer of the Gendarmerie approaching, accompanied by a man in European dress whom I thought might possibly be an American—the United States not then having declared war. As soon as they were within earshot I commenced to yell out in English at the top of my voice, continuing until I had attracted their attention, despite the threats of the sentry.

The Westerner said something to the officer, who shrugged his shoulders and appeared to be telling him to take no notice of us. Fearing that they would pass out of sight without coming to us I yelled out, "For God's sake get us out of here, we are Englishmen."

When he heard that the Westerner came over to us, followed by the officer.

"What are you in there for?" he asked us.

We told him that we were escapees, prisoners of war from Kut-el-Amara.

When he said "Mein Gott!" my heart sank, for then I

knew that he was a German and not, as I had thought, an American.

Rapidly I told him of the state of the prison we were in, of the sick and dying men, of the daily deaths and our entire lack of food.

"If you cannot help us, then ask that police-officer to have us taken out and shot," I begged him. After all, such a death was preferable to one by neglect and starvation.

The German held a brief conversation with the officer, who finally ordered the sentry to unlock the door and let us out. We lost no time in getting out, and when the German saw the state we were in and caught a whiff of the fetid atmosphere of our prison, he looked shocked. He kept repeating, "Poor dears, poor dears," as I enlarged on the few details I had already given him, and he promised to do what he could for us.

We were taken to a small room near by in which a Chaoush and two Onbashis of the police were apparently in detention. The room was quite clean and had a raised platform inside on which to sleep or sit. The Onbashis were quite friendly and gave us some bread to eat as soon as we got inside, as they had heard all about us from the sentry of the prison. They were Arabs, but had served long terms of service in the police force of Adana. The Chaoush was an elderly chap who took no notice of us, but spent his time on his knees, praying and occasionally letting out a deep sigh and a very earnest "Alla-a-a-h!" Raoul Onbashi, the livelier of the two Onbashis, said that the disgrace of his punishment weighed heavily on the Chaoush, that was why he was continually in prayer.

Just before sunset we received a bundle of *chupattis* and a bowl of thick mutton stew, and, to our great surprise, a lira note. The soldier who brought those good things said that the food came from the *Dowlat* (Government) and the money from the *Alliman* (German).

We were too hungry to care who had sent which and in a twinkling were feeding like famished dogs, and about as daintily! Later on we discussed the kindness of the Germans whom we had met since we had become prisoners of war, and agreed that it was a great pity that they were now our enemies.

We asked Raoul Onbashi how we could purchase fruit and cigarettes with the paper money that we now had. He told us that if we wanted to change it into cash we should only get sixty out of the hundred piastres that it represented, but if we spent a quarter of it and got the change in paper then we should get full value for the quarter. So we decided to spend a quarter and Raoul called a sentry and told him what we wanted.

Our new prison boasted a hurricane lamp, and as we sat and chatted in the light of it we felt much better, and began to forget the nightmare existence of the past two days, especially when the sentry had brought the things we had ordered and we could puff at a cigarette.

We received a great kerchief of grapes and figs, bread-rings, and packets of tobacco and cigarette papers for our twenty-five piastres, and there appeared to be an amazing amount for the money. I asked Raoul how I could reward the sentry and was told not to worry about that as the stuff I had received had only cost twenty piastres, or less, and the sentry had taken the balance of the quarter lira for himself!

We sat and rolled cigarettes and offered some to our fellow prisoners. It was then that I discovered that we had forgotten all about matches. Raoul produced what he called a *chekmuk*, a flint and wool-cord lighter. It was the first we had seen of this novelty—a war-time product—and we little dreamed that even in England those economical lighters were in use and were to be the forerunners of the now universal petrol-lighter.

For several hours we smoked and chatted and I learned

many things from Raoul that proved useful to me during the frequent sojourns I subsequently made in various Turkish prisons. I was surprised to learn that Turkish N.C.O.'s did not necessarily lose their rank when they were put into prison, as apparently good N.C.O.'s were hard to come by, and there was no other form of punishment for them.

The old Chaoush continued to call on Allah and did not join in the conversation. Neither did he join us when we feasted on the bread and fruit we had bought, though the two Onbashis made up for his absence!

The following morning we each received three loaves and were told that they represented the three days' rations we should have had since we had arrived at Adana. Someone was evidently looking into things on our behalf.

All would have been well had not the Sergeant begun to get pains in the stomach and bad headaches. Fortunately we were allowed out as often as we liked so that he was able to walk up and down outside when his pains became particularly bad. He became so bad that I asked the sentry to send for a doctor, though the Sergeant protested that he would be all right in a couple of days, and did not want any Turkish doctor messing him about! During the afternoon of the third day—after I had sent for a doctor—an official of some sort came to take particulars of our names and our fathers' names, etc. I pointed out the condition of the Sergeant, and said that he needed attention more than the Turks needed to know our fathers' names. Without any argument, and much to my surprise, the official sent for a sentry and told me to assist the Sergeant, and the sentry would take us to the doctor.

The doctor's surgery was not far away and in getting to it we had to pass through a rose garden. For a few moments we stopped and inhaled the fragrance of flowers that brought memories of England to us. It seemed to me a profanity that roses—of all flowers—should grow in such a corrupt land!

We passed on and, after a short delay, were admitted into the presence of the Hakim Effendi (Doctor). After a brief examination the doctor told me that the Sergeant must go into hospital, and, when I said that I had better go with him, informed me that there were many British soldiers in the hospital in Adana. That was news indeed, as we had no idea that any Britishers were within miles of us. I begged the doctor to send me along with the Sergeant, saying that I, too, was very sick! He examined me and smiled, and shook his head. It was no use, we had to part; I to return to prison and the Sergeant to go to hospital. I was very sorry to see him go alone, but I knew that he would never get better unless he had some sort of treatment, and he would have the company of other Englishmen also.

The following morning I was taken from the remand prison to the *mappus khana* (prison house), the main prison of Adana. I made the journey by *arabah*, the Turkish equivalent of the *arabana* of the Arabs, a flat-bottomed, springless, four-wheeled cart, held together by odd bits of wire and string and of uncertain age. I was rattled and jolted along at a breakneck speed through the streets of the town, and was very pleased when we arrived at the prison on the outskirts.

I was at once surrounded by soldier-warders and pretty thoroughly searched. The Chaoush in charge took from me the broken crucifix that I had—for no apparent reason—carried all the way from Jezerieh-ibn-Oman.

The prison was a large mud-built thatched building similar in shape and design to the familiar "army huts" of war days. Down the centre of its length was a roof-high partition, which divided the sleeping quarters of the warders from that of the prisoners. A small wicket-gate gave access to the prison through the partition, and an armed guard was posted on either side. Through this gate I was led and introduced to the inmates by the Chaoush bellowing out "Ingleezi!"

I was immediately surrounded by a gaping crowd of civil prisoners of many races and many degrees of uncleanliness. I pushed my way into the centre of the long room and stood undecided what to do next. Suddenly a voice shouted in English, "Oh, there! are you English?" I turned and saw someone waving to me; I went up to him and said, "Yes, I am English."

"Cripes! but you certainly don't look like one!" said the speaker; and I certainly did not in comparison with him. He thereupon introduced me to two others who were his companions and I learned that they were Australians, would-be escapees from a working camp in the Taurus Mountains, called Belamadik. They proved to be rare good fellows, and it was fortunate for me that they had been long enough in prison to have learned all the schemes and wangles that go to make life easier in a Turkish prison.

Among other things they told me that they were daily expecting to be released and sent back to the working camp. That did not cheer me up at all, as their release meant loneliness for me. However, by the time they did go, some nine or ten days later, I was fairly conversant with all that went on in the place.

By some means or other they had got into touch with the American Consul at Mersina who had sent them money, clothes, bedding, and sundry other things. They promised that they would get the same for me; meanwhile they were good enough to share what they had with me.

I speedily realized that those three "Aussies" had established a tiny bit of the Empire in that foul prison. The other prisoners held them in great respect and all the warders were very friendly towards them and allowed them many privileges.

They sent for a barber and paid him to give me a shave and a close-crop haircut, after which they helped me to have a good wash down—using real soap!—and, when it was all over, I both felt and looked a different man.

For dinner the "Aussies" had a huge bowl of fruit salad, the chief ingredient being chunks of luscious watermelon. This, they told me, was their weekly luxury, and I had been fortunate enough to arrive on that auspicious day.

As that prison was as unlike any civil prison I had ever conceived, and was certainly unlike any English institution of a similar nature, a detailed description of it will help the reader to understand the conditions.

The actual prison was a room about one hundred feet long by twenty feet wide and contained a raised platform, seven feet in width, that ran along the four sides. This platform was to sleep on and to stow such kit as any of the prisoners might have. The place was well windowed, though bars took the place of glass, which was removed during the summer and only replaced during the winter. A loaf of black bread was issued in the mornings and vegetable soup in the evenings, and this was the only food provided. Food could be handed in through the windows by any of the friends or relatives of the prisoners—after it had been searched, and oftimes sampled, by one of the warders—and most of the inmates of that prison received all they required in that way. Smoking was permitted and a general shop was attached to the prison from which almost anything could be purchased. A barber came in daily and all who needed his services had to pay in advance. No one was aware of the length of time he had to serve and everyone appeared to be treated alike. There was no exercise beyond what one could get by walking about the room, and no one was put to work other than to very occasionally sweep the beaten-earth floor or help the warders to tidy up their sleeping quarters. As a general rule, prisoners were only allowed to the latrines at sunrise and sunset, when they were marched there in a body. If any wished to go out during the night they could only go in two's, handcuffed together the whole time. Unfortunately I was subjected to the same treatment for the first two weeks, and the degradation I suffered on the occasions I was obliged to go out at night can be imagined. During the period I was in that prison the men who had served their sentences only knew it when they were taken out under escort to become soldiers or were posted to a labour battalion. There was one custom that amused me greatly. A dirty old Greek, known as Katib Effendi (Clerk), plied a brisk trade in letter writing, the letters always being addressed to the Commandant of the prison. These letters contained, for the most part, appeals for release and were after this style:

"Favoured of Allah. I have been in this prison for six long months and now I desire to return to my family, who are loyal supporters of the Sultan and Islam. My wife's father has been taken away to join the army, and he has taken all the money which I had saved to pay the taxes to the Vali. I think also that six months is long enough imprisonment for whatever you are honoured to think I did wrong."

Funnily enough, very often these appeals were successful and proved a good advertisement for the letter-writer, whose charge was five piastres a time.

Very often a prisoner had no idea whatever of his offence and many had received no sort of trial. For that matter, neither had I!

Through the medium of Arabic I learned a lot of Turkish from that old Greek letter-writer.

One end of the room was occupied by a ruffianly gang of Kurds and Arabs who were heavily chained together. Their spirits were neither chained nor broken, and they were a gay, laughing crowd, and were very friendly towards me. Very often they performed a communal dance at night and on several occasions I joined in with them. This dance consisted of holding hands and forming a circle around one of the pillars that supported the roof. One man would chant and the rest would join in the refrain, very much like the old sea-shanty singing; the circle moving two steps to the right and one to the left in rhythm to the chant. The pace gradually increased and the dancers stamped their feet and shouted the refrain at the top of their voices as they became more and more excited. The clanking chains added to the resultant din and the flickering light of a solitary wick—suspended from a tin of oil hanging on the pillar—added to the weirdness of the scene. The dance usually came to an end when the verses of the chant contained obscene references to some official or other who was particularly disliked by the prisoners. Then the warders would come in and break up the circle. It used to relieve my feelings on the occasions that I joined in the dancing to bawl and shout, "Osman Effendi, chok fenna!" though I had no idea whom he might be or why he was "very bad."

The opposite end of the room was occupied by the élite of the prisoners. Here were one or two Beys, besides other well-to-do people, and they received their rank or Effendi from warders and prisoners alike and were treated with great respect. Wall-mats covered the walls round their particular part of the room, and rugs and carpets covered the platform and many gaily coloured cushions were there for them to lounge upon. All these things were supplied by themselves, of course. They dressed in silken dressing-gowns, and several times a week were taken to the town baths. All their meals were brought in from a restaurant in the town and, what with one thing and another, they had a very soft time of it. It must have been a very expensive time for them also, and I often wondered why they were in prison at all, knowing as I did that money could do most things in Turkey, including buying oneself out of prison. I was told that one of them—Tekki Bey—was serving a portion of a hundred years' sentence imposed on his father, who had died in prison. It was expected that when Tekki Bey died that his son would take his place in prison!

The rest of the room was occupied by all types of near Easterners, good, bad, and indifferent.

By the time my Australian friends were taken away I knew most of the warders by name and lots of the prisoners. A retired warder, one Abdullah Ahmid, acted as runner for the prisoners and, I should imagine, found it lucrative employment. I became very friendly with him, and in consequence found life much more tolerable as he would often take me outside to sit and chat in the shade of the building, and he did his best to get me what I required at the cheapest price from the prison shop.

As the "Aussies" had promised, I received money and clothes from the American Consul's agent, and was raised thereby to the status of Effendi! The blow of being left a solitary Englishman in a Turkish civil prison was considerably softened by my possession of decent clothes, bedding, and money.

After I had been in prison about sixteen days the Chaoush —a friendly enough chap—came and inquired after my health. Suspecting nothing unpleasant, I replied that I was quite all right, but should be much better when I was released He smiled and left me, soon to return accompanied by two warders, one of whom carried a rifle equipped with a sling and a rawhide whip. The Chaoush called me into the middle of the room and told me to lie on my back. All talking stopped as soon as the Chaoush called to me, and I had a sense of impending disaster. When I was told to lie down and hold up my feet I knew what was to happen, and a chill of fear crept over me. I broke into a cold sweat and I asked the Chaoush why I should be treated like a criminal.

I was to be bastinadoed, whipped on the bare feet, a fearful punishment for any man but a positive torture for an Englishman. More than once I had heard men—whose feet were as hard as iron—scream in agony as the green sticks or whip lashed their feet.

There was no escape for me and I was forced into position and my feet secured by having the sling of the rifle dropped over my ankles whilst the two warders twisted the rifle until my feet were as in a vice.

I have no idea how many strokes I received as I fainted before the Chaoush had finished, but I shall never forget the appalling agony of it. I returned to consciousness feeling the exquisite stinging of salt being rubbed into my bleeding feet. A fellow-prisoner gave me a drink of water as I lay sobbing and trembling and wondering what hell I had been flung into.

It will be remembered that I had had no sort of trial, nor had I been interviewed officially by any official, yet I had been imprisoned and brutally tortured. What might I expect *after* I had been tried if that was a foretaste of my punishment?

I was not the only English prisoner to receive the dreaded bastinado in Turkey. After my return to England I met Company Sergeant-Major R. Richards of the Norfolk Regiment, who told me that he had received ten lashes a day for ten days—one hundred strokes—for daring to write to the Grand Vizier for better treatment for the men of his party who were working on the roads at Eskir-shehir. At Afion-Kara-Hissar a Staff-Sergeant had the soles of his feet beaten to pulp with a bicycle tyre. Nice people, the Turks!

Evening came but I had no appetite for the usual ration of vegetable soup. I just wanted to lay and recover from the mental and physical hurt that I had received.

The oil-cruse lamps were lighted and it was dark outside when someone touched me and softly said, "Inglis." I opened my eyes and saw the Chaoush sitting by my side, rolling cigarettes and forming them into a little pile.

"Jigara?" he inquired, and gently put one into my mouth. Then he went on to explain that he had received orders to beat me and, although he had protested against giving me the *di'ak* (bastinado), he had been compelled to do so. He was very sorry for me and promised to give me every consideration that was in his power.

I certainly had no cause for complaint of his subsequent treatment of me, for he was as good as his word. He was a gruff old Arab who had seen many years of service with the Turks, but he proved to be a kindly soul and often went out of his way to do me a kindness. Sometimes he would call me into the warders' quarters to hear a travelling musician or to watch some itinerant dancers. Before he left me, on the day of my punishment, he pushed the pile of cigarettes over within reach of my hand and told me to ask for anything I wanted during the night.

It was many days before I was able to walk in comfort but I quickly threw off the depression that had taken hold of me, and once more joined in the social round of the prison. I was invited to eat with both the élite and chained gang at different times and, in that way, managed to eke out the money I had received.

In order that I should receive full value in hard cash for my paper liras, Abdul (Abdullah Ahmid) taught me a good dodge. I would purchase half a lira's worth of tobacco or grapes or tomatoes and divide them into one-piastre lots. Those lots I would arrange in front of me on my bit of platform, and then I sat and waited for customers! As the prison shop only gave half-value in hard cash for paper, unless the full amount was expended, the short-time prisoners—or those who thought that they *might* be short time—and newcomers did very little dealing there, so I had very little trouble to dispose of my stock.

With the hard cash that I thus received I could buy elsewhere than at the prison shop and I often used to send into Adana for baked meats and invite my friends to a meal.

There was another character in that prison who deserves mention. He was a very old and partially blind Arab whose name was also Abdullah, though he would never answer to

Abdul like the runner did. He was very proud of his few words of English and would air them on every possible occasion, particularly when he wished to impress new arrivals. At one time he had been a bumboat-man and sold oranges to the passengers of liners, from whom he had learnt his half a dozen words of English.

One day the prison *katib* (clerk) came in to get some particulars off me and, instead of coming straight to me, bawled out in Arabic for the services of anyone who could act as an interpreter for me. There was a general cry for Abdullah, who was only too willing to shine in that capacity. I smiled to myself for I knew the extent of his English, but I decided to play up to him for as long as it would last. The following is the way it went:

Clerk: "Ask him his name."

Abdullah: "Johnny, nice orong, sweet orong."

Myself: "Long."

Clerk, writing laboriously and spelling out the result: "Longha. Now his father's name."

Abdullah: "Whatcha wan, ten a shillin?"

Myself: "Long."

Clerk: "Longha! No, no, I want his father's name."

Abdullah: "Six a shillin, ten a shillin, Jack, Bill, Bob, what say?"

Myself: "Long."

Clerk, getting irritable: "Longha. I have got that. If that is his father's name what is his name?"

Abdullah: "Nice orong, sweet orong, Johnnie."

Myself: "Walter."

Clerk, triumphantly "Ah! Longha Wilcher."

And so it went on, a crowd of gaping prisoners sitting around us and repeating every answer I gave. When I was asked the name of the town I lived in I answered, as always, "Londra" (London) as no other place-name would convey intelligence to the majority of clerks that I had to do with in Turkey.

Henceforward I was known officially as Longha Wilcher ibn Longha, meaning Long Walter son of Long, though I was normally addressed as Inglis. The joke of it all was that Abdullah normally chatted to me in Arabic and knew that I understood all that the clerk had asked me and could have answered direct had I have wished. I had no desire to lower poor old Abdullah's prestige and it was good fun for me.

On another day there was much sweeping and furbishing of the prison and, for the first time, I saw the place really clean, or as clean as it was possible to get it. I inquired the reason for all the activity and was told that the Governor of the Vilayet, Ramsi Pasha, was coming on a tour of inspection.

The Pasha duly arrived accompanied by the usual retinue of popinjays complete with clanking swords. He was a smart, soberly dressed man wearing a neatly trimmed brown beard. The prisoners were called to attention, which meant for them kneeling upright on the platform. At a word from the Pasha they dropped back on to their heels and remained in that posture. I continued to sit and watch until he reached me when I stood to attention and saluted him.

"Kim der bu?" ("Who is this?") he asked in Turkish. Before anyone could answer I replied, "Inglis ysir, Kut-el-Amara don" ("English prisoner from Kut-el-Amara").

"Ingleezi?" he asked in surprise, and then turned to one of his staff and asked a lot of questions which at that time I was unable to understand as my Turkish was of the sketchiest. When he had finished he turned to me again and asked if it were true that I spoke Arabic. I answered him in that language, and he asked me then if I were comfortable or in need of anything. I told him that I had been bastinadoed by the order of some official I had never seen, but beyond that I had no complaints as the Chaoush and his staff had treated me very well, at the same time I should be better pleased if I were to be sent to where I could join my own comrades. He smiled at the latter part of my remark and said that I should, no doubt, soon be joining them. Then he told the Chaoush that an *eshon* (27 inches) of space should be kept clear of me on either side of the platform and that no other prisoner was to be allowed to interfere with me. With a smile and a salute he passed on.

The order about the space that was to be kept on either side of me did not have any significance for me at the time it was given, as up to that time I had always had plenty of room. Two days later I understood and was grateful to the Pasha for his foresight. To the accompaniment of much yelling and shouting of orders over a hundred new prisoners were suddenly herded into the room filling up every inch of space. They were certainly a motley crowd: Kurds, Arabs, Turks, Greeks, and Albanians, besides others of mixed nationalities, and dressed in all manner of clothes. One old chap had a long strip of carpet—very much like stair carpet—wrapped around his middle in such a manner that it reached to just below his chin, and gave him the appearance of being in a barrel. The place became like "bedlam" as they fought for the few places left on the platform and for places on the floor, and they shouted and yelled in a dozen different tongues. In vain I attempted to retain my *eshon* of space and I had work enough to keep the little bit of space that was taken up by my clothes, etc. I sat tight until the hubbub subsided somewhat and then yelled at the top of my voice for the Chaoush. The sentry on the wicket heard me and sent for that worthy, who proceeded to kick his way through the prisoners on the floor until he reached me. There was no need for me to tell him what I wanted, for, as soon as he saw the space around me packed to suffocation, he began at once to kick it clear of prisoners. When my *eshon* had been restored to me he gave out to the remainder strict orders for them to keep clear of me under pain of the *di'ak* should any disobey. I breathed a sigh of relief and thanked the Chaoush for that favour.

During the first night of the arrival of those newcomers I awoke to find that an Arab had taken advantage of my being curled up asleep to stretch himself on the platform at my feet. I sat up and saw that the whole of the floor space was packed with sleeping figures and that not a few could only find space to sit. Laying down again I put my feet up to the Arab who was poaching my space and, straightening my knees, shot him off the platform and on to the sleepers on the floor. There was plenty of cursing and grumbling from those who were so rudely awakened, but no one attempted to sleep near me after that.

The following day I learned that these men had been rounded up from among the mountains in the vicinity, where they had been in hiding to avoid being conscripted into the army. I was told that as each one was caught he was roped to the remainder until the Gendarmes had completed their circuit when they were driven along into Adana roped together like cattle. The unfortunates who had been among the first to be caught must have had a very thin time of it, as it had taken several weeks to get that particular bunch.

Every day after that several names were called out and the owners left the prison, perhaps to be thrown into a worse one or to be drafted into the army or a labour gang. Within a week most of them had gone, but it was a most unpleasant time whilst they were there, as it was impossible to walk about and it was not wise to leave one's kit unguarded for two seconds.

On another occasion a Corporal and two privates of a Turkish infantry regiment came in late at night, and were allotted a space next to me that had been recently vacated. As they were soldiers and appeared decent enough fellows I quickly struck up an acquaintance with them. They had served in Gallipoli and were there during the evacuation by the British, and were able to tell me much that was of great interest about that campaign from the Turkish point of view.

They were without food or extra clothing so I gave them some bread and salt and lent them an old overcoat that I had bought for a few piastres. The three of them lay close together that night and spread my overcoat over themselves, hanging it on a nail over my bed space the next morning. The following night I lent it to them again as I was quite warm enough rolled up in my padded quilt, though the nights had become very cold at that time. During the afternoon following the second night they had had it I lay talking to the old Greek *katib*—who had moved into the space on the other side of me—with my feet to the wall, a position all of us had now adopted in order to attempt to foil the voracious attacks by the monster bugs that had begun to emerge every night from the many cracks in the mud walls. Suddenly the Greek ejaculated, "Ne dir or, kaput 'der?" ("What is that on the overcoat?"), pointing to my coat hanging on its nail. I could see nothing amiss and said so, whereupon the Greek got to his feet, gave one close look at the coat, and yelled, "Beetlar, beetlar!" ("Lice, lice!") and, turning to the soldiers, swore and cursed them in a shocking manner. I got up and looked at the overcoat and found it swarming with lice so that it was almost literally alive! It was truly amazing how quickly it had become like that as it was perfectly free from vermin before I had lent it to the soldiers. Meanwhile the Greek had run to the sentry at the wicket, shrieking and complaining at being compelled to sleep in the same room as "lousy soldiers." An Onbashi and two warders came in to investigate matters. The Onbashi removed my coat on the end of his rifle, taking care to keep it at great length from himself, and the warders kicked the soldiers to their feet and ran them out of the building. I have no idea where they were taken, but they did not return to the prison. The Chaoush had been sent for and when he arrived he ordered everyone outside the building. I followed the remainder, but he called me back and said that I need not go out as he was sure that I was free from lice. As a matter of fact I was, strange to relate! So I stood in the doorway to watch events. The prisoners were formed up in rows with about five yards between rows and kerosene oil tins were placed at intervals between them. Everyone was then ordered to strip off their clothing and de-louse, the vermin to be dropped into the tins! I was asked if I wished to have my overcoat fumigated at a cost to myself of twenty piastres. To that I replied that I would have my quilt fumigated just "in case" and that the overcoat could be burnt as I could never fancy wearing it again.

And so the days passed, and I gradually lost hope of being released before the end of the war. The day or the date I never knew, nor how many weeks I spent in Adana civil prison.

Came a great day when I was told that another Englishman was being sent to the prison. I had no idea whom he might be and the Chaoush could only tell me that he was a *koshdiji* (runaway) like myself, which meant that he was an escapee.

At last he arrived and pushed his way through the gaping crowd at the wicket. He was ragged and unshaven and looked most unhappy as he stood and gazed about him. Under other circumstances it would have been very difficult to have recognized in him an Englishman. I shouted from where I sat, "Hi, there! Are you an Englishman?"

"Thank Gawd!" was his only reply, uttered very fervently as he came over to me. I told him who I was and he told me that he was a Pioneer Corporal of the West Kent Regiment, Cpl. A. E. Dade.

After I had got him settled beside me he told me how he came to be where he was. Together with six or seven others he had attempted to escape from a working camp called Entilli, in the Amanus mountains, and on the Constantinople to Baghdad railway. The party had been recaptured after a day or two of freedom and had been sent to Adana. For some reason unknown to Cpl. Dade—henceforth to be known as "Micky"—he had been separated from the others and sent down to join me. He had no kit whatsoever, nothing beyond the rags he stood up in, and I was glad that I was in a position to give him something to eat and a share of what I had.

I was overjoyed to have a companion of my own race, and we talked for hours and hours for the first few days. I was so unused to speaking in English that I could not help interjecting Turkish or Arabic adjectives into my conversation. We chatted on every conceivable subject until at last we dried up and used to sit or lay on the platform in silence gazing up at the roof for hours at a time. Micky had bouts of neuralgia which used to drive him half crazy with pain, and he would pace up and down a beat of half a dozen yards all night long on those occasions.

About that period the prison bugs had become increasingly active, and nothing I did prevented me from being badly bitten every night. My body, and even the palms of my hands, and my face became covered with big red blotches. Several of the native prisoners remarked on my appearance and suggested that I ought to see the doctor. They had no idea what had caused the blotches but thought that I was suffering from some malignant disease or other. The fact that bug bites were the real cause of my condition did not enter their heads, as they were apparently too unsavoury for even bugs to feed on! Thinking that the doctor might also be deceived I decided to see him on his next visiting day.

The Chaoush had been told that I wished to see the doctor so when that man arrived I was duly taken outside to see him. He was sitting at a table and, several yards before I reached him, I halted and exposed my body to his gaze, saying that I had better not approach too closely in case I had contracted a contagious disease. He was quick to swallow my hint and ordered me to be taken to hospital without delay, and did not bother to examine me at all. I was taken completely by surprise, so easily had I managed to hoodwink him, and regretted that I had not attempted something of the sort previously.

I re-entered the prison and told Micky that I was being sent to hospital, which meant that he would be left on his own. We laughed together at the absurdity of it all and he said that, though he was pleased for my sake, he was sorry to see me go, and hoped that either he was quickly released or that I soon returned. His hopes were realized within a week as he was taken out and sent to Afion-Kara-Hissar. So I said good-bye to Micky and little dreamed that we were to meet again and experience some extraordinary adventures together.

CHAPTER SEVEN

LIFE IN ADANA HOSPITAL

ONCE again I sat on the floor of an *arabah* and was jolted through the streets of Adana. The *arabanchi* (driver) was a loquacious sort of chap and kept up a running commentary about everything and nothing, interspersed with questions about myself and the English, which he did not wait for me to answer. Indeed, I had very little breath with which to answer questions, and long before we reached the hospital I had lost any inclination to talk I may have had. At last he waved his whip in the direction of a large rectangular building and said, "Khousta Khana" ("Hospital"). We clattered through the main entrance and into the quadrangle and halted at the foot of a flight of stone steps that led to the first floor of the building. I climbed wearily out of the bone and nerve-shaking vehicle and looked around me.

It was the usual type of building: two storied, flat-roofed and with a balcony running round the inside of the first floor. I looked up at the balcony and saw twenty or more patients leaning over the rail and regarding me with great interest. They wore nightgowns and skull-caps of white linen and were not recognizable as Englishmen from where I stood, but I discovered later they were.

An Armenian girl in the uniform of a Red Crescent nurse came up to me and told me, in excellent English, to follow her. I followed her up the stone stairs, on to the balcony of the first floor and into a small office, where sat another Armenian nurse. Without any preliminaries she said—also in English—"Give me your name, home address, and any other particulars please."

I complied and then asked whether Sergeant R. was in the hospital.

"Yes, and he has told us all about you," she replied.

"Then please let me see him," I requested.

"First you must be taken to the bath and then change your clothes, after that you will be able to see him," replied the nurse.

An orderly led me to a Turkish bath outside the hospital building, where my clothes were taken from me to be fumigated and stored. Then I was alternatively parboiled and frozen, shaved from head to foot—less my eyebrows and upper-lip—dressed in skull-cap and nightgown, shod with heelless red slippers, and led back to the hospital. By this time I had a violent headache and felt decidedly out of sorts.

Again I climbed the stairs and, as soon as I reached the balcony, was surrounded by English patients, all clamouring for news as to who I was, where I had come from, etc. I answered scores of questions before I got a chance to ask a few on my own account. When I did I learned that there were about one hundred and eighty of the Kut Garrison there, all that were left of a party of several hundreds that had been working on the railroad at Bagtchi, in the Amanus mountains. Apparently the treatment meted out to them at that working camp, coupled with the criminal negligence of the Eurasian Assistant-Surgeon in charge of the sick quarters, had so decimated the party that even the Turkish officials had become alarmed and had removed the remainder to Adana hospital. Our conversation was interrupted by a nurse who requested me to accompany her to the hospital office, where the Assistant Matron was waiting to interview me.

I followed her, greatly intrigued by being "requested" to do something—after being used to receiving peremptory orders—and by a female, too. As I entered the office I was greeted by a cheery "Good morning, Englishman," given by a good-looking Armenian woman. She asked me a few questions and then proceeded to enlighten me as to the routine of the hospital in so far as it affected the patients. I was not particularly interested as I did not expect to find any different routine there than I had done in any other Turkish establishment. She went on to tell me that the Matron was an English lady, by name Miss Davies (actually she was a Welsh woman from Flint, North Wales), who worked with an American doctor, named Cyril Haas, in looking after the welfare and interest of the British and Indian prisoners in the two hospitals under their charge. For this privilege the Turks claimed their assistance for the Turkish sick and wounded, many of whom were in that same hospital. The Matron resided at an American Mission hospital in another part of the town, where the Indian Mohammedan sick prisoners and Turkish officers were, and where Doctor Haas had his surgery and operating room. I was told that both the Matron and the doctor paid frequent visits to see the British sick, but that they were greatly hampered and restricted in all that they did by the Turks. An Arab doctor, who was a Christian, was the regular doctor for that hospital, and she—the Assistant Matron—was responsible for the care and conduct of all the patients, both British and Turks. I listened attentively to all that she had to say, and when she concluded I asked after the Sergeant.

"He is very ill now," she said, "but we are putting you into a bed next to him, for the time being."

I thanked her and followed the nurse to the ward where I was to stay. This was a large room, almost the full length of the building, and contained upwards of one hundred and fifty beds, in four long rows. I was led to one end of the room, to an empty bed next to one occupied by my friend the Sergeant. He greeted me with a wan smile and I was deeply grieved to see how obviously ill he was. The nurse left me, with instructions to get into bed quickly. I related all that had happened to me since he had left me to the Sergeant, and he told me that he had had another very bad bout of malaria and was now ill with dysentery. He had great difficulty in talking so I refrained from asking him any questions, merely contenting myself with letting him ramble on as he liked. I got into bed and experienced the delight and luxury of clean sheets once more, something I had not had for over two years.

Soon after I had got into bed two uncouth-looking Arab orderlies came along bearing large wooden trays on which were basins of vegetable soup, very much similar to that which had been my fare in prison. I received a basin and a hunk of wholemeal bread. It was all very well cooked and palatable, but not very filling. The Sergeant received a small quantity of *yaghourt* (curdled milk). As I was eating my meal the patient in the bed on the other side of me uncovered his head and asked me in a very feeble voice whether I was an Englishman, if so what was my name and regiment. Before I could tell him he had covered up his head again and I was left wondering what was wrong with him. Later on, one of the "up" patients came along to chat with me, and he told me that my end of the room was known as the "dead end," because patients who were not likely to recover were moved there to fill the beds left vacant by others who had "passed on"—which was all too frequently. Not very cheerful news for me, but I knew that I had been put there only to be near the Sergeant. My cheerful visitor told me further that it was certain that very few of the patients would live to get out of hospital, as the Turks either could or would not supply medicines for the Arab doctor! My headache was worse after he had gone, and I was pleased to lie down and try to sleep. In the evening I received a bowl of very thin *libn* and that was the last meal of the day. During the night the Sergeant moaned quite a lot and several times I got out of bed to assist him, and on those occasions I felt bad myself, so much so that I began to regret that I had got into the hospital.

The next morning two or three corpses were removed, and, so far as I could see, none of the patients took the slightest interest in them! No one inquired who they might be or where they were to be buried, to such a pass had the men of the Kut Garrison been brought. The occupants of all the beds in my immediate vicinity appeared to be very sick men, and I had no one to talk to except the Sergeant, and he was almost beyond it. The convalescent patients avoided our end of the room as much as they were able, and who could blame them? During the morning the Arab doctor arrived, accompanied by a Turkish Chaoush. In due course he arrived at my bedside and inquired after my health. I told him that I was a new arrival and beyond a bad headache felt quite all right. He felt my pulse and then said, "You have a temperature, my dear. Read so-and-so (here he quoted a verse of Scripture) and you will be quickly better!" He went on to tell me that he was a Christian from Mount Lebanon and had been trained in his profession at "Bart's" in London. After he had left me I wondered how the other patients fared if they got no other treatment than I had. To my amazement I discovered that they got very little else. All that doctor had in the way of medicines was a very small quantity of quinine and some powdered chalk! If a man was suffering from malaria he received a dose of quinine solution from a bottle carried by the Chaoush. As the solution in the bottle became less it was replenished by the addition of more water, so that the last patients to receive doses got practically pure water! Most of the men suffered from stomach complaints and they received any number from four to ten chalk powders, wrapped in bits of newspaper or pages torn from a book. Each and every patient was exhorted to read certain passages of the Scriptures which, when read, were certainly applicable to the occasion but hardly likely to effect a cure. No wonder there was a daily collection of corpses.

A nurse told me that fresh milk was brought for the British patients who were very ill, out of the private purse of Doctor Haas, and that most of the other food was paid for out of a fund administered by the American Consul, though the amount that could be purchased was strictly limited by the Turks.

By nightfall of that first day I was feeling very seedy, and continued so far about three days, after which my fever left me and I recovered my usual good health. During those days I was haunted by the vision of the dead being carried out and by the knowledge that I was lying in a bed in the "dead end" of the room.

A night orderly was on duty in the hospital, but he was rarely in attendance, with the result that patients crawled along the floor in an endeavour to reach the primitive latrines on the balcony rather than soil their beds. Many were unable to make the journey and collapsed on the way, with disgusting results. The condition of the place in the mornings was appalling, and the wonder is that anyone survived them. Shortly after dawn each day a party of Armenian charwomen came in to scrub out the place, and the stench was so bad that they invariably stuffed up their nostrils with aromatic leaves.

The Sergeant became worse and was removed to one of several small wards under the direct supervision of Doctor Haas. Only the more serious cases were taken to those wards —if they lived long enough to get there. A Sergeant of the Artillery was put into the Sergeant's bed next to me, and he told me a good deal about the treatment our men had received at Bagtchi before he died, which was four days later. The man on the other side of me—he who always had his head covered—died the same night, from what cause I have no idea. After the corpses had been removed the following morning, I got out of bed and went in search of a nurse.

Those poor girls rarely visited the big room as they had all they could manage in the smaller ones. They had had no training as nurses, other than that Miss Davies and Doctor Haas had given them at odd periods, but had been compelled by the Turks to accept the work or the alternative of exile—or worse. Most of them had lost all their male relatives during the 1914–15 massacres of the Armenians, and the fate of their female relatives was unknown in most cases. No praise could be high enough for the manner they performed the arduous and, in many instances, disgusting work, especially as they were open to, and often received, obscene insults from the Turkish and Arab staff and patients.

I found one of them and pleaded with her to get me removed from my present position in the big room, where I was becoming most depressed and in great fear of contracting some sort of illness from which I should not recover. I spoke to her in Turkish and she was delighted to find an Englishman who could talk to her in, what was to all intents and purposes, her own language. She took me to the Assistant Matron and told her excitedly that I could speak Turkish and had pleaded to be taken out of the big room. That good woman kept me chatting for half an hour and promised that she would do what she could for me. That same afternoon I was removed to a smaller ward containing only eight beds. Two of the patients there were suffering from old wounds that had become full of maggots, a result of neglect and inability to obtain treatment.

Doctor Haas came round the next day on one of his visits and was greatly amused when I told him how I had managed to get into hospital from prison. He promised to keep me in hospital as long as he could, but was afraid that I should be turned out during one of the periodic visits of the Turkish Chief Medical Officer. I asked if he could do anything for my badly smashed nose. After carefully examining it he said that it would take an operation to put it right, and, as the Turks carefully doled out the necessary anaesthetics, he only used them on urgent cases, so that he would not promise to perform one. Nevertheless, he said that it was a card we could play if necessity demanded and was something that we could show to the Turks if they wished to turn me out. If they became insistent he would operate, but not until. Eighteen years later Doctor Haas was still in practice in Adana and I wrote to him and reminded him of the incident and thanked him for his many kindnesses.

For three more days I remained in bed, and the only relief in the awful monotony of the time spent between meals was to watch the bugs come out in the evening and climb the whitewashed wall to the ceiling. Those fellows were as big as sixpences, and my neighbour and I would select our fancy and wager impossible sums on the result of their journey up the wall! Whoever won the imaginary stake would note the amount, which would be added or subtracted from the wager on the following night, according to whether he won or lost.

When I was allowed up I went in search of the Sergeant and found him in a ghastly condition. Doctor Haas made a great fight to save his life and fed him with small doses of brandy and yolk of eggs which, it is needless to say, he paid for himself. His efforts were in vain, and my friend, Sergeant R., died a few days after I was allowed up. Another victim to swell the rising number of deaths among the men of the Kut Garrison.

The days dragged slowly by, but I made friends with the nurses and the Armenian women and girls that did the menial work about the hospital, and was well content to remain where I was in preference to returning to prison. I had clean linen and a sheeted bed, and by careful expenditure of the small sum of money still remaining from that I had received from the Consul, I managed to supplement the rations with fruit and an occasional egg. Fruit was still very cheap—particularly oranges—and radishes as big as turnips were to be had at a farthing apiece. I did not smoke much at this period, and a small packet of tobacco lasted me a long time.

Quite a number of patients were now convalescent, and we used to sit and yarn on the balcony, warmed by the December sun. One day we were thus engaged when an orderly came along and inquired whether any of us wished to see the dentist who would be visiting the hospital that morning. If so we were told to sit on chairs on the balcony and the remainder were to get back close to the wall. Here and there a Turkish patient was sitting waiting, but none of the English would risk the adventure. The dentist arrived, followed by an orderly who carried a kidney bowl which contained a solitary pair of forceps. Several of us moved closer to the nearest Turk awaiting treatment in order to watch and criticize the technique of the dentist. The Turk began to yell long before the dentist reached him and he received a box of the ears from one of the orderlies to quieten him. When the dentist asked him which was the tooth he wanted extracting he pointed to one of the front lower incisors. Carefully picking out the forceps—in a manner suggesting that he was selecting the right pair!— the dentist took a grip of the offending tooth and gave a tug. To our amazement, and no little horror, the whole row of teeth came away attached to a portion of the jawbone! We crowded round the dentist to get a closer look at the results of his efforts. He was just as amazed as we were and readily showed the teeth to us. I asked him what was the reason they had come away like that and was told that in all probability it was the result of a neglected disease. Whatever the cause may have been we all decided that we had no wish to see the dentist professionally.

A few days after this incident the doctor received orders

to clear all the British out of the hospital in order to make room for a large party of wounded Turks that were expected from the Palestine front. Both Doctor Haas and Miss Davies carefully examined what patients still survived, including the convalescent ones. I was told to get into bed before the Turkish C.M.O. arrived. When that officer came he examined all the bed patients, after saying that every man marked "up" must go out, and he made another dozen get out of bed though the doctor protested that they were not fit. He examined me and agreed to let me stay until after my operation. The party was mustered two days later and Miss Davies came to say good-bye to them, bringing with her clothing, quilts, cooking-pots, shoes, and cutlery for each man. They were bound for Afion-Kara-Hissar, and we learned later that many of them perished before they reached their destination. A week later the Turkish C.M.O. paid another visit and ordered all but six of us to be sent out. We who were left were told that we should shortly be moved to another hospital.

It was about that time that Ramsi Pasha visited the hospital and he spoke very kindly to the patients, both British and Turkish. I saw him stop one orderly and order him to undo his tunic. The man did so and when the Pasha saw lice on his shirt he knocked him down and ordered the Chaoush to have him arrested. There was no reason why the orderlies should have been unclean as there seemed to be no lack of clean linen for both patients and staff.

After the second party had gone a large party of sick and wounded Turks arrived, and we were taken to the American Mission hospital, where we found twenty odd other Englishmen of the first party who had collapsed before they had been out of the military hospital an hour. Things were vastly different in that hospital, where Miss Davies lived and ruled the roost. There were no Arab or other orderlies, and the only sign of the Turks was a sentry on the gate.

Armenian nurses tended the sick and an Armenian woman cooked the food. One wing of the hospital was occupied by Indian Mohammedans and the other by Britishers, whilst in one side ward was an elderly Bimbashi and in another were two Mulazim Thanis (subalterns). A week or so before Christmas several of the English patients were sent out and we that were left were put all together in one room.

The food was well cooked if not as plentiful as we should have liked, and we were as happy as circumstances allowed us to be. I, being a fit man, helped in the preparation of the food and assisted the nurse in charge of the dressings-room and operating theatre. Hosannah Avsharian, the nurse whom I assisted, was a very beautiful girl who had been studying at the American College in Adana at the outbreak of war. All her relatives had been either butchered or exiled, and she, together with the other girls, had been protected by Miss Davies and had taken up nursing. There had been two girls at the college named Hosannah, so she had been nicknamed by Miss Davies "Susie," because she was so like an English girl.

Miss Davies had been a member of the Armenian Relief Commission during the massacre of 1908 and had remained in Adana ever since, being attached to the American Mission. She was beloved by practically everyone in Adana, and when England declared war against Turkey she was allowed to carry on her work unhindered, certain Turkish officials giving out that she was in reality an American woman! After America had entered the war she was still permitted to carry on. Miss Davies is one of the unsung heroines of the Great War—a great-hearted Welsh lady.

Christmas Day came and was celebrated in the evening by several of us English attempting to give an exhibition of ballroom dancing, with the nurses forming an interested audience. As the "music" was supplied by the bed-patients whistling or humming and we danced in stockinged feet, the exhibition came to a speedy and unsuccessful end. We sang a few carols and the nurses sang to us in Armenian. Food was too scarce to permit of increased rations, but for all that we managed, with the aid of oranges and nuts, to get a little Christmas atmosphere. It was to be the happiest one we were to experience during the years of our captivity.

The days passed happily enough for me as I helped Susie in her work or sat and received lessons in Turkish from her. In addition to her other work she made the beds and tidied the rooms of the Turkish officers, and, by reason of certain things she had told me, I always made it a practice to be in the corridor when she was in the room of the two junior officers. During a period when Miss Davies, the Assistant Matron and Doctor Haas were ill with typhus, and the discipline of the hospital was relaxed somewhat, I heard Susie call my name from behind the closed door of the two officers' room. I flung open the door and caught one of the despicable hounds molesting the poor girl. In Turkish I told Susie to leave the room, which she did without interference, as the officers were too amazed to do more than stare at me. When she had gone one of them lay down on his bed and laughed, but the other came up to me and started to swear and threaten me. Without the slightest hesitation I hit him as hard as I could, full on his foul mouth. In two seconds there was an uproar in that room that must have been heard in the street. Both officers shouted at the top of their voices and attempted to grapple with me. I hit out right and left and was not too particular where my blows landed. Suddenly the door was thrown open and in strode the Bimbashi in his nightgown and skull-cap.

"Dur, dur!" ("Stop, stop"), he bellowed. "What is all this about and what are you doing in here?" he asked of me. I explained what had happened. He must have known his men for, without giving them time to make excuses, he began to curse them and call them most unprintable names, concluding by ordering them to get ready to leave the hospital! The following day the two officers left and the Bimbashi sent for me to thank me! He was in bed when I entered his room, and he told me to sit down and help myself to cigarettes and chat to him. During our conversation he told me that Susie had looked after him very well, and that he had a fatherly affection for her and was very sorry for all the unfortunate Armenians. He was a kindly old chap and quite out of tune with the Turkish officers of that time.

During the illness of Doctor Haas our friend the Arab doctor took charge of the patients. He performed a delicate and painful operation on a Farrier-Staff-Sergeant, one of our number, without instruments other than a probe and a pair of nail scissors and without anaesthetics. Four of us held the Farrier down whilst it was being done, and, though he screamed in agony, the operation undoubtedly saved his life. One morning I asked that huge Arab—he was well over six and a half feet tall and as broad as a door—why he quoted Scriptures instead of giving out medicines.

"I have no medicines to give," he answered. "The Turks will give me neither medicines nor instruments, and I am in daily fear of my life." (The instruments belonging to Doctor Haas had all been locked away.) "Oh, God! when shall I see my family and my beloved Lebanon again?" he cried, as tears streamed down his face. I was genuinely sorry for him as there was no shadow of doubt but that all he had said was true, and we had found him to be a kindly and considerate man.

During that period when the Matron and doctor were ill I was summoned to attend the police court. The nurse in charge, Victoria Danilau, sent a message to Doctor Haas and asked what she had better do. The doctor sent back to say that I should have to go, but for me to remember what arrangements we had come to. He also sent along his

Armenian dispenser to act as interpreter for me. I was taken by *arabah* to the military hospital clothing store to get my clothes. After a long search we found them tied up in a linen bag and labelled "Wilcher Longha." It can be imagined what they looked like when it is remembered that they were fumigated before they were stored, and I should imagine that they were put into the bag still full of steam! I changed from my hospital rig-out and got back into the *arabah* and was driven into the same quadrangle that I had often gazed into from the window of my first prison in Adana. As I passed that tiny window I could discern faces crowding it and I wondered what life was like in there then.

We reached the court and climbed the stairs to the first-floor landing, where we found a crowd of police and natives. Apparently we were in good time, so my escort—a Chaoush— and I squatted on our haunches at the top of the stairs. One or two warders from the town prison were there and they came and shook hands with me, asking after my health and telling me that Micky had long since left the prison. After we had been there about half an hour an under-sized Bimbashi came up the stairs, his sword scabbard banging metallically on every step. The collar of his tunic was so high as to endanger his ears! Neither the Chaoush nor I took any notice of him as he strode—or rather, bounced— by us, so he turned round and boxed the ears of the Chaoush for failing to salute him.

"Kim der bu?" ("Who is this?") he asked, indicating me with his foot. When he was told that I was English he spat on the floor in disgust.

At last my name was called and I was shepherded into a large room and stood facing seven officers seated on a dais. One of the officers was the strutting Bimbashi, but I was pleased to notice that he was not the senior officer present. That did not prevent him from glaring at me as though he would willingly support a motion for my execution. The

proceedings opened by the senior office telling the interpreter to ask me if all the particulars he was about to read
were correct. Then followed the particulars that I had given
to the prison *katib*, followed by particulars of Sergeant R.
The court seemed nonplussed when I told them that the
Sergeant had long since died. It is not necessary to relate
the numerous questions—mostly futile—that were put to
me, nor the answers that I gave. By having an interpreter
I was able to frame my answers so that I could give them
without hesitation, as I was able to understand them before
the interpreter did his part. I gleaned one useful piece of
information that stood me in good stead on subsequent
occasions when I was being interrogated. That was that
no record seemed to be kept by local administrators or
Commandants of the misdemeanours of prisoners of war.
For instance, on this occasion I told the court, in answer
to their query as to why I had attempted to escape, that
I had done no such thing. I stated that a party of us were
being escorted from Islahie to Mamourie and in the night
the escort had deserted us, and that we had wandered about
for several days, trying to find our way in the mountains.
I gave as the reason for the Sergeant and I being alone a
yarn that we two were the fittest of the party and had
pushed on ahead of the others, and they had not overtaken
us when we were attacked by the Gendarmes! I also stressed
the fact that I had suffered permanent injury to my nose
when we were attacked by the police. After all that had
been duly interpreted to the court there ensued an excited
debate, to which I listened intently whilst looking extremely
vacant. I could not understand all that was said, but I
gathered enough to know that they had been unable to get
any information concerning us from the Commandant at
Mamourie, and also that it was becoming a prevalent practice
for soldiers to desert when on escort duty. When the jabbering had subsided somewhat I begged permission to ask

who had given authority for me to be bastinadoed and why I had been kept in prison for several weeks without being given a trial. That caused more excited jabbering and gesticulating and I began to be amused. At last the senior officer turned to the interpreter and said, "Tell him that we have considered his case and have decided that he was not to blame and that we shall not punish him. Tell him also that he is to understand that he must never again wander about the country alone, as he may be attacked and killed. If he remains with the Turks he will be well and properly cared for. He can now return to hospital, and we hope that he will soon be fit enough to join his comrades."

All but the Bimbashi of the high collar smiled at me during the time the interpreter was conveying those remarks to me. I saluted smartly, turned about and marched out, inwardly exulting that I had won my case by colossal bluff and against seven officers. I did not forget, though, that I had already been punished, despite the fact that I was found not guilty. The interpreter bade me good-bye, and the Chaoush and I returned to the clothing store to collect my hospital kit. I would not leave my other clothes there, but took them with me to the hospital.

Life went on as serenely as before and I actually began to develop a "tummy," a fact that caused no little amusement among the nurses. I spent a good deal of my time in the kitchen, sitting at the fire and chatting to the nurses who were off duty. They would listen for hours to my tales of England, the home of the free. I have the happiest recollections of those days and of the little acts of kindness performed for me by those poor Armenian girls. My knowledge of Turkish was greatly increased, and I was able to teach Susie a great many colloquialisms that she would never have learnt at college!

All good things must come to an end, and one fine day Miss Davies—who had now returned to duty—said that

Other Ranks of Kut   M

she had been ordered to make room for more sick Turks from the front, so that she was compelled to send out those of us who were fit. There were six of us to go, and she granted us a great privilege. We were allowed to go into Adana, accompanied by a nurse and a soldier, to try and find hats that would fit us, as none of us possessed hats of any sort. We scoured the town but were unable to find more than two, and they were rusty old bowlers. Still, we thoroughly enjoyed the outing. We all received a brand new outfit, myself included, and we made ready to leave. The nurses cried as we bade them good-bye, and there was not one of us that couldn't quite easily have done so. Half a dozen Indians and a Russian Pole came with us, and we were taken to a building next door to the town prison called the *sokiet khana*. It was a kind of distribution prison, where all discharged prisoners and hospital patients were kept until such time as they were drafted into various units of the army. We had been supplied with plenty of food before we left hospital, and we hoped that we should be sent on to our next destination before we had to rely on the prison diet.

CHAPTER EIGHT

GUESTS OF THE SULTAN ONCE MORE

THE prison was exactly the same as the last I had been in and was fairly full, though we managed to find sufficient space on the platform where we could all sleep together—that is, we English and the Russian. That first night we amused ourselves and the rest of the inmates by singing choruses, of which *John Brown's Body* was received with greatest applause by our prisoner audience.

The following morning I received permission to visit the town prison next door, to see if any of my old friends were still there and to recover my kit if any were left. The Chaoush was on leave and most of the warders were strangers to me, but old Abdul the prison runner was still there and he made a great fuss of me. We entered the prison together and were immediately surrounded by a howling mob, who no doubt thought that I was a newcomer amongst them. The place was packed and it was several minutes before what was left of my kit was brought forward. Had it not have been for Abdullah the Orange Vendor I should have had nothing to collect, as he had looked after it right up to the day he had been taken out, which was only the day before my arrival. As it was, I had little use for what remained, and gave it away after I had seen the state it was in. I had several glasses of tea with Abdullah in the warders' quarters before I returned to the *sokiet*.

On my return I chatted to the sentry on the wicket, and he told me that as soon as there was room enough for us on a train we should be sent to Tarsus. From there we should have to march over the mountains until we reached the railway at Bozanti, where we should entrain for Afion-Kara-Hissar. That meant that we should have to carry all our kit, so I suggested to my party that we ought to practise arranging our kits into a pack-like bundle, ready for when we should have to march. This was agreed to be a good plan, so we opened up our spare clothes and the things that we had received from Miss Davies. I had opened out my quilt and was packing everything neatly upon it when a crowd of rowdies gathered around, laughing and passing rude remarks. One of them persisted in picking up every article I put down, the more closely to examine and criticize it. I told him repeatedly to leave things alone and to let me get on with my job, but he took not the slightest notice. At last I lost patience and temper and jumped off the platform and hit him a clout on the nose, immediately drawing blood. Pained and amazed he stood with his legs apart and his body bent forward, allowing the blood to drip from his nose and form a small pool on the floor. His pals stood round in a circle gazing, as though fascinated, at the blood. I had returned to the platform and continued to arrange my kit, with an alert eye for the next move that I expected would be made. It was not long in coming. Suddenly the crowd made a rush at me and I was seized by a dozen pairs of hands. I managed to kick myself free for a few moments and to get in several punches that loosened the teeth of the recipients, but the odds were too heavy against me. Dozens of shoes and slippers were used as weapons, wielded by as many hands, and I was well and truly belaboured about the head and shoulders. Then I was grabbed from behind and lifted off my feet and the clothes were torn off me. How I should have fared further I shudder to think, had not the sentry have come to my aid. The Russian Pole had rushed to the wicket for him when he saw me off my feet, and he arrived, smashing his way through the crowd with a clubbed rifle. He was followed almost immediately by an Onbashi who helped me to my feet from where I had been dropped. The Onbashi demanded an explanation, and I was

THE START OF A CARAVAN

[*See* p. 346

KIRKUK

[*See p.* 72

A KURKDISH VILLAGE

[*See p.* 188

accused of an unwarranted and brutal assault, my accusers producing the victim as evidence. Blood was still upon his chin and clothing, and I had to think of a convincing yarn to explain my action, as the truth would certainly not be appreciated. I told the Onbashi that when I had told the man to leave my things alone he had attacked me with a knife and I had struck him in self-defence! After that the whole of his party of friends had attacked me. The Onbashi could see for himself what sort of handling I had received and, fortunately for me, he believed my story. He ordered the sentry to fetch a posse of policemen from their billets and then ordered all the prisoners to stand by their kits. When the policemen arrived he posted them at different points of the room and commenced a search among the kits of my attackers for the knife I had alleged had been used. I knew that knives were strictly forbidden and did not dream for one moment that the search would be successful—but it was! Several knives were discovered and the owners immediately protested their innocence of any attack upon me. It was no good, my story had been proved to the satisfaction of the Onbashi, who spat upon them and jabbed them with the muzzle of his rifle. When the search was over the whole unsavoury gang was tied together, wrist to wrist, and marched out of the *sokiet* and into the town prison. By this time I had donned my old fumigated suit and had collected what remained of the other one that had been torn off me. It had been a hectic five minutes for me and I was not so sure that I had come off best, though I consoled myself with the thought that I had retained my independence. The other five Englishmen had been taken completely by surprise by the sudden action and, in any case, had been so utterly cowed by the treatment they had had at Bagtchi that they could do no more than stand helplessly looking on at the mêlée. I had only the Russian to thank for the fact that I had escaped with nothing worse than scores of bruises. My head was covered with bumps and looked as though it had been attacked by a swarm of infuriated bees.

Just before sunset on the day of that disturbance the sentry at the wicket yelled out for the "Ingleezi Terjiman." I went over to him to see what he wanted and he said that a girl had come to see me and was outside the building. Wondering who it could be, I stepped outside and found Susie waiting for me with a basket of food; bread, and boiled eggs. She told me that they had learned at the hospital that we were still in the *sokiet* so she had volunteered to bring us some more food. The sentry and several other loungers outside the building passed obscene comments at the unusual scene of an unveiled female talking confidentially to an English prisoner. Inwardly foaming, I told Susie that it was unsafe for her to come and see us, and that I felt ashamed that she was subjected to insults on our behalf. She, brave girl, only laughed, and said that no harm would come to her and that she was used to hearing obscenities from the Turks. That was all very well, but I was not used to it, and I was greatly relieved when she bade me good-bye and left me.

We still had food left, but we were glad enough to get the extra, as we knew, from past experiences, that we should need all we could get.

That night we again sang choruses, and there were many shouts of encouragement and much clapping of hands in rhythm by our fellow prisoners.

Morning brought the news that we should be leaving for the station before noon, so we joyfully packed our kits into handy bundles. For once the news was true and it was not long before we were on our way to the railway station at Adana. We were not the only ones to be leaving the *sokiet*, as our party was made up to about fifty by the addition of sundry Kurds, Arabs, Armenians and Turks. At the station we were taken to a siding and entrained into goods wagons, with one sentry to each wagon. The doors were left open on either side and we were not unduly crowded. After half an hour's wait we were shunted on to the main line and attached to a passenger train that was due to start within the hour. To my great surprise, Susie arrived again with another basket of food, just after we had got on to the main line. The sentry allowed me to get out of the wagon in order to talk to her and she told me that she had got to know the day and time we were leaving by the aid of the Bimbashi, and had determined to come and see us off. There were many curious eyes turned in our direction as we stood laughing and chatting by the side of the train. The passenger coach to which our wagon was hooked was one reserved for women, and there was an excited babble coming from the veiled occupants all the time we stood there. I was unable to catch any of the remarks that they passed, but Susie must have done, as she blushed furiously at something that was said that caused those women to laugh uproariously. The whistle blew, and I—reckless of Turkish conventions—kissed Susie a hurried good-bye before I climbed back into my wagon. With a whispered "God protect you," the brave little girl hurried out of the station without once glancing back.

I distributed the food that she had brought, not forgetting to give the obliging sentry a share.

It was only a short run into Tarsus, though it was not until late afternoon that we reached there. We detrained and were marched to a building which our escort described as *medressah Ermin* (Armenian school), and where we were to spend the night. In a large room with a boarded floor —something unusual—we found nearly a hundred men who, like us, were to march over the mountains sooner or later. They were singing and dancing as we entered, and they appeared in no wise depressed by their immediate prospects.

We British were immediately surrounded and put through the usual catechism. Everyone was friendly, and in a very short time we were all laughing and talking and swearing about the *Dowlat* (Government). Two "star" dancers gave an exhibition of folk dancing for our benefit, accompanied by the raucous chanting and rhythmical clapping of the onlookers. Apparently one of the dancers represented an elusive damsel and the other her ardent swain. Both performers used castanets and did a fair amount of stamping, which latter caused clouds of dust to rise from the unswept floor. The dance continued until the performers were tired of it, but the conclusion did *not* bring the capture of the damsel by her swain!

We made our beds on the floor near a wall and discussed the future as we ate our frugal supper. It was extremely cold and we were very glad of the quilts with which we had been provided by Miss Davies. I chatted for a time with a man who claimed to be a "Tarsusli," a native of Tarsus, although he could tell me very little about the place other than it possessed a river called Tatli Su (sweet water), which was *chok tatli* (very sweet) and the best in Turkey. I was unable to dispute his statement and, having learned to value a good drop of water, found nothing funny in his oft-repeated, "A-a-ah! Tarsu-u-us, memliketi, Tatli su; chok, chok, tatli." ("Ah! Tarsus, my home town. Sweet water; very, very sweet.") Ever afterwards, when I heard the words *chok tatli*, I was reminded of the night I spent in that Armenian school at Tarsus.

The next morning we set off towards the Taurus Mountains, which we had to cross in order to reach the railway to carry us on to our destination. As we marched over the plain that led to the foothills we passed several parties of Armenian road-menders; men who had obviously had a very rough time of it and were terribly emaciated and ill-looking. Most of them were old men and were crying piteously as their overseers beat them in an effort to get them to work faster. It was a very depressing sight for us, as we had heard all about the tribulations of the Armenians from our nurses in Adana. There seemed to be little that was good in the Turkey of those days.

We entered the foothills during the afternoon and marched into a military encampment. Here most of our party—those who had joined us at Tarsus—were taken elsewhere, whilst those of us from Adana were told to sit where we were until food was ready for us. We were on the edge of a fair-sized parade-ground, which was bordered on three sides by roughly built stone huts. Behind the huts were rows of bell-tents, making a fairly large camp. We had not been waiting long when someone blew a whistle and orders were shouted among the tents, which brought several hundreds of soldiers on to the parade-ground where they took up a—to me— peculiar formation. They were in long double lines, each pair of lines being about four yards apart and the front rank facing the rear rank, thus forming long avenues of men. Down those avenues came other men carrying steaming ration-tins—copper dishes about eighteen inches diameter by four inches deep—which were placed on the ground at intervals of five files of men, i.e. between every ten men. Each man on parade carried a spoon. At the end of the parade-ground stood a Bash-Chaoush (Sergeant-Major) who, when all was ready, blew a whistle. At the sound of the whistle, the whole parade moved to their respective dishes and squatted down, each man being just able to get his right arm into the circle around each dish. They lost no time in delicate feeding but shovelled the mess into their mouths as hard as they could go, each man trying to get an odd spoonful ahead of his neighbour. In what seemed to me an incredibly short time the Bash-Chaoush blew his whistle again and every man stood to his feet at once! I could see into those dishes nearest to us and they were perfectly clean, not a vestige of food remaining. It was one of the most amazing features of a Turkish soldier's life I had seen to date, and I was greatly amused to think that they had to eat literally "by numbers."

After the Turks had marched back to the tents we were told to send one man of each ten to the cookhouse to draw our rations. There were only six of us English and one Russian, so I went for a tin for the seven of us, as I had no intention of feeding "by numbers" with natives floundering about in the same dish. At the cookhouse a Chaoush was supervising the issue of rations and I asked him for a dish for seven Englishmen. He wore the red and white ribbon of the Dardanelles campaign, and as soon as I said "Ingleezi" he took me to the huge cauldron and ordered the cook to serve me first. I received ten rations, the same as the remainder, so for once in a while I was lucky. We shared out our feed—a wheat *pilaff* called *burgrll*—into our own enamel food containers, leaving a goodly share in the ration-tin for the Russian. As long as we were able we intended to eat in the manner to which we were accustomed, as to gallop our food, feeding from a common dish, was no acquirement of British soldiers. The natives of our party had eaten like the Turkish soldiers and had finished before we had even started!

We spent that night in one of the stone huts, huddled together for warmth as the windows were barred but un-glazed and the floor was very damp, the whole atmosphere of the interior being like that of an unused riverside cellar.

We were up and off early the next morning without re-ceiving anything to eat, being told that we should receive rations at our next camping-place. The morning was bright but intensely cold, and we were glad to be on the move. Slowly we toiled along the road that led upwards to the pass through the Taurus Mountains. I tried to recall all I had read of this famous pass; perhaps it was the one where

Saul had come through on his journey to Tarsus. I knew that legions of soldiery had passed that way during the centuries from the days of the Hittites, but surely those towering crags had never witnessed English soldiers in such a state, marching into captivity. Under other circumstances we might have appreciated the grandeur of the scene, but now we were too intent upon the climb.

Before I had left Adana I had become the proud possessor of a pair of boots—if the contraptions I was wearing could rightly be called such. They had been made without the aid of lasts so that the right was indistinguishable from the left! Owing to the metal shortage in Turkey no rivets were available, so the soles had been secured to the uppers by wooden pegs. Pieces of string served for laces and were threaded through eyeletless holes. When I had bought them my feet had become soft again, and I thought that they would serve me better than the Turkish slippers I had received from the American Consul. As I plodded up the steep road I very much regretted my choice, as blisters formed on my heels and toes and I could feel the points of the pegs sticking through the soles.

High above us the mountain peaks were hidden in fleecy clouds and snow lay in the ravines and crevices on either side of the road. As we climbed higher we became enveloped in clouds and it began to snow. Nothing could have added more to our misery than snow and I, for one, wished that I was under a scorching sun again. One of our party, a Sergeant-Major of the Royal Garrison Artillery, began to weaken and required assistance. Our escort were not unduly harsh but they rarely allowed us to halt, saying that we should not get to our next camp before the next morning if we dallied. Parties of soldiers, on their way to the plains, passed us occasionally, and we noticed how spiritless they appeared and how poorly dressed and equipped they were. The road became more difficult when the snow began to settle, and my boots began to show signs of falling to pieces. Hour after hour we plodded our miserable way upwards, too utterly fed up to talk to each other. At last we reached what appeared to be an elevated valley between two ranges of mountains.

To the left of us was a huge mechanical-transport park belonging to the Germans, the neat layout and uniformity of the rows of vehicles vividly reminding us of similar scenes in our own Service; reminding us, too, of the miserable plight we were now in as prisoners of war. To our right was a Kurdish village built of rocks and rough timber; just off the road—where it took a sweeping bend round the German encampment—were some half-dugouts, crudely roofed over with mud-covered logs. Into those we were herded and told that there we should stop for the night. Everything lay under a mantle of snow, but even snow could not disguise the squalidness of those rude hovels. That into which my particular party entered was lit by a single smoky hurricane lamp and, to our horror, we found it carpeted with snow. We scraped a place clear where we thought to lay our quilts for the night, only to find that the snow concealed a deep layer of cattle droppings, now become a wet and stinking mass. I went to the doorway and shouted for the Chaoush, expecting the Chaoush of our escort to appear, instead, a foul-looking Arab *askar* came up and asked what I wanted. I requested that we be put into a dry dug-out as, not being cattle, we could not sleep in wet dung. For my pains I received a stinging cut across my face from a whip he carried, and was knocked back into the hovel. I rejoined my party and helped them rake back the snow over the dung and then sat down to await rations. We had nothing left of the food that Susie had brought to us before we left Adana and we were now both cold and hungry. When rations eventually arrived they proved to be in keeping with everything else in that inhospitable camp: lukewarm, watery, meatless *kurrawanna* (stew), and a loaf of sour black bread. The best that could be said of it all was that it filled our empty bellies.

Meanwhile, some of the Arabs who were sharing the hovel with us had been out foraging for firewood and had brought in a considerable quantity of dead branches. These they piled up on the floor and lit, speedily filling the hovel with smoke and acrid fumes which, however uncomfortable it was for our lungs and eyes, took the deadly chill off the atmosphere. When at last the branches broke into a blaze we were greatly comforted even by the sight of them. The Arabs had only the clothes they wore to keep them warm, so they huddled around the fire until early morning, shouting and cursing and constantly awakening us with their raucous singing. We curled up in our quilts and endeavoured to sleep, but the heat of our bodies melted the snow beneath us and the wet mass beneath the snow quickly soaked through to our bodies, so that sleep did not come easily.

Morning brought brilliant sunshine and we were only too pleased to hear the familiar "Yellah, yellah," that meant we were to get outside and on the move again. From the whole party fifteen of the natives had vanished during the night, and the officer in charge of that dismal "half-way house" jumped up and down and screamed at the sentries like an hysterical woman. Our start was delayed for more than an hour whilst the immediate neighbourhood was searched for any sign of the escapees. When we did move off we climbed without a break until the summit of the pass was reached. Long before that the soles of my boots had parted company from the uppers and, once more, I was barefoot. The Chaoush would not let me stop to tie bits of rag around my feet, saying that he intended to reach the next camp early and would not allow anyone to halt except when he gave the order. That resulted in my feet becoming very sore and lacerated and my gait slow and painful. Several times during the morning we heard the "crack" of rifle shots and I was informed, by one of the Arabs, that in all probability patrols were hunting the fugitives from our party. My informant told me also that, in addition to deserters, there were many Armenians and bandits roaming the mountains in that district. As I gazed at the gloomy and formidable crags on either side of me I found no difficulty in believing them to be the haunt of lawless and desperate men.

The road, at one point, entered a ravine that seemed to be the result of a slice having been carved out of the mountain. On either side rose, in gaunt majesty, the raw sides of the "cut." Hugging the perpendicular side on the left was the road on which we were travelling, and on the right a stream splashed its way among the boulders. The gorge gradually tapered until it seemed as though we were marching along a gigantic corridor at the end of which we might come to the entrance of an ogre's castle! The Cilician Gates! Unfortunately, at that time I had but a hazy knowledge of the history of those parts, otherwise I might have been more interested in the writings we could see, cut high up in the mountain face. As it was, I was impressed by the overawing majesty of the place.

Issuing from the ravine we began our descent to the valley, and ere long I was unable to continue without assistance. I had stumbled and fallen many times as a more than usually sharp flint cut my half-frozen and bleeding feet, and now I had come to the end of my endurance. One of the Englishmen and the Russian helped me to my feet and supported me between themselves for the remainder of the journey. It was the first time—and the last—that I was assisted on the march during my captivity.

At the foot of the pass we reached Bozanti, the terminus of the Anatolian section of the Constantinople to Baghdad railway. We were taken into a barrack-like hut and told that we should have to wait there until we could get a train going north to Afion-Kara-Hissar. Further along the mountainside a tunnel was being constructed and, at a place called Belemedik, was a prisoners of war labour camp. Most of the prisoners were naval ratings and soldiers taken at the Dardanelles; the Australians that I had met in Adana civil prison had been working there when they made their unsuccessful attempt to escape.

The hut we occupied was a pole and brushwood affair without windows. It was certainly clean inside, compared with our last lodging, but it provided little shelter against the cold. We were given more bread and *kurrawanna* and instructed not to go outside for any purpose whatsoever, unless we wanted trouble. I managed to get water to bathe my feet and, after I had bandaged them with strips torn from my shirt, and had had an hour or two of rest, I felt considerably better. We remained in that hut until the evening of the following day, when we were taken to the station and locked into a goods wagon of a waiting train. About midnight we felt the train moving and conjectured that we were off on the last stage of our journey to Afion-Kara-Hissar. It was impossible to sleep because of the continual jolt and rattle of the train, which seemed to come to a stop every half an hour or so. We had no idea what was happening outside, but it seemed as though the train had left the rails and was taking a short cut over the mountains!

After several hours of extreme discomfort the train came to another of its many halts and the door of our wagon was opened and we were ordered to get out. It was barely dawn, and, as we stood and shivered in the half-light and peered about us, we wondered what was going to happen. None of the Arabs and Kurds, etc., of the party had been allowed out—just the few English and Indians, and the Russian, who had come from hospital in Adana. So far as we could see there were only two buildings at the place, the station

and a house, so we concluded that it couldn't be our destination. The sentries were a churlish lot and would tell us
nothing.

Dawn came and with it the sun, and we were very grateful
for its warmth as the night had been bitterly cold. We found
that we had stopped on a bare featureless plain and it was
not until we saw a party approaching from the horizon that
we had any idea why we had stopped there. The party
eventually reached the waiting train and they proved to be as
desperate a crowd of men as we had seen so far. There were
about two dozen of them securely roped together and guarded
by ten Gendarmes. They were helped into the truck we had
vacated by vicious blows from the escort, as they experienced
difficulty in getting in because of their bonds. Then the
train moved off, leaving us standing in that desolate spot.
A Chaoush and two *askars* had remained and I asked them
what was going to happen, having visions of another painful
march. I was told that we should have to wait for another
train, which might arrive that day or the next!

For three days we waited at that wayside station and the
only food we got was what the Chaoush could beg from
occasional troop trains that halted there. There was no
shelter of any sort and we were lucky that it neither rained
nor snowed in those three days, though it was certainly cold
and miserable enough at nights.

On the fourth day we were picked up by a passing freight
train and continued our journey to Afion-Kara-Hissar without further untoward events. We arrived at our destination
late at night and were taken to a building just outside the
station until daylight, when we were taken to the local
hammam (bath). There our clothes were taken from us to be
fumigated and we were shaved from head to foot before being
parboiled in the bath. The bath entrance opened on to a
large walled-in quadrangle and it was there—I learned later
—that several hundreds of Bulgarian prisoners of war were

massacred when the news of the fall of Adrianople came through, during the second Balkan War.

When we came to collect our clothes we found that the bath attendants had helped themselves to anything they had fancied from our bundles.

From the bath we were marched up a hill and through the town to a large house, where we were to stay. Before we went in we were counted several times and had to give the usual particulars of our home towns, etc. The Indians and the Russian were taken elsewhere and we six Englishmen were admonished to keep the place clean and not to walk about the rooms with boots on! Then we entered and a Turkish sailor—the first we had seen—was mounted as sentry at the door and we were left to our own devices.

After inspecting the house from cellar to garret we chose a large bay-windowed room on the second floor, overlooking the street, as our quarters. There was ample room on the bare floor for the six of us and we each picked a place to call our own. When we had spread our quilts and put out our few belongings we crowded to the window to see what we could of Afion-Kara-Hissar (Opium Black Rock). The rock was the most prominent feature and dominated the whole town. Perched right on the top of it was the remains of an ancient castle. We counted forty minarets from our window and concluded that the Mohammedans hereabouts either were very devout or fanatical or both. Directly opposite us across the street was a house similar to ours which, so far as we could see, was occupied by two Russian officers. To our left the street was bisected by a cross-road and above that we could see British and Indian officers exercising up and down the street. I went on to the roof and saw a woman in the house that backed on to ours playing on a sort of zither. I continued to stare until she noticed me, when she gave a squeal and vanished. Although I had done no harm I left the roof, sensing that she might make trouble. I was right!

Other Ranks of Kut   **N**

As I re-entered our room a *posta* (sentry) came in and demanded to know which dog among us had been spying on the woman next door. It was on the tip of my tongue to explain, but the attitude of the man was so threatening, and his abuse of us so vile, that I thought discretion to be the better part of valour and kept my mouth shut. We decided that if that *posta* was a sample of Turkish sailors, then they were a particularly nasty brand, and subsequent events proved that we were not far wrong.

During the day we received a loaf of bread and *kurrawanna*, the bread being quite good but the stew being very watery and insipid. It was the sort of ration that we were to get all the time we were at Afion. Sometimes the stew was made with broad beans—still in the pod!—and at others of grape-vine cuttings and olive oil! Hunger made a fine sauce and whatever we got we ate without question and with avidity.

During our second day at Afion a Cypriote came into our room and announced himself as the *terjiman* to the Commandant. He led each of us in turn to the window and carefully scrutinized us. What he wanted or for whom he was searching we were unable to guess, but he was apparently unsuccessful, for in the end he said to the *posta* who had accompanied him into the room, "Kimsa yok" ("No one"), clicking his tongue and giving the short upward jerk of the head that signifies negation to the Turk. For a long time I debated in my mind the reason—or lack of it—for the Cypriote's action, and it was not until other Englishmen, from another place in the town, had joined us that the riddle was solved. Then we learned that Musloum Bey had committed unnatural practices on certain of the younger members of the Kut Garrison. From that we conjectured—no doubt rightly—that his *terjiman* was seeking a fresh victim from among the new-comers when he had inspected us. We were to hear more about the brutal degenerate Musloum Bey.

Surely no nation in the world had sunk so low as the

Turkey of those days. We had encountered little but bestiality, brutality, bribery and corruption wherever we had been. Civilization was at a very low ebb in that accursed land.

For the first five days after our arrival at Afion we were confined to our house, and the awful monotony of our empty lives was having a bad effect on our nerves. We had absolutely nothing to do but lie about or look out of the window. On the sixth day we were allowed into the roadway for an hour's exercise. That hour we spent playing leapfrog and generally acting like school-boys let out at playtime. Four days later we were taken to a large field outside the town, where we met, for the first time, the other "rank and file" prisoners of war, who were billeted in an Armenian church in the town. In the intervals of exchanging yarns we played every kind of game that we could think of—games that required no sort of equipment, of course. Many of us searched our memories for clues as to games that we had played as schoolboys, and, to the onlooker, the scene that day must have been most ludicrous. Actually to us it was starkly tragic. That was the only occasion during my stay at Afion that we were allowed so much liberty.

Two days after our "organized games" a party of three British officers arrived next door from the Palestine front. I was asked by our senior member, Sammy Field—Sergeant-Major of the Royal Garrison Artillery—to act as servant to them during the fourteen days of quarantine that they would spend in the house next door. I gladly consented, as it would give me something to do, and moved my odds and ends into my new billet. One of the officers was a Lieutenant of an Indian cavalry regiment and wore the '08 Indian Frontier Medal, the other two were Second Lieutenants, youngsters of war-time vintage, and all three were attached for flying duties to the Royal Flying Corps. They had been brought down behind the Turkish lines before Gaza. All three were very affable and took things in great good humour, though they cursed all things Turkish. From what they told me afterwards I learned that the Lieutenant and one of the subs. had been on patrol over the Turkish lines when their engine gave out and they were forced to land. Unfortunately for them, they were dressed only in pyjamas, and it was not until a German pilot dropped a message for them into the British lines, in answer to which a suitcase full of clothes was dropped for them, that they were able to get dressed! Even then the sub. was unlucky, as the only shirt they dropped for him was a "boiled" one! What he was doing on active service with a dress-shirt I never discovered. By the time he had reached Afion it was in a pretty dirty state and he was still cursing the stupidity of the person who had packed his kit before it was dropped for him.

My first duty was to get in a stock of food and fuel for them. They supplied me with some cash and I was given an amiable old Turkish soldier as an escort into the town bazaar. There I thoroughly enjoyed myself, bargaining with the shopkeepers and generally airing my Turkish. When I returned I found the Cypriote and Kolassi (Assistant Commandant) taking particulars from the officers, and I noticed that the Lieutenant was not favourably impressed with his questioners. Apparently they had brought some money for the officers, for the Lieutenant was counting out a few Turkish lira notes and he said something about the robbing, blankety-blank Turks. The Cypriote murmured something about reprisals which caused the Lieutenant to indulge in a real outburst of profanity which continued until the Cypriote and Kolassi had left, much to my great amusement. I went "below stairs" (literally) and made a fire preparatory to cooking the officers a meal. I had purchased cooking-pots, crockery, and cutlery, and I got as much fun out of cooking the meal as the officers did pleasure when they received it. Fortunately for them I was no novice in the kitchen. They insisted that I sleep in the same room as themselves and tell them of the siege of Kut-el-Amara and other happenings on the Mesopotamian front. I well remember the Lieutenant saying, apropos of the R.F.C. dropping food into Kut during the siege, that he would guarantee to drop a crate of eggs from an aeroplane without breaking one! I very much doubt whether that feat could be done even now—twenty years later.

That first night was the last that I slept in the same room with them, for I was kept awake all night by the hideous noise the Lieutenant made, grinding his teeth!

The following fortnight was an easy one for me. Each day I went to the bazaar on a shopping expedition and was very soon on good terms with the shopkeepers, who let me taste their foodstuffs before I decided to purchase. One of the subs. was taken away to hospital, suffering from a mild attack of typhoid, and I took that opportunity to wash his only shirt as well as his other linen. When he was due to come out I took his clothes to him and he complained bitterly that the Turks had shaved him all over! I told him that most of us had suffered that indignity and that he had really nothing to complain about—yet. That was the last I ever saw of him, as I had to leave his clothes with him and then return to the house, and he was posted from hospital to the officers' quarters farther up the road, where the other two joined him a day or so later. On one occasion during my period as batman I managed to pay a visit to the officers' quarters up the road, and I was amazed to see how comfortably they had managed to fix themselves up. They all seemed to be very busy with some job or other; one was making a "stick and string" bed, another was busy making a table, whilst a third was patching up some books. I passed into the kitchen and found everything in full swing preparing for dinner. To me it was an eye-opener, that visit to the officers' quarters. Compared with what the "other ranks" had and the conditions under which

they lived, the officers had a life of luxury. I have no doubt
that they themselves thought that they were in pretty low
water and were having a devilish rough time. It is not for
me to criticize unfavourably the tremendous disparity in the
treatment of the officers and men in those bad days, but it is
well to put on record that only a very few of the officer
prisoners had any idea at all of the vile conditions and brutal
treatment that was the lot of the "other ranks." There were
instances where officers got into trouble with the Turks for
attempting to assist the men when they did get to know a
little of the truth, but those instances were rare. Undoubtedly
the ingenuity and skill of the officers themselves did much to
make life easier for them, but they had to have the *means*,
otherwise they would have been unable to contrive all they
did. The "other ranks" had neither the means nor the
opportunity, and only they can speak with authority on the
ghastliness of life as prisoners of war with the Turks. This
is written in no spirit of churlishness or rancour, for I know
that there were some very gallant officers at Afion and other
camps, and some most amazing attempts to escape were
made by some of them, attempts which entailed the possession of indomitable courage and the ability to endure great
hardships. But nothing they suffered under the normal state
of captivity can be compared in the slightest to the suffering,
degradation and hardships that were the portion of the
"other ranks."

I had only been back with my party one day when three
more officers arrived in the quarantine house, and I went
back to look after them. They, also, had been taken on the
Palestine front, at Gaza. One was a Major and the other two
were Lieutenants, all were of a war-time battalion of the
Essex Regiment. Unfortunately, I found things not quite so
pleasant this time. I was kept very much in my place and the
prices of all the commodities I bought for them were carefully checked and recorded. To say the least of it, I was not

very happy with those officers and was not at all sorry when
they departed for Kastamuni or some other officers' camp.
They were quite obviously "temporary gentlemen" and had
a lot to learn about many things, and I am quite confident
that they received adequate tuition when they got among the
type of officers with whom I was used to serving.

Very shortly after this we received news that a working
party was being formed of prisoners from the Armenian
church, and that it was quite possible that several of us who
were fit would be chosen to join them when they were ready
to leave Afion. When the time came four of us were chosen,
and we marched away to the station to join some twenty
others, taken from the church. In addition there were a dozen
Russians and about the same number of Indians. Among
the Englishmen was Corporal Dade—Micky of my Adana
prison days. Speculation was rife as to our ultimate destination and no one could be found who could or would tell us.
I did not care very much as I was heartily sick of being
cooped up in a house and longed for a change of scenery.

Once more we found ourselves locked into a goods wagon
and being jolted along Turkey's single-track railway. Nothing
worthy of note occurred on the journey, it was just another
series of jerk, rattle, and stop until we were ordered to de-
train at a place called Oogla Kishla. There we were marched
into a huge barn-like structure and securely locked in.
Several hours later we received a meal of *chourba* (rice soup)
and bread, and were told that on the following day we should
be going inland to a place called Bōr. None of us had any
idea where that place might be nor of what we should be
expected to do when we got there.

All that day it poured with rain and we found that our
lodging was in the same ruinous condition as every other
place in Turkey, for we were constantly moving around the
building to dodge the drippings from the leaky roof. For
some unaccountable reason we did not start off until the

evening, so that it was impossible to see what sort of locality we were in. It was not a long march as we understood the term, but it was arduous because of the long time that most of us had been off the road. During the night we passed a fair-sized place which, I was told by the escort, was called Nigda, and shortly after we reached our destination—Bōr.

CHAPTER NINE

AT BŌR AND ANOTHER MOVE SOUTH

BŌR seemed to be a place right off the map; a peaceful little village. We were still wondering why we had been sent there, when we marched down a narrow alley that terminated in an entrance to the courtyard of a fairly large house. Through the entrance we went and were surprised to find half a dozen other Englishmen and four or five Frenchmen already there. We were allotted various rooms in the house according to nationalities; the English into two, the Russians into one other, and the Indians into a fourth. When we had settled in we gathered round the other Englishmen and asked for news. They told us that the Turks had decided to prepare another concentration camp for the many prisoners that they had taken on the Palestine front, and that it was to be at Bōr, the place we were now at. We, it seemed, were to form the camp, though what we were expected to do they could not tell us. The house had belonged to a wealthy Armenian, who had been killed off to make room! The Turks certainly had a unique method of relieving the pressure of house shortage! This particular house was in reality several houses, forming three sides of a square round the courtyard. The third side was taken up by a wall in which was a built-up entrance to an apricot grove. Water was supplied from a foot-wide stone conduit that entered the yard from the garden, crossed the cobble-stoned courtyard and left through an aperture near the entrance. The entrance was guarded by a very ancient one-legged *posta*, whose "bayonet" consisted of a bar of iron *welded* on to the muzzle end of the barrel of his rifle! We speedily discovered that all the sentries were either very old or disabled men, a sure indication that even at that date—1917—the Turks were getting short of trained men.

The first party of officers I had looked after in Afion had generously given me two lira before they had gone to join the other officers in the camp, and but for that money I should have had a very thin time of it during my short stay at Bōr, for rations were very meagre there. We were allowed to purchase what we wanted from the local bazaar, but only one man of each nationality was permitted to do the shopping each day. It was decided that each man should have an opportunity of the change a visit to the bazaar afforded, so we took it in turns to do the shopping. That was a perfectly fair arrangement but *I* wanted to get out more often than that so I looked around for a means of exit. On one side of the courtyard the house adjoined others and I thought that if I could get on to the roof I might possibly find a way of getting down to the streets outside. The normal way on to the roof had been nailed up by the Turks but I succeeded in making a hole in the ceiling of the top room, big enough to let me through. As I thought, it was an easy matter to gain access to the roof of the house adjoining, and, as is usual in the East, I was able to travel along a series of roofs until I found a place where I could climb down to earth. I proceeded very cautiously the first time I ventured abroad, but when I found that my presence in the village, without an escort, went unnoticed, I threw caution to the winds. In the open space in the centre of the village was a fountain that supplied water to the inhabitants and there I made many friends among the children who used to draw water. There was a noticeable absence of adult males in the village. I have never been sure whether my young friends were Turkish or Kurdish but they were a merry crowd. They used to make all my purchases for me from the bazaar, as they usually got things at half the price that was being charged us, which made me think that there was some system of graft going on between the *postas* and the shopkeepers. My luck was too good to last and my little jaunts came to a very sudden end.

One morning, I crawled through the hole in the ceiling as usual and, to my great surprise, was confronted by two *postas*, who immediately jumped on me. They very soon had me securely bound by the arms and I was led over the roofs and down the stairs of one of the houses. One of the *postas* was armed with a huge felling axe and he led the way, holding his axe at the "ready." I was taken straight to the Commandant's office and haled before that official to answer for my misdeed. That was the first time that I had seen the Commandant and I was pleased to notice that he seemed an amiable sort of person. The *posta* with the axe told his story, and before he had finished I hardly knew whether to laugh or to be alarmed. According to his account he had long suspected that an attempt to escape was to be made so, in consequence, he and his companion had continuously watched, unseen, on the roof-tops, with the result that they had caught me red-handed making an attempt to escape. I had fought desperately when they had caught me and they had had to bind me up! When he had finished his rigmarole the Commandant asked me why I was smiling, and what had I to say for myself. Greatly daring I asked the Commandant whether he believed the story he had just heard.

"Why should I not believe my soldiers?" he asked. I had no ready reply to that, so I said that I had discovered the hole already made in the roof and had frequently used it in order to do my own shopping, as the shopkeepers were charging extortionate prices to our official shoppers. I told him, further, that had I wanted to have escaped I could have done so on the first occasion that I had used the hole. I did not worry about being punished for my offence but I certainly did not want to be charged with the relatively serious offence of attempting to escape. After a few questions had been put to me and answered, apparently satisfactorily, the Commandant told the *postas* to release me and take me back to the house. He said, before I went, that he did not believe that I was trying to escape but I had no business to break the rules he had laid down and if I were caught at it again he would have no hesitation in having me shot!

I considered myself very lucky and, needless to state, I did not again attempt to visit the village on my own.

The walls of the rooms of our house had been whitewashed and Micky—being no mean artist—had decorated several of them with huge charcoal sketches. One of them was a life-size representation of the god Mercury, and when this was seen by one of the ancient *postas* there was a terrific hulla-baloo. The *posta* brought in the Chaoush to see the sacrilege committed by an infidel *Nosrani* (unbelieving Christian).

The orthodox Mohammedan will not tolerate any photo-graphs, drawings, or other pictorial representations of the human form, as they hold them to be man's attempt to usurp the powers of God.

The Chaoush was enraged and I had a difficult task to convince him that the drawings were not intended to be an insult to the Mahommedans or anyone else, but were just idle drawings. In the end I was successful but we received strict orders not to do anything else of the kind.

About this time, sickness was on the increase among us, and we were greatly amused when we were informed by the Turkish doctor that we brought about our illnesses by constantly washing our bodies! It was our habit to strip to the waist at least twice a day and have a thorough wash in the water-conduit that passed through the courtyard, and we had often been told by the *postas* that that was the reason why we were so white and weakly. We little dreamed that a doctor would tell us the same thing and we laughed outright when he got a *posta* to demonstrate how we ought to wash if we wished to keep our health. According to the accepted Turkish fashion we had to push our hats to the back of our heads and wipe our faces with our wetted hands. To wash the neck, etc., was simply asking for trouble. Needless to say, we took not the slightest notice of the doctor's advice but continued to keep ourselves as clean as we could.

Since the ban on charcoal drawings, Micky had become possessed of a toy box of paints, bought in the bazaar, and these were to prove useful in another way. One day an order was issued that everyone was to be vaccinated and we were to "fall in" with one sleeve rolled up to the shoulder. The idea of being vaccinated by a Turk was extremely repugnant to me, and, when I saw the entire lack of precautions against infection that were being taken, I determined to avoid being done if it were at all possible. The doctor sat on a low wall and performed the operation and the Chaoush mustered those that had been done into a separate party. If he saw a spot of blood in the appropriate place the Chaoush was satisfied that the man had been vaccinated. Micky and I observed all this and we had an idea. We would paint some drops of "blood" on our arm with vermilion from Micky's paint box! This we did and, screwing up our faces as though our arms were smarting, we joined the party under the Chaoush. He was completely hoodwinked, much to our satisfaction and amusement. We were not always able to avoid injections and the like but that was not the last time that Micky and I managed to dupe the doctors.

Life became terribly monotonous in that crowded court-yard, so it was with feelings of tremendous relief that I was chosen to be one of a party of twenty that were picked to be sent as a working party farther down south. Micky was of the party and from that time forward we were inseparable and our subsequent adventures together form the most amazing feature of our lives as prisoners of war in Turkey.

We left Bōr late one night and arrived at Oogla Kishla early the next morning, where we entrained for Bozanti after a short visit. From Bozanti we were marched to Belemedik, where we fully expected to remain. There we found naval ratings of the submarines that had performed

such epic deeds in the Dardanelles—the A.E.2 and E.7.—
as well as a good number of "Aussies." They were all
employed on the Taurus tunnel, or in the workshops attached
to that construction. Those "old-timers" gave us a great
welcome, which included one of the best meals we had had
for a long time. As I was still bare-foot they gave me a pair
of boots. True, they were first cousins to the weird contraptions that I had got in Adana, but none the less they
were better than nothing.

A Chief Petty Officer was in charge and he was detailing
us for various jobs when we received a message that we were
to leave the following day for work on the Amanus tunnel!
That was near the camp of Bagtchi of ill-repute and Micky
had already had one experience of the conditions there, and
he had no wish to repeat it. I had heard all I wanted to about
it, so we discussed the possibility of escape, finally deciding
to give it a trial and then, if conditions were too bad, to make
our plans accordingly.

The following morning we left Belemedik and crossed the
mountains at the point where the tunnel was being constructed, eventually regaining the railroad track on the other
side. Gangs of Kurds and Arabs were making gigantic
cuttings on that section of the line, and they were heavily
guarded against any possibility of their escape. It was
interesting to see them cutting into a bank of shale or earth.
They faced the bank in a long line, wielding spades, shaped
like mattocks, in perfect unison as they chopped and hacked,
chanting the while in rhythm to the shrill piping of the chant-
leader, playing on a reed. Every few minutes the leader would
give a loud "Hah!" and they would all stop at once, as though
they were controlled by machinery. After a few seconds'
"blow" the piping would recommence and the human
machine would start chopping and hacking again.

At the camp of one of those labour gangs we received a loaf
of bread as the day's rations, and at another we spent the

night, sleeping out in the open. Three days later we reached
a station on the line between Tarsus and Adana, and once
more we found ourselves locked inside a goods wagon. The
sun was just setting as the door was unlocked and we were
ordered to get out. We found ourselves once more at Mamourie but were given no time to look round; setting off at once
for our destination. Marching alongside the railway we came
to where a narrow-gauge line was laid between the broad-
gauge track, at a place called Injilli. Here we were given a
lift, as a train was just about to start. We sat in an open truck
behind an engine that puffed and snorted and belched out
showers of red-hot ashes that kept us jumping about like
demented creatures as we vainly tried to keep them from
burning through our clothes. Actually, we would have much
preferred to have marched the whole way, after we had had
a taste of that ride, so we were relieved when we felt a horrible
jolting and realized that the engine was off the rails! The
driver and fireman were Germans and they cursed and swore
as they tried to lever the engine back on to the rails. We were
supposed to help but we only simulated exertion as we
"heaved" and grunted along with the engine crew. After
half an hour our escort decided that we had better leave the
engine and continue on our way. We still kept to the track
as we made our way slowly to Yarbagtchi, and then on to
Bagtchi, where we stopped for the night, once more sleeping
in the open. Apparently Bagtchi was not our destination so
we marched out early the next morning and on to Iran, at
the mouth of the tunnel, where we were taken to a bell-tent
occupied by some officials of the Turkish Commandant.
A *katib* came out and proceeded to take our particulars but
he would not tell us what we were to do or whether we were
to be handed over to the German construction company
or not.

We were not long left in doubt. The tunnel was completed but the broad-gauge track had not yet been laid, and

our job was to be unloading goods and munitions from the
heavy railway trucks and reloading them on to those of the
light railway. The worst feature was that we were to work
under the Turks and not for the German company. That
meant poor and insufficient food, long hours and vile treatment generally. We should be treated just as we had seen
other "slave gangs" treated farther up the line.

Our fears were certainly realized. We slaved at our job
from dawn to sunset with only half an hour off at midday,
when we received a small loaf of black, gritty bread. Before
we commenced work and after we had finished each day, we
received a bowl of "target paste"—boiled flour—nothing
else at all, neither meat nor vegetables. Our overseers were
soldiers, who relentlessly kept us hard at it from the time
we started until we finished. It was as much as they would
allow to let us go to a rusty boiler occasionally to get a drink
of lukewarm water. All day long we were tormented by
millions of fleas. To lift one's arms or open one's legs was to
release swarms of those active and voracious insects. During
the whole time I was a prisoner in that land of vermin
pestilences, I never encountered anything quite like the fleas
of Iran. The very air was alive with them. When we drew
our "target paste" the surface of it, in the cauldron in which
it was cooked, was black with fleas that had fallen in and we
got our share of them. Tired as we were after each gruelling
day at our job, we found it next to impossible to sleep so
viciously were we bitten. The outlook was hopeless and the
future seemed to hold nothing for us.

There were three other Englishmen in the camp, and they
had good jobs under the Germans and were comparatively
well off. One night, Micky and I managed to slip away
from our party without being observed by the sentries and
we visited those men. We were out to find out what assistance
they could render us in the event of us trying a getaway.
Unfortunately, there was little they could do as bread or

flour was unprocurable, and getting rations for our pro-
spective flight was our chief concern. They were able to
give us a few piastres to add to those I still had left, and
promised to save us any bread they could—even if it was
only a slice. We were able to rejoin our party unnoticed and
lay discussing our plans until morning.

As Micky and I had decided not to take either of the
other Englishmen of the party along with us, we had asked
the three employed by the Company not to say anything to
them should they have an opportunity to speak with them.
I had already sounded the others of our party and they had
scouted the very idea, preferring the hardships of their
present existence to the hazards of another.

In the days that followed we exchanged our quilts, and
most of our other possessions, for bread. I went about barefoot for the most part, in order to harden my feet, as I did not
expect my cardboard boots to last very long once we got on
the road again. On the Fridays, our days off, we got permission from the Chaoush in charge to visit the other labour
camps in the vicinity, and we spent the time in trying to buy
bread. It was little enough we could get as bread was so
scarce that money could hardly buy it. We had hoped to get
enough food to last us for two weeks, the time we reckoned it
would take us to get through to our troops on the Palestine
front. Bit by bit we accumulated a little store, which we kept
in the hut of our three friends on the Company. They added
several tins of foodstuff that they had received in parcels
from home. Unfortunately they had no idea what those tins
contained as the labels had been ripped off by the Turkish
censors.

At last the conditions under which we were working
became so intolerable that we decided to go at once, food or
no food. Two of the other Englishmen in our party had
collapsed and the others were in little better shape, and we
were afraid that we too should be too ill to start if we delayed

further. We decided that the next Friday night would be the
best time to go, as we should have all day in which to pack
our rations and few belongings, and we should have had a
whole day's rest.

The "Day" duly arrived, and, to celebrate the occasion
of our departure, Micky thought he would indulge in the
luxury of a shave in the camp barber's shop. He had not had
a shave for many days, so that the safety razor and well-used
blades that he had were unequal to the task. I accompanied
him to the barber's to act as *terjiman*. The barber, a villainous looking Greek, was busy shaving an Arab when we
entered the little shop, and I soon saw, by his actions, that
he was very much "under the weather." I pointed that out
to Micky, who said, "Well, now I am here I am going to
have a shave, so tell him to be careful."

The Arab left and Micky sat in the chair.

"Aha!" Ingleezi, eh?" said the barber.

"Yes," I answered, "and be careful what you are doing, or
you will cut him."

The Greek looked hard at me with his bleary eye, but
evidently he was unable to collect his wits sufficiently to give
me the answer he would have liked, so he proceeded to
lather Micky's chin, using his hand in lieu of a brush.
After making several ineffectual attempts to strop his razor
he commenced to scrape away at Micky's beard. After a
minute or so Micky pushed his hand away and said
fiercely, "Yowash!" ("Steady!"), then, turning to me, said,
"Tell this drunken swine that if he cuts me I'll knock his
damned head off!" I knew Micky well enough to know
that, regardless of consequences, he was likely to attempt to
carry out his threat, so I warned him not to do anything that
would upset our plans. Meanwhile the Greek had stood
glaring from one to the other of us, and when I had finished
speaking he said, "Ne di'or?" ("What does he say?") "He is
afraid that you will cut him," I explained. That seemed to

amuse the drunken barber greatly. "A cut! Afraid of a cut?"
he cackled. "Ho! ho! look at this." Then he made three or
four slashes with his razor at the lobe of his ear, laughing like
a maniac as he did so. The blood poured on to his shoulder
and down his white shirt-sleeve. "There you are," he said,
"a cut is nothing," and made as though to continue shaving
Micky, but that worthy had seen enough and jumped out
of his chair and told the barber, in terse Cockney, just what
he thought of all Greeks and a certain Greek barber in
particular, before he kicked open the shop door and strode
out, leaving the bleary-eyed barber cackling inanely.

We made our way to the hut of our three friends, where
Micky completed his shave and I made our packs ready
for our move that night. Our friends had arranged to put
the packs where we could find them after we had eluded our
sentries, so that we should arouse no suspicion if we were
seen moving about after dark, which we most certainly
should have done had we been carrying packs. We remained
with our friends until it was time to report back to our camp,
and then they bid us good luck and good-bye, adding that
they still thought that we were mad to make the attempt.

Our camp lay on the side of a 4,000-foot high mountain,
and we intended to make our way to the summit of that
rather than take the easier way down the valley, where the
risks of being caught were greater. So we lay and waited for
the opportune moment. As is the case on such occasions,
everything seemed fated to delay that moment. The Indians
sat up later than usual, chattering away, and two of the other
Englishmen came over to where we lay to talk about the
prospects of a change of work. Had they known, we were
even then waiting the opportunity to make a change for
ourselves. We were all "keyed up" with excitement and
they chattered on, suggesting that I should see the Commandant and ask for other work, etc., until I was ready to
scream. At last they left us, and the rest of the camp gradually

212 AT BŌR AND ANOTHER MOVE SOUTH

became quiet. I lay watching the solitary sentry, and it
seemed as though he would never lay down, as was his wont.
When at last he did so I nudged Micky and we prepared to
move. We gave the sentry time enough to get off to sleep
before we made off in the direction of our friends' hut, where
our packs had been placed under the verandah.

We were off!

As silently as we could we commenced our climb up the
mountain-side. After half an hour we abandoned caution and
climbed more rapidly in consequence. Hour after hour we
sweated and scrambled; slipping back one pace in every
three as we tried to negotiate banks of loose shale or pine
needles. It was pitch-dark, as the moon had not yet risen,
and we were unable to find any sort of track. It was a tortuous
climb and one that I shall not quickly forget. The slope was
very steep but not continuous, there were two valley-like
depressions to overcome, and descending those in the darkness was infinitely worse than climbing. We slithered and
stumbled down, not knowing whether we should suddenly
fall over the edge of some gorge or drop into a pit. The
mountain-side was thickly wooded with pines and scrub
oaks and they did not help us at all, for, as we descended the
depressions, we continually bumped into them or tripped
over their roots. The false dawn came just as we reached the
summit and we could dimly discern the camp we had left
far below us.

We were dead-beat but we had to find a place of concealment in which to hide up during the day, as there was almost
bound to be a hue and cry after us. Fortunately, the summit
was strewn with crags and boulders and covered with thick
scrub, and we were able to find a hiding-place under an overhanging boulder and behind a bank of ferns and bracken.
We opened our packs in order to have one meal before we
went off to sleep, and, to lighten our loads a little, decided to
eat our tinned stuff first, at the rate of one tin per day and

without bread. We selected a tin that we judged to be
salmon, but, to our disgust, proved to be tripe! Imagine it.
There were we, two tired and hungry fugitives, sitting on a
mountain-top in the chilly dawn, eating cold tripe with our
fingers.

I can imagine no more depressing meal at any time than
cold tripe, but at that particular time it was simply awful.
We could not afford to open another tin of stuff so we had to
make the best of it, and, after that uninspiring meal, lay down
to sleep until sunset.

We were awake by mid-afternoon and crawled out of our
hiding-place to take our bearings. There was not a soul to be
seen in the valley down which we had to go to get out of the
mountains. Micky said that he recognized the place as the
valley where he had been working, at a place called Entilli,
when he had made his first attempt to escape. He suggested
that we should cautiously advance to the labour camp, as
perhaps there might still be someone there that he knew. I
could see nothing against the plan so we shouldered our
packs and commenced the descent. Luck was with us and we
reached the huts of the camp without seeing anyone, or being
seen. Not knowing the lay of the camp, I lay concealed with
the packs whilst Micky went off to reconnoitre. In a very
short time he was back, to say that the coast was clear and
that it was safe to go into one of the huts. There were only
two Englishmen there, employed as storemen, and Micky
had been fortunate enough to see them as they were returning
from work, finished for the day.

The tiny hut where they lived was away from the main
camp and we were able to slip into it unobserved. Our
friends told us that most of the other huts were empty now,
as the labour gangs had been moved elsewhere. They could
not afford to give us anything to eat, but, after we had told
them of the "tripe" incident, offered to help us eat the rest of
our tinned stuff and provide us with a bag of crushed oats in

exchange. Funny though that may seem, it was really an advantageous exchange, as we were hopeful of being able to cook up a meal of the oats, which would provide us with a far more sustaining meal than anything the tins were likely to contain. The two good fellows gave us, in addition, several Oxo cubes, which would serve for the meat element when we cooked our porridge. Although they were uneasy at the thoughts of harbouring us—in case we were discovered, when the consequences to themselves would have been serious—they insisted that we stay with them for at least a day, saying that we should be the better for a long rest before proceeding on our way. We did not require much persuading as we were still tired from our climb, coming as it did on the top of several weeks of real hard labour.

Early the next morning, our friends went off to work and we were left to our own devices. They had not been gone long when one of them returned, bringing with him a length of thin wire and a bunch of wild flowers, and he requested us to make a wreath for a Eurasian who had just died in the sick quarters there. The poor fellow had been a member of the Bombay Volunteer Artillery, and was of the Kut Garrison. We gladly agreed to make the wreath, as it would give us something to do to while away the time before nightfall, as well as being a little act of remembrance for a comrade. It was certainly a peculiar situation. There were we, on a most desperate venture, with our lives as a possible forfeit, sitting in a hut calmly making a wreath for a dead comrade!

It so happened that I knew the lad who had died. He had been one of my party from Mosul to Islahie, and had gone into hospital at the latter place, suffering from dysentery, the complaint from which he had just died. I well remember him telling me about his home life on one occasion. I remember him telling me, also, the difference between a *chupatti* and a *purri*. A *purri* was a sweet pancake and was eaten with sweet-meats, whereas a *chupatti* was used in the same manner as we used bread. By such trivial memories do we remember our dead.

By noon the wreath was finished and our friends took it away and went to perform the last rites over the unfortunate Eurasian. During the afternoon we slept and by the time they returned we were much refreshed and anxious to get on. We opened our last two tins of food—salmon and cherries— which we shared with them as a farewell meal, before slipping quietly down the valley.

It was quite dark by the time we reached Islahie, and we passed by without any trouble, on our way to the open plains in the direction of Aleppo. All night long we marched and I speedily became footsore from the horrible boots I was wearing, until, at last, I threw them away in disgust. My feet were not so hard as they had been during my march up from Samarah, so I was pleased when the first glimmer of dawn warned us that we must look for a place to hide in.

We could still plainly see the towering mass of Kurd Dagh (Kurd Mountain), the highest peak in the Amanus range, and were surprised at the apparently short distance we had come during the night.

Unfortunately, we were unable to find a suitable spot near water where we could hide, so that we had to lay all day in a place without water, a great hardship. We became so thirsty that we started out before dark in order to find water, and saw a company of soldiers marching towards the east, from the direction of Islahie. We found a small, smelly stream where we slaked our thirst and waited for dark before continuing.

Night fell and we plodded on once more, on a road that became gradually very rough and stony, which caused me to limp along on bleeding feet before very long. We continued on after dawn and until we came to water, as neither of us could contemplate another long day without a drink. Summer was not far distant and the sun was becoming uncomfortably

hot again, and to lay in it all day without water was far from
pleasant. Before we went to sleep we cut all our bread into
slices and lay it in the sun, for it had gone mouldy. When we
were ready to start again that evening, we found the bread
swarming with ants, and it took us a considerable time before
we got rid of them all.

We had reckoned on getting to Aleppo within three days
from Entilli, but we still seemed a long way away from that
place. We trudged along in silence that night, each busy with
his own thoughts. I was not so optimistic as I had been,
principally because of the state of our bread and secondly
because of the state of my feet. We had little enough bread
to start with and if we had to throw any away because of it
going bad—and it would have to be pretty bad before we
did that—things were going to look bad for us. In addition
to that, Micky had developed a touch of gastritis, and
mouldy bread was not going to do him any good. I mused
over all those things as I stumbled along that night, and,
when morning came, discussed them with Micky.

Looking to the south we could see a line of hills and
judged that somewhere beyond them lay Aleppo, our
immediate objective. We had neither maps nor compass and
very little idea of where Aleppo was in relation to anywhere
else. We only knew that it was on the road to Palestine,
where we hoped to connect up with our own troops, and we
thought that we might be able to get food or assistance there.
The more I thought of it the more I thought that we were on
a mad escapade and one that was likely to prove disastrous.
I said as much to Micky, and, to my surprise he said that
he was thinking the same thing and had been thinking so all
night. So for an hour we discussed possible alternatives to
going on with our march towards Palestine. Eventually we
decided to retrace our steps and try and reach Adana, where
perhaps we might get assistance from Miss Davies or Doctor
Haas. At least we had got away from the slavery at Iran, even

if we had not done anything better, and it seemed madness to wander about as we were doing, without maps and with insufficient food. So, as soon as it was dark, we set off back in the direction from which we had come, both of us quite happy in the decision we had made, despite the fact that the consequences were likely to be just as bad for us whichever way we went.

In two night marches we were back in the valley at Islahie and we decided to take the road over the mountains to Mamourie, as we knew that road and it was, besides, the shortest way to Adana. During the day, whilst waiting for darkness before we continued on our way, we made a fire of dried grasses and cooked a meal of porridge and Oxo. By feeding the fire with small quantities of grass we avoided making a smoke, which would have caused our discovery had it been seen. The porridge was very tasty and a welcome change from the mouldy bread that we had been eating for the past two or three days.

At nightfall we made our way cautiously to the mountain road and reached it without mishap. We intended to keep to the road as much as we possibly could, only to leave it for cover when we heard someone coming. For about three hours we marched along in complete silence, our ears strained for any sound that might portend danger. So far, luck had been with us and we hoped to reach the other side in two days and without trouble. After a short rest we started off again and the moon, rising above the peaks, lighted the way for us. I was thinking of the first time that I had come this way when, on suddenly rounding a bend, we were confronted by a solitary horseman. My heart leapt to my mouth but I managed to say "Mahubbah emishary" ("Greetings, friend").

"Greetings. Where are you going?" came the reply and question.

I moved closer and saw that the horseman was a Turkish

officer, which meant that I should have to be very careful in what I said, so playing for time I said,

"Oh, we are going to Mamourie."

"Who are you and why are you going to Mamourie at this time of the night?" was the next question.

As the officer did not bully or bluster my confidence returned and I began to lie like blazes. I told him that we were telegraphists working for the *Compania*—the German Railroad Construction Company, known colloquially as the *Compania*—and had been inspecting the telegraph lines between Bagtchi and Islahie, along the rail track. To his query as to why we did not return in the daylight I replied that we wished to avoid journeying in the heat of the day. He agreed that that was a very sensible plan, then he said:

"But you are not Germans."

"No," I replied, "we are prisoners of war, but have been working for the *Compania* for over a year."

"Aren't they afraid that you will escape?" he asked next.

I laughed and asked him where we could go if we did escape, and why should we wish to escape anyway, seeing that we were being well treated and looked after.

After that he told us that he had fought at the Dardanelles and had conceived a great admiration for the fighting qualities of the British soldier. He continued in that strain for some time and I became uneasy, suspecting that he was merely killing time. I spoke to Micky—who had, of course, been unable to follow what had been said—and told him to be prepared for trouble. Then I turned to the officer and said that we had better be getting on our way, as we had a long march in front of us. To that he replied, "Oh, there is no hurry. Have a cigarette." We accepted cigarettes and were just lighting them when his next words put me in a flutter.

"I have my regiment coming along behind me and we can chat until they come."

Phew! So that was it, he was waiting for assistance. Well, we had no desire whatever to chat until his regiment arrived, so, at the risk of arousing his suspicions further—if he was indeed suspicious—I insisted on getting on our way. Bidding him an affable "Good night," we left him, sitting puffing slowly at his cigarette.

We hurried up the road, and, just before we turned a bend, turned to see that the officer had not moved but was sitting watching us. The bend concealed us from his view and we fled precipitately up the mountain-side. Sitting high above the road, among the bracken and at the foot of a giant pine, we watched the road below us for signs of pursuit. We had not been waiting more than five minutes before we heard the tramping of many feet, and shortly after there came into view a regiment of Turkish infantry. In silence we sat and watched them as they passed, followed by their transport and a string of camels. We sat on for another half an hour before we judged it wise to get back to the road. That midnight encounter had shaken us somewhat, though we laughed at the ease with which I had bluffed the officer. Nothing else happened that night and we continued to march until dawn, when we descended into a small valley and cooked another mess of porridge, after which we slept.

Night came and we returned to the road and again plodded along in the dust. In great trepidation we crept through the villages, fearful that the barking dogs would rouse the villagers. Probably our fears were groundless, as those villagers who had avoided conscription, or the butchery of the Turks, had no doubt long since ceased to pay attention to people travelling through the pass by night.

We reached the highest part of the road and commenced the gradual descent, gasping for a drink. There was no sign of a spring, or water of any sort, except the mountain stream that mocked us as it splashed its way onwards far below us. For hours we heard it; sometimes in a musical tinkling, at

others in a continued roar as it was forced between boulders
in the narrowing gorge. Once we endeavoured to reach it, so
harassed with thirst had we become, but after descending a
couple of hundred feet we were stopped by a precipitous
drop that barred further progress, and we were compelled to
return to the road.

At last we saw the lights of Mamourie station twinkling in
the valley below us. I remarked to Micky that in another
two or three hours we should be lying concealed in the
scrub through which Sergeant R. and I had escaped, when,
without the slightest warning, a voice commanded "Dur!"
("Stop!")

Micky ejaculated a single "Christ!" and was silent. A
soldier stepped into the road in front of us and asked,
"Nair elli, sis?" ("Where are you from?")

"Bashi Bazouklar, Islahie don," I replied, thinking that I
was telling him that we were civilians from Islahie. At that
time I was under the impression that *Bashi Bazouk* was
Turkish for civilian and it was not until several months later
that I learned that a *Bashi Bazouk* was a bandit, or, alternatively, a member of a band of guerrilla fighters of sanguinary
reputation.

The soldier shouted "Onbashi" and was immediately
joined by a corporal, who asked us who we were. I told him
that we were American civilians making our way to the
station at Mamourie. He ordered the *askar* (soldier) to take us
along. We were pushed through a gap in the bushes bordering
the road and into a small clearing, whereon stood a bell-tent.
Then followed a long interrogation by the Onbashi. The gist
of my story was that we were Americans who had been
working in Baghdad when that city fell to the British, and
we had fled up country in our search for work. We had
subsequently worked at Nisibin and Ras-el-Ain but wished
to get to Constantinople, so, not being able to afford the
railway fare, had decided to walk there, and here we were on

EVERDAY SCENES ON THE OUTSKIRTS OF ANY TOWN OR LARGE VILLAGE

A LARGE RIVERSIDE ARAB VILLAGE, SHOWING THE HUDDLED MANNER
OF GROUPING THE HOUSES: DENS OF VILENESS

[See p. 69

KURDS OF THE TURKISH BORDER MOUNTAINS

[*See p.* 219

KURDS OUTSIDE A GOAT'S-HAIR TENT

[*See p.* 255

our way. The Onbashi seemed to believe me but he said
that we were in danger of being shot as deserters if we
wandered about without an escort, so we had better remain
where we were for the rest of the night and he would send
an *askar* with us to Mamourie in the morning—for our
protection. He was quite pleasant and gave us cigarettes and
a mat to sit on, but we felt far from happy, as can be imagined.

To one side of the tent we could dimly discern a group of
figures and rightly conjectured that they were the night's
"bag" of that police-post. We chatted about our predicament
and I gave the opinion that, in all probability, we should not
be connected with the disappearance of two prisoners from
Iran. I doubted whether the fact of our escape had been
reported from that place. We were still chatting when once
more we heard the command "Dur!"

In a few minutes two Arabs were pushed headlong into
the clearing, loudly protesting. The Onbashi commenced his
questioning by soundly smacking their faces. That, no doubt,
was to ensure that they spoke the truth. The questions and
answers were very rapid, and in a guttural dialect unknown
to me, so that I was unable to follow them. Apparently the
answers were unsatisfactory, for, in a few minutes, the
Arabs were on their backs and receiving the *di'ak* (bastinado),
administered by the Onbashi, who used a hefty cudgel for
the purpose. At each "thwack" the victims yelled "Oman,
oman Effendi!" ("Mercy, mercy, sir!") I shuddered to think
that we had just missed a like punishment, for there is not
the slightest doubt that had my story not have been sufficiently convincing, the Onbashi would have had no hesitation
in bastinadoing us.

After their punishment, the Arabs were kicked over to the
group by the tent, where they lay audibly blubbering.

"Nice fellow, the Corporal!" was the caustic comment
of Micky.

It is as well to mention here that Micky had no know-

ledge of either Turkish or Arabic, so that every decision that
had to be made or yarn invented had to be made or said by
me. The only advantage to this was, that any story I might
tell was not likely to be upset by Micky telling a different
one. Fortunately I possessed a vivid imagination and was
able to tell a plausible yarn to fit all circumstances, as events
will prove.

Daylight came and we and the rest of the "bag" completed
the journey to Mamourie. The "bag" were securely roped
together, and a more miserable gang of toughs could not
be imagined. We ambled along behind them and I chatted
cheerily to the Onbashi, until we came to the stream in the
valley, where we stopped to wash, and quench our thirst and
eat the last of our now very mouldy bread. Shortly after our
halt we arrived at the station buildings and the "bag" were
taken elsewhere whilst we followed the Onbashi to a tent set
up some distance from the station. We followed the Onbashi
into the tent and an official of some sort was seated at a
table, whilst two others stood at his side. The Onbashi told
his story and I was asked to repeat mine. When I kept
repeating that we were *Bashi Bazouklar*, all three laughed,
and at last the seated Effendi said:

"Are you sure that you are not escaped prisoners of war?"
That I emphatically denied, and said that we were workmen
and had never been soldiers.

"Well, then," the official went on, "would you like to work
here?"

I quickly replied that we were prepared to work anywhere,
and that Mamourie would suit us well enough for the time
being. The Onbashi was dismissed and the three officials
held a whispered consultation, meanwhile I explained the
situation to Micky. Eventually, the seated official said that
we should be given work for which we should be fed and
paid at the normal rates. We were then motioned to get outside. One of the officials accompanied us and took us to a

large engine shed. We wondered what our chances were of being immediately fed, rather than of what work we were likely to have to do. Our rations had been very scanty for the past few days and we thought that we could not possibly do any work until we had been fed. Our employers thought differently. Outside the engine shed our guide called to a ragged little man who bore the chevrons of a Corporal on his filthy tunic. The official whispered something to him and then walked off, leaving us in charge of the Onbashi. That dirty little chap said a single word, "Gel" ("Come") and led us to a truck-load of coal standing next to an engine, and motioned us to climb on top. Before we did so I asked the Onbashi about food, but the only answer I could get was an oft-repeated "Sonra" ("Later)." There was nothing we could do but to climb on to the coal and commence our job. We had to load up the engine tender, throwing the big lumps in with our hands and shovelling in the "smalls." Long before that awful day was over we were as black as soot and our hands were as raw as meat. Our backs ached terribly from the constant stooping and rising, and the sun, which beat upon our uncovered heads mercilessly, added to our tortures. As soon as we had loaded up one engine tender we pushed that on to a turntable and on to a different set of lines, whilst another one was pushed by other workmen alongside the coal trucks ready for us to load. At noon we had half an hour "break" and sat and watched the Onbashi eating his black bread. He had worked steadily all the morning, without any sort of complaint; perhaps thinking that he was much better off where he was than in the firing line. He told me that all his previous assistants had run away after a few days on the coal trucks. We didn't blame them in the least. Our pay, he said, was to be the same as a *nuffer's* (private soldier's), five piastres a month (the equivalent of ten pence at the normal rate of exchange), and that it would be paid in arrears, which meant that we should have to work for a month before we

received anything. He told us further that we should become
entitled to rations on the following day. We certainly had
food for thought that afternoon, even if we had none to eat.
Unfortunately, our tortured bodies would not permit our
brains to function properly, and we were unable to think of
any way out of our predicament.

Sunset brought cessation of work and issue of rations to
those entitled. Coal-grimed, aching in every limb, hands
like raw meat and hunger gnawing our vitals, we were on
the point of collapse when the harsh clanging of a piece of
suspended rail announced that our tortures were over for
that day. Climbing wearily from the coal truck, we followed
the Onbashi across the lines, between rows of workmen's
huts and to a log shack, where men of many races, colours,
and creeds were receiving a ladleful of steaming *kurrawanna*.
As we had only one pot between us I joined the queue, and,
when I reached the cauldron, said, "Ekki tenna" ("Two")
and held out my pot expectantly. The huge, bearded cook
looked at me and said, "Haidi, git" ("Get out") and served
the next in the queue. I sought out the Onbashi and told him
that, as he was our boss, he had better see about getting us
some food if he wanted us to work the next day. He continued
to eat his meal leisurely and took no notice of my excited
protests beyond saying gently, "Yuwash, yuwash, arkadashm."
("Slowly, slowly, my brother.") At last the long line of workmen were served and the Onbashi very quietly and humbly
asked the cook whether he could spare a little *kurrawanna* for
us. Waving his hands in the air and bawling at the top of his
voice, the cook demanded to know where he could get extra
rations from, and was he expected to feed a thousand men
with rations for a hundred, etc. The poor little Onbashi
wilted under the storm of words and expressively shrugged
his shoulders at me as he moved away. Blind rage seized me
and I swore and cursed and damned the Turks and all
things Turkish to eternity. The workmen sitting around

applauded and shouted, "Offerim, Ingleezi!" ("Bravo, English"). I begged and threatened and finally grovelled for food
until, to get rid of me, the cook yielded and gave me a measly
pint of his precious *kurrawanna*. A sympathetic bystander
gave me a piece of bread, and we had to be thankful for what
we had.

The Onbashi was waiting to take us back to the engine
shed and was all smiles as we approached him.

"Now that you have food you are all right, eh?" he queried.
I could have strangled him, though it was not his fault that
we had had to fight for such small commons.

We sat on a grassed bank outside the engine shed and
discussed what we were to do next. To carry on in the job
we had been given was unthinkable, and our main idea was
to get away while we still had strength left; that very night
if it was at all possible. But how?

The Onbashi would not leave our side, and we soon
discovered that he had no intention of losing his new
assistants as he had lost his others. I stood up and announced
our intention of having a bath.

"A bath!" gasped the Onbashi, "whatever for? You will be
just as dirty to-morrow."

I explained that to Micky who exploded into profane
Cockneyese, to my great amusement. We went to a small
irrigation ditch behind the engine shed, followed by the
Onbashi, who, when we stripped off our blackened rags,
moved off a little way and sat waiting until we had finished.
The cold water went a long way towards refreshing us, though,
without soap, it did little to cleanse the sweat and grime from
our bodies. We did our best to wash the coal-dust from the
burst blisters on our hands, but it was a painful and not very
successful business. All the time we were bathing we were
discussing ways and means to elude the Onbashi and vanish
from Mamourie. We were no nearer a solution to our troubles
when we had finished and were being led back to the engine

shed. Our docile but alert little "boss" piloted us into the shed and right to the far end of it, away from the doors. There the Onbashi had his *pranda*, a folding bed made on the principle of a camp stool. He said that we could sleep beside him, on the ground, where we should be nice and warm and sheltered. We lay down and closed our eyes, too utterly "fed up" to do anything else, but sleep in that inferno was an impossibility, tired as hounds though we were. Engines were whistling and blowing off steam, and men on night shift were shouting and hammering and making a frightful din. I pulled my ragged shirt over my head in an endeavour to deaden the noise somewhat, but it was no use. Micky was almost frantic as well, and, when I could stick it no longer, I stood up and said, "Come on, Micky, I'm going outside and the Devil take the Onbashi." As we moved off, that little chap shouted after us to bring us back. I told him that if we were to work the next day we must sleep that night, and we were going outside where it was quieter. We went outside, followed by the protesting Onbashi carrying his *pranda*, and selected a spot near the main line which was covered with dried grass; there we lay down again. The Onbashi said that we should die of exposure where we were, and begged us to go back inside again. I took no notice of him, as I had got an idea and was busy turning it over in my mind. When I had thought it out a bit more I told it to Micky, who voted it a good one and worth trying out. It was this. We were to wait until we heard a train coming and then dash in front of it and into the scrub on the other side of the line. We reasoned that pursuit would be difficult in the dark and delayed until the train had passed, so that we should have a few valuable seconds start. Failing the coming of a train we would wait— if we could remain awake—until the Onbashi had fallen asleep, and then make off into the scrub. It seemed the only possible way out of our troubles, and we determined to try it. Our greatest problem was to remain awake, as we were terribly tired after our racking day, following on the march of the night before.

Having settled on our plan we lay quiet, simulating sleep, in the hope that the Onbashi would the more quickly cease to watch us and go to sleep himself. For a long time I lay, fascinated by the glowing tip of the Onbashi's cigarette, and wondering whether I should fall asleep before he did. The moon rose above the distant mountain-tops and flooded the valley with its pale light, but still the wiry little Turk puffed away at his cigarette. No sooner had he smoked one than he lit another until I began to think that he required no sleep at all, but made tobacco smoke suffice. At last he turned over and composed himself for sleep. His face was in a shadow, so we were unable to tell whether he was watching us or not. The minutes dragged by, and, since the Onbashi had put out his cigarette, I had become wide awake and greatly excited. I could not tell whether or not Micky was awake and I was afraid to move or speak in case the Onbashi was still watching us. Far away in the mountains towards Bagtchi I heard a whistle of an engine. My heart began to pound against my ribs and I braced myself for the effort to come, when we should have to dash in front of the train. The rumble of revolving wheels came into earshot and I put out a tentative hand and touched Micky. He touched my fingers as a sign that he had heard and was ready. The train was barely twenty yards away when we made a wild dash over the lines, in imminent peril of our lives should we have the misfortune to stumble. With a roar and a rattle and screeching of brakes— for it was pulling up as it neared the station—the train passed by and effectually blocked us from the vision of anyone who may have witnessed our getaway. We had plunged headlong into the scrub, and, panting and puffing, strove to put as great a distance as possible between us and possible pursuers before we halted and listened and took breath. How like my first dash from Mamourie. We could hear no signs of pursuit, so we made a wide detour that brought us back to the main line, which we intended to follow in the direction of Adana.

After about three hours of shuffling along the permanent-way we were too tired to go any further, so we crossed the line and crept into a thicket of "tiger" grass and promptly fell asleep.

The sun was well up above the horizon when we awoke the following day, and we stretched our aching limbs and cursed our hunger, for had we had food we would have rested where we were for another day. We had not forgotten to pick up our bundles when we made our mad dash across the line, and now we searched the corners for any stray crumbs of bread that may have been adhering to the inside. The tiny meal we had had overnight had done nothing to appease our hunger, and thoughts of food dominated everything. We did not feel inclined to go on to Adana without food, as it was quite likely that we should have to hang about for two or three days before we got an opportunity to get into touch with Miss Davies or Doctor Haas. Having met with a kindly reception the last time I had entered a village in this locality, I decided to try it again, though this time I had no sick companion. I told Micky of that last experience of mine, and he agreed that it might work again, so, picking up our bundles, we set off, determined to boldly enter the first village we came to, meanwhile keeping a sharp look-out for anyone wearing any sort of uniform.

We had not proceeded far when, far away at the foot of a low range of mountains, we saw a village, surrounded by poplars. Viewed from where we were it presented a pretty and peaceful sight, and, if in imagination one substituted a church steeple for the minaret peeping above the roof-tops, was remarkably like an English village. It lay away from the main track and thus suited us better, as we thought it most likely to be free from soldiers or Gendarmes.

Keeping under cover as much as we could, we made a bee-line for the village and reached it within an hour. As we neared it we saw, to our great disappointment, soldiers entering and leaving the place, so once more we had to change our plans. We were so hungry that we eventually decided to give ourselves up to the military, in the hopes that we should get something to eat. Even a Turkish civil prison would offer more comfort—we thought—than a job at coal-heaving for an elusive wage of tenpence a month. And the chances were that we might not survive to draw even that amount.

Having made up our minds we marched boldly into the village.

CHAPTER TEN

LIFE IN BARRACKS AT OSMANIA

No one accosted us or took the slightest notice of us as we passed into the bazaar and between the lines of booths with their stacks of water-melons, apricots and other fruits. The sight and smell of so much to eat made us feel quite faint. I ventured to beg here and there, off the fruit vendors, and occasionally I was successful in getting a few small, unripe apricots or a couple of over-ripe figs. Whatever it was and whatever its condition, we took it and were thankful. We even picked up the discarded skins of melons from the dust of the road and bit off the tiny fragments of fruit that still adhered to the bitter outer skin.

At the top end of the bazaar we saw a gaudily dressed young officer sitting in a booth and eating grapes, and I decided that he was the man who would "recapture" us. I approached him and gave him an elaborate salute and said, "Zabout Effendi" ("Officer, sir"), "we are runaway prisoners of war (*ysir coshdilar*), and we wish to be taken to the Town Commandant."

He looked at us as though we were something loathsome and then said, "Go away and find an *askar* and tell him to take you. I am busy." That was something entirely different, and I was rather at a loss what to say next. I conferred with Micky, who saw the humour of the situation and laughed, though he had little enough to laugh about, goodness knows. I tried again, this time insisting on being taken, otherwise, I said, I would find the Commandant myself and tell him that an officer had refused to accept our surrender. That roused the young puppy, and he spat at me as he got to his feet and said, "Gel" ("Come").

We followed him through the narrow streets of the village

until we came to a *serai* over which flew the Turkish military flag. Through the domed entrance, past a sleepy-eyed sentry, up a flight of stairs to the balcony of the first floor we followed the strutting Mulazim Thani. Outside a door he stopped and motioned us to sit down before he knocked and entered, not because he wanted us to be comfortable, but sitting or kneeling on the ground was the correct position for inferiors to meet their overlords in those days. We sat down on the dusty boards and waited. In a few minutes the officer came out, accompanied by a thick-set, bearded Turk in the uniform of a Colonel. We scrambled to our feet and saluted. He gazed at us—not unkindly—for a few seconds and then said, "Turcha belirmi sis?" ("Do you understand Turkish?") I replied that I did and, without waiting for the flood of questions that I knew would follow, begged for food, saying that we were positively starving. To my surprise the Commandant turned to the officer and gave him some whispered instructions and then told us to be seated and gave us each a cigarette. We leaned back against the balcony rail and wondered what would happen next. The Commandant paced up and down the balcony, apparently waiting for the Mulazim Thani, who had gone down the stairs. We had not long to wait, for, within five minutes, an *askar* appeared, bearing a large bowl of grapes and several bread-rings. The Commandant took the food from the soldier and placed it on the balcony in front of us, with the injunction "Haidi, yere" ("Go on, eat"). We needed no further telling but "got busy." We tried to eat rationally, but I am afraid it was only too obvious to the Turk that we were famished. Before we had finished all that there was, the kindly Commandant brought out of his room a jar of ice-cold water, and when we had finished he gave us another cigarette.

When we were sitting comfortably puffing at our cigarettes, the Commandant brought out a chair and seated himself before us and began to question me. Omitting all mention of our experience at Mamourie, I told him of our escape from Iran and the reason for it. I let him think that we had come from that place to Osmania—the village we were in—and said nothing of our recapture since, as I had no wish to be sent back to Mamourie, whereas it was unlikely that we should be sent back to Iran, or so I hoped. In any case, Iran was preferable to Mamourie, under the circumstances. At the conclusion of my tale the Commandant sent for a clerk, who took down our names and other particulars, and an *askar*, who was to take us elsewhere. As we stood to our feet the Commandant said, "This soldier will take you to the barracks, where you will be looked after until I decide what is to be done with you. Don't worry, you will be able to have a good rest and no one will interfere with you."

To say that we were amazed is to put it very mildly. Here was a Turk of all Turks; kind and considerate, and able to appreciate our condition as unfortunate soldiers. What a pity there were not more of his sort in the Turkey of those days.

After thanking him for all his goodness we filed down the stairs in the wake of the *askar*, who took us to some huts on the edge of the village, near a cultivated area. Into one of the huts we were taken and handed over to a Bash Chaoush, a young and smartly dressed man who received us with a smile. The *askar* took him on one side and gave him certain instructions from the Commandant before saluting prior to his departure.

All non-commissioned officers in the Turkish Army received the salute, and whenever a person was addressing his superior officer—of any rank—or delivering a message, that person remained at the salute until he was dismissed. N.C.O.s generally were invested with great authority, even to the extent that they could, without reference to an officer, inflict corporal or other punishment.

The room in which we found ourselves was very similar to the prison at Adana; a long room equipped with a platform running around two-thirds of its length, the other third being occupied by *prandas*, for the use of N.C.O.s and the permanent staff of the barracks. We were given a *pranda* each, which was considerably more comfortable than the hard boards of the platform. Besides the Bash Chaoush we were the only people in the room when we entered it, as the recruits were out on parade. We dumped our bundles on to our *prandas* and sat down and laughed. The humour of the situation appealed to us greatly—and does even now, when we recall it. We had been extraordinarily lucky in our tactics so far, and we considered that we had fallen on clover.

The Bash Chaoush came and sat beside us and gave us cigarettes as he asked us questions about ourselves. He was entirely different from the usual type of Turkish soldier; gentlemanly and very considerate to his men—as we soon found out. In the weeks that followed we became great friends with Bash Chaoush Raoul Effendi—his full title. He told us that we should get the same rations as the recruits, bread in the morning and *kurrawanna* in the evening. It was little enough, but seemed to be the usual ration throughout Turkey for all men in the pay of the Government. Those with money supplemented their rations with food bought privately. In normal times that was no doubt an acceptable régime, as food and fruit were very cheap indeed in all parts of the country. Even in 1916, when I was in Adana, prices were very low when compared with those that I had been used to, either in India or England. At the time we reached Osmania, however, Turkey was beginning to feel the pinch pretty badly, and the fact that tons of food was being sent out of the country to feed the Germans made things much worse. That latter point became a very real and deep grievance with the population before the war was over.

Raoul left us and we managed to get several hours of sleep before the return of the recruits. With them came an Onbashi who told us that we could go to the cookhouse and draw our own ration of *kurrawannna*, and he offered to show us the way there and then. As we had still only the one pot, we decided that it would be better if I were to draw rations, as, being able to converse with the cook, I might be able to get an extra helping sometimes. *Kurrawanna* that first night consisted of tomatoes, egg-plant and a very small amount of mutton. With a single exception that was to be our diet—with a small loaf of bread—for several weeks.

When I returned I found the recruits—who had had their meal—sitting on their platform gazing at Micky in great curiosity. They were very young for the most part, and it is doubtful whether any of them had ever seen an Englishman at close hand before, even if they had ever seen one. I took the opportunity to study them as I ate my *kurrawanna*. Not one of them had a complete uniform, and no two were dressed alike. Their footwear beggars description, as they wore anything that remotely resembled boots or shoes, and some had only rags upon their feet. Other than a belt and bayonet they appeared to have no equipment, and their pitifully few personal belongings they kept in all sorts of dirty bags, which they used as pillows. Of bedding or blankets they had none. Several of them had pieces of straw matting or a sheep-skin to lie on, but their overcoats—such as they were—did duty as blankets.

Raoul came in and barked out an order. At once every recruit scrambled to the edge of the platform and knelt upright. At a second command they dropped back on to their heels and relaxed. Raoul paced up and down the intervening space and gave them a short lecture. For the most part the lecture was about the necessity for paying proper respect to their N.C.O.s. The following is one of the points he stressed, giving an instance.

"For instance, when you see an N.C.O. about to smoke, it is proper for you to hurry up to him with a *chekmuk* (lighter) and remain at the salute until he has his cigarette properly alight. Then again, if an N.C.O. says 'Su' ('Water'), at once dash off and bring to him a drink of water, and remain at the salute until he has finished drinking."

He concluded his lecture by referring to us, saying that we were "Ingleezi Chaoushlar" (English Sergeants—my fiction) and exhorting them to be respectful towards us, as we were soldiers of our country and volunteers to boot, which was more than he could say of them. With that he left them and at once set them a good example by coming over to us, and, saluting, said, "Mahubbah, Chaoushlar," before sitting down and proffering his cigarettes.

From thenceforward we were treated by those youngsters as their superiors, and they never forgot to salute us or address us as Chaoush or Effendi. I used to chat with them very freely and delight them with tales of England and the lot of an English soldier. They were greatly intrigued every time we scraped our chins with Micky's safety razor and called it a *trash makina* (shaving machine). They were only allowed out of barracks alone on one afternoon each week— on Fridays, their Sabbath—and at all times a sentry was posted on the door of the barrack-room. Under no circumstances were they permitted to leave the room during the night. Sometimes when I went outside after dark, I would disturb the drowsing sentry, who, not recognizing me, would shout, "Nairdair gitior sen?" ("Where are you going?"), to which I would reply, "To Baghdad," or "To Stamboul." Invariably there came back, "Chok eyi, Effendi." ("Very good, sir.")

One Friday morning, after I had been there a couple of weeks, I was sitting on my *pranda* when I felt the need for a drink of water. I called one of the youngsters by name and asked to him to get me some water.

When he returned, Raoul came over and said to the lad, "What is your name?"

The lad told him the same name as I had used. Raoul then

asked me how I came to know his name, and was greatly surprised when I told him that I knew everyone in the room by name. He called half a dozen of the recruits to him and asked me their names, asking them if I were right. When I had proved my word to his satisfaction, Raoul said:

"Offerim!" ("Bravo!") "Why I don't know them myself!"

About that period I asked Raoul if we could get a bath anywhere, as we found it very difficult to keep clean with only a cup or two of drinking-water to use. He immediately detailed one of the recruits to escort us to a place where we could bathe ourselves. That proved to be a stream in an orchard about half a mile from the barracks. It was a great treat to be out in the open and among the trees. We still had a piece of soap remaining from some that Raoul had given to us shortly after our arrival, and with this we were able to wash the scanty clothes that we wore, putting them on the grass to dry whilst we sat naked up a fig-tree, gorging ourselves on the luscious fruit. Every day after that we went out to the orchard to bathe and sometimes to wash our clothes, though the fruit was as much a lure as the water.

One man of the permanent staff was the depôt trumpeter and had fought at the Dardanelles. He told us a very interesting story of how he was so very "fed up" on one occasion— at the Dardanelles—that he determined to go over to the British. On the night that he chose to go he arrived at the British trenches only to find them empty. He returned to his own side again but was afraid to tell his officers in case they questioned him too closely as to why he had been over to the British lines. On the following day it was discovered that the British had withdrawn.

The trumpeter became a good friend of ours and kept us supplied with tobacco and cigarette papers for a long time. He was also a help in another way. One day Micky had an urge to sketch, as a means of breaking the awful monotony of his empty days, so I asked the trumpeter whether he could get paints or crayons in the bazaar. I told him that if he could, Micky would be pleased to draw his *resim* (portrait) for him. He was delighted with the idea and, as soon as he was off duty, went off to the bazaar to see what he could get, returning with two pencils of the "red one end and blue the other" variety, one blacklead, and a dozen plain postcards. All those things he gave to us on condition that we did him one or two *resims*. Micky got to work at once but instead of portraying the trumpeter in the ragged uniform that he wore, sketched him in the blue with red facings of the Stamboul Guards, complete with knee-boots, spurs and a beautiful trumpet with cords. By the time the sketch was completed we had quite an audience, and they all said what a marvellous likeness it was—though several of them held it upside down to inspect it. The trumpeter was well pleased and asked to be portrayed in company with a *guzel guz* (beautiful girl). Nothing loth, Micky got busy again and produced a masterpiece. The trumpeter exhibited his pictures with great pride to all the recruits and men of the permanent staff, with the result that we were snowed under with orders. That was more than we had bargained for, so Micky and I closed the business and went into committee.

I warned him that if he did sketches for nothing he would be pestered by every vain fool in the barracks and we should not get a moment's peace. He agreed, so we decided to turn things to good account and make a charge of five piastres, paper money, for each *resim*. I called over the trumpeter and told him that in England Micky would get a big fee for making *resims* and, although he would like to do one for everybody, it was not fair to ask him to work for nothing, so that if anyone else wanted one they would have to pay five piastres for it. The trumpeter went among the men in the room and told them what I had said, with the result that most of the orders were withdrawn.

We knew that most of the recruits received money from

their homes occasionally and that the permanent staff had their own methods of getting cash, so we were not asking impossibilities.

Those who still wanted *resims* came and "sat" for them straight away, although I demanded payment first. It was great fun whilst it lasted, besides bringing in money to supplement our meagre rations.

Our fame quickly spread, and we got more and more orders. Micky used to draw the figures—with no attempt at portrayal of the subject, of course—and I used to colour and shade them. The criticisms and instructions we received kept us laughing, at times, until the tears ran down our faces, to the blank astonishment of the recruits. At first, Micky sketched the figures three-quarter face, which gave a fore-shortened view of one foot. That would not do at all. The whole of the feet, hands, arms, and legs had to be shown, and some even insisted on having both eyes and ears in the picture. It can be imagined what the result looked like. It was great fun to watch the pictures being passed round for inspection. They were viewed from every possible angle and admired whichever way they were looked at. Our little business was to be closed down very suddenly.

One day a very arrogant Bash Chaoush—a man we had not seen previously—came in and demanded that we do his *resim*. I insisted that he paid for it, the same as the others, cash first, and until he had paid we would not start on it. When we did get started we decided that he should have special treatment, more because he was a Bash Chaoush than because we liked him. After all, it was policy to keep on the right side of the seniors. So he was portrayed as sitting in a beautiful room, with black and white marble floor, and urns of flowers on either side of him, whilst he was dressed in a magnificent uniform complete with sword. Through the open windows of the room he was sitting in could be seen the domes and minarets of a wonderful Oriental city. It was really a work of art, that picture, and worth more than the five piastres we got for it. However, the Bash Chaoush was as pleased as though he had been promoted to Pasha and carefully pointed out all the various details to Raoul and another Chaoush who was Raoul's friend. That picture was our undoing.

The next morning we were busy sketching a few pictures for stock when in walked a Yuzbashi of the medical service. "So," he snorted, in good English, "you no doubt think that you are clever, eh?" He managed to get a fair amount of scorn into his words, and it was obvious that he was very angry. He waved the picture we had done for the Bash Chaoush under our noses and said, "You would make a fool of my Bash Chaoush and cheat our soldiers, would you?" We were too taken aback at his attitude to make any reply, so he continued to rave and storm and ask questions that he knew we should not answer.

"You think that a good game, eh? Bloody damn fool Turk know nothing, eh? Pah! I spit on the ground for you (suiting the action to his words) and I am a Greek and a Christian. The Turk he is better in all things than the English. Bah! I spit again. No more of this foolishness you will do. No more you make damn fool of our brave soldiers. Yessok, yessok." ("Forbidden.") And with that he stormed out of the room. We sat dumbfounded. Not a word had we managed to say in defence of our action. Fortunately the recruits were all on parade and we were alone in the room, so that no one witnessed our discomfiture. Micky broke the tension by spitting on the ground and saying:

"Bah! Bloody damn-fool Greasy Greek no want it picture. I spit for you." Then we roared with laughter.

It was all very funny—viewed from one angle—but we had to shut up shop and go back to our diet of bread and *kurra-wanna*, for we dare not make any more *resims* in case the Greek Yuzbashi got to hear of it.

One evening, shortly after this incident, I was drawing our ration of *kurrawanna* when I was greeted by an *askar* I recognized as one of the men on duty at the Adana Police Courts on the day that I was tried. I called him to one side and cautioned him not to tell anyone that he knew me, otherwise the Commandant might get to know and that would make things bad for us if he discovered that we had been in prison before for wandering at large. The *askar* was quite a good sort and said that he understood and would not give us away. It was several days later that he saw me and told me that he was going to Adana for three days' leave. Here was an opportunity not to be missed. I asked him if he would take a note to the American hospital for me and bring me back an answer. He willingly agreed to do so, so I ran back to the barrack-room and wrote a note to Miss Davies asking her to get us some money from the Consul in Adana who might then be acting on behalf of the prisoners of war for the Dutch Legation. I told the *askar* that, in all probability, there would be money with the answer, so to be careful and not lose it.

It may appear strange that I so readily trusted a Turk after what I have written, but I had a happy knack of being able to judge those whom I could trust, and I found that the Anatolian Turkish soldier was usually a very likeable sort of chap, despite his bad treatment by his superiors.

My trust was not misplaced, for, four days later, the *askar* handed me an answer to my note. Unfortunately it contained no money. Miss Davies pointed out what I ought to have realized myself, that it would be extremely dangerous for her if it was discovered that she was helping runaway prisoners. She went on to chide me for again attempting to get away, after all I had suffered the first time. The letter was very carefully worded, in case it got into the wrong hands. Naturally, I was disappointed at not receiving financial help, but I quite understood the attitude of Miss Davies. It was something to have made contact again with her, and besides, I received verbal messages from Susie and the Armenian staff at the hospital. Susie had wanted to send me a parcel of food but Miss Davies forbade her to send anything at all.

During the four-day period of waiting for an answer, a minor sensation was caused in the barracks by the desertion of our friend Raoul. We were very sorry to lose him but we sincerely hoped that he would evade recapture. His friend the Chaoush was promoted to Bash Chaoush and took his place in our room. One day, the new man was entertaining a couple of lively pals to a light luncheon—on an upturned box —and he called me over to tell him what was written on a tin of stuff that he had got from a German. The tin was un-opened and had just one hyphenated word stamped on it— *Schweine-fleisch*—and that word was just enough to make its contents taboo for Mohammedans. I smiled as I read the word and said, "Doongus" ("Pork"). None of them would believe me, chiefly because they didn't want to, and they tried to make me say it was something else or at least to say I was doubtful. At last the Bash Chaoush opened the tin and tasted the contents. The others tasted it and they all continued to taste it until it was all gone.

"Well," said the Bash-Chaoush, "I don't believe it was *doongus*, but whatever it was it was very good and in any case we cannot bring it back now." Which was one way of getting round the taboo.

By this time our fame had spread around the camp and village, and I was regarded as the world's most wonderful *terjiman*. This was due, in the main, to a little leg-pulling that I had indulged in. One of the Indian deserters that I mentioned earlier in this narrative had reached Osmania and was brought to see me—introduced as an *askar arkadash* (brother in arms). I had no wish to see him but I took the opportunity of telling him in Hindustani my opinion of deserters. The N.C.O.s who had brought him to me listened intently, and, after he had gone, evinced admiration at my linguistic abilities and asked me how many languages I could speak. I mentioned the two or three that I knew and then went on to add all the English-speaking countries that I could think of, such as America, Canada, New Zealand, Australia, etc., and included Ireland, Scotland and Wales. The eyes and mouths of my listeners opened wide as I demonstrated each one—in a weird made-up jargon—and they repeatedly ejaculated "Ma'shallah!" or "Offerim!" or "Ockoli sen." ("Praise God," "Bravo," "You are wise"). They went off, animatedly discussing the learning of all Englishmen and myself in particular, and were, I have no doubt, responsible for an incident that occurred the following day.

Micky and I were having an afternoon nap when an *askar* wakened me to say that a certain Zabout Effendi (officer) wished to see me. Wondering what was afoot I followed the soldier and was taken to a small whitewashed room, the officer's quarters, and introduced to three young officers of junior rank as the Terjiman Chaoush. They were dressed in their best and most foppish uniforms complete with extraordinarily high collars—after the German pattern —and, after I had seen them in all their glory, they undid their tunics and removed the collars—which were fastened to the tunics with press-studs. The room reeked of scent, and the complexions of the officers were a beautiful pink and white. I knew their type, and I have no doubt that they considered themselves very smart young fellows. One of them addressed me in Turkish, and, as I was answering him, another spoke to me in Arabic. I was answering the second one, when the third rapped out something in French. I did not understand French, and said so. They took no notice of me but continued to fire questions at me in all three languages. It did not take me long to tumble to their game. They were trying to make me admit to a knowledge of

French. For what reason I have no idea, unless they thought that I was a French spy masquerading as an English prisoner of war. In the end they *insisted* that I knew French and vowed that they would find means of making me talk in that language, and they assumed a threatening attitude. I was not in the least frightened of them and told them—in Turkish— just what I thought of them and ended by threatening to report them to the Commandant. Their expressions, when I had finished, were most comical. All their conceit and waggishness had vanished, together with their blustering attitude, and they looked very sheepish. Obviously they did not expect such an outburst from a ragged prisoner of war. Among other things I told them that a year or two of campaigning on the Mesopotamian front would do them the world of good; then they would dress more like soldiers and would certainly not underrate the spirit of the British soldier, whether in the field or as a captive. I refused their proffered cigarettes and strode out of the room, returning in high dudgeon to my own barrack-room, where I related to Micky all that had taken place.

About this time Micky was feeling very queer and was unable to eat his nightly allowance of *kurrawanna* or his daily ration of bread; a sure sign that he was really ill. He was afraid to report sick as he would have to see the obnoxious Greek doctor. Eventually he was compelled to go, and I accompanied him to see that he got fair play. The doctor examined him and then ordered him to lie down and not eat anything until he felt better. Micky told him that he had not eaten for several days and asked that he might be given either milk or *yorghurt*, as he must have something unless he were to starve to death. He was told by the Greek to sell his ration of bread and buy what he wanted. Two days later he was taken to hospital suffering from typhus.

I missed Micky's company dreadfully. The hours dragged slowly enough when we were together, but then we managed to find something to amuse us. We saw humour in the most trivial events and took life very much as it came and not at all seriously. We were eminently suited to be partners in the kind of life we were leading: both of us were carpenters; both had some artistic ability; both of us were full of "ideas" and we shared the ability to sum up a situation at once and act accordingly—our summing-up was invariably the same. Whereas he was undoubtedly the better craftsman and artist, I had the gift of languages that he did not possess in the slightest degree, otherwise our attributes were uncannily alike. One other thing he could do that I could not was to play a tune by rapping on his skull and opening and closing his mouth to graduate the sound and form the notes. He could do the same by holding a pencil between his teeth and tapping it with his finger-nails.

The nights became very chilly, and it became the custom of the guard to light a fire of brushwood and branches in the middle of the barrack-room floor—which was of beaten earth. The acrid smoke thus caused, combined with the incessant chatter of the sentries, lost me many a night's sleep, and on those occasions I would stroll up and down outside listening to the sentries on duty calling out the numbers of their respective posts. All night long they called out, "Bir," "ekki," "uch," "dirt" (one, two, three, four), and so on up to twelve, the total number of posts. I once asked the sentry on our door what would happen if number six—for instance—did not answer. He replied that he did not know. Occasionally a visiting N.C.O. would yell out from the darkness, "Nobutchi yeddi tenna" ("Sentry number seven")—or whatever the number of the post was—and the sentry would reply, "Borda" ("Here.") "Peck oli" ("All right"), the N.C.O. would yell, and pass on.

At the foot of my *pranda* was a rifle-rack, and, one day when I lay idly gazing at the rifles and wishing that Micky were back with me, I noticed that a good many of the bolts of the rifles were only partially in and had been secured with string. I got up to examine them more closely and took one up to see why the bolt would not enter properly. I found that they were all Russian rifles—probably captured on one of the Russian fronts—and, of course, the numbers were in the European adaptation of Arabic figures, and so unintelligible to the illiterate *askars*. This had resulted in all the bolts being mixed up and not being fitted to the proper rifles of the same number. The Bash Chaoush had observed me looking at the rifles and came over to me and asked if I could read the numbers and sort them out for him. He knew what was wrong but was unable to put the matter right himself or get anyone to read the numbers for him. I willingly agreed to sort them out for him, as it was something for me to do to break the awful monotony. When the recruits returned from parade I organized the whole affair. I sorted out all the bolts and fitted them to their respective rifles and placed them into the rack. Above each rifle I wrote a number from one to the total number of rifles, in Arabic. I recorded the number of each rifle and the number each occupied in the rack beside the names of the recruits to whom they were to be issued. The recruits were "fallen in," told the number of their rifles in the rack, and then ordered to get their own rifles. After one or two mistakes they were able to take and replace their rifles in the correct places in the rack. I showed the Bash Chaoush how to compare the Russian numbers with the numbers I had recorded, so that, in the event of the bolts becoming mixed again, he could readily sort them out and know which recruit had been at fault. I had just finished, and the Bash Chaoush was expressing his delight at my demonstration of a little "system," when in strode the Officer Commanding the Depôt and demanded to know what was going on. The Bash Chaoush explained what I had done and got the recruits to take their rifles from the rack and replace them in their proper places.

The O.C. was very pleased and said, "Many thanks, Engleezi Chaoush. I have often been told that all the English soldiers can read and write, and that their N.C.O.s are very wise (*chok ockle*). Now I know that is true." He gave me a cigarette and lit it for me before turning to address the recruits this wise. "You have all seen? Well, take good notice of how a soldier behaves. This English soldier is our prisoner now, but he has not forgotten that he is still a soldier and his example is a good one for you all to follow." With that he saluted me and strode out of the room.

My prestige was high and my privileges many, but nothing could compensate for my loneliness, and no one was able to authorize extra food, so that my days were just long hours of half-starved boredom for the most part during the time Micky was in hospital.

On one red-letter day I received a message that I could visit Micky, as he was getting better. I at once called for a soldier to accompany me and hurried off to the hospital. Micky looked very thin and ill when I saw him, but he assured me that he was quite all right and getting rapidly better. He was full of praises for the hospital staff, of which both doctors and nurses were Armenian. One of the doctors had even procured for him a couple of bars of chocolate, an act of great magnitude, as sugar, or sweet stuff in any shape or form, was practically impossible to obtain and cost a great deal of money. Micky was telling me how good the nurses had been to him when into the ward rushed half a dozen of them. The news had just reached them that another Englishman was in the hospital. They crowded round me, and great was their delight when they found that I could talk to them in Turkish; they knew no English. They asked me a great many questions, some of them extremely embarrassing, and held my hands and generally treated me as though I were some long-lost brother. Those girls seemed quite happy and chattered away like birds at nesting time, despite the fact that they were all exiles and had suffered the loss of male relatives during the massacres in 1915. This, I was told, was because they were working under doctors of their own race; also, the Commandant treated them with great kindliness and consideration. No one molested them and they were allowed to live their own lives. Money or material was supplied to them for their clothes, and, in addition to adequate rations, they received a few piastres in hard cash every month. I envied Micky his comfortable bed and clean sheets—not to mention the company of the nurses—and suggested to the doctor, before I left, that it would be a good idea if I too were to be admitted to hospital. He laughed and said that were the place not so crowded he would have been only too pleased to have had me in. I stayed with Micky until it was time to draw my evening meal of *kurrawanna*.

A few days later Micky was out of hospital and back with me in barracks. He had only been back a couple of days when we received a visit from the Commandant. He had heard of Micky's illness and was anxious to know how we were both getting on. He told me that we had to report sick immediately we felt the slightest bit unwell, as he had no wish for anything serious to happen to us. Then he asked whether we had everything we wanted. That was a very difficult question to answer, as there were many things we wanted—more food, clothes, and money—but as we were getting the same food as his men, and they were in rags and received no pay, I could only say that, all things considered, we were very comfortable and wanted for nothing. He emptied his cigarette-case on to my bed and told the recruits in the room that it was their duty to see that we did not lack for a smoke.

It was a great pity that there were not more Commandants of his kidney in Turkey in those days, then there would have been more "other ranks" of the Kut Garrison to attend the annual reunion now than there are. Because of that particular

Commandant, Osmania was one of the few bright spots in
Turkey, and, I imagine, the recruits that were lucky enough
to pass through the training depôt there thought so too after
they had left it.

One afternoon the recruits returned earlier from parade
than was usual, and I told Micky that something must be
afoot. There certainly was. The Bash Chaoush followed the
recruits into the room and ordered them to "sit to attention"
on their platform. Then he proceeded to rave and threaten
and exhort them to inform him who had stolen some ammunition. From what I could gather, the lads had been on
musketry practice the day previously, under the charge of one
Ahmed Onbashi, and twenty-odd rounds of rifle ammunition
had disappeared. When no one volunteered information the
Bash Chaoush asked each of the youngsters individually to
swear that they knew nothing of the matter. That part over,
Ahmed Onbashi was sent for and arrived under armed escort.
The Bash Chaoush told him that all the men had sworn that
they knew nothing of the missing ammunition, therefore he
—Ahmed—must know something of the matter. Ahmed
protested his innocence and said that undoubtedly the
cartridges were taken when his back was turned. "All right,"
said the Bash Chaoush, "we shall soon see. Take off your
boots." Everyone knew what was to follow, and the recruits
looked uneasy and frightened. Without further parley the
Bash Chaoush commenced to administer the bastinado to
the Onbashi, using the horrible "rawhide" whip that I have
previously mentioned. The victim screamed in agony and
pleaded for mercy. After half a dozen strokes the Bash
Chaoush asked the Onbashi whether he still knew nothing of
the matter, continuing the punishment as soon as knowledge
was denied. The Onbashi could not keep up his attitude of
ignorance in the matter for very long, and eventually
screamed out that he would tell the truth. He produced the
missing ammunition from the folds of his capacious cummer-

bund. Drastic detective methods but certainly effective. The Onbashi was taken away, and I trembled to think what his ultimate punishment would be.

The big feast after the fast of Ramadan came along, and we received a ration of *pilaff* in lieu of our usual *kurrawanna*, the exception to our diet that I have mentioned. Following the feast came the news that a Pasha was coming to inspect the men under training. I forget the Pasha's name, but I remember that he was a man of some importance and that everyone was in a state of great excitement as the great day came nearer. Extra drills were the order of the day, and fatigue parties worked long hours in an endeavour to make the camp clean and tidy. There was an issue of new uniform to the recruits, and that issue was one of the most surprising and amusing events that we witnessed at any time during our captivity. I will attempt to describe it, though I fear that it will be impossible to convey the ludicrousness of the scene.

The recruits were made to "sit at ease" on their platform and wait until one of the permanent staff arrived, bearing a sack full of boots and clothing on his back. This he emptied on to the middle of the floor and said, "Get what you can."

In a moment there was a wild scramble; recruits fighting like a pack of wolves to get an article of clothing or a pair of boots. Micky and I roared with laughter as we watched the scene. The scramble was soon over and the men returned to the platform with whatever prizes they had managed to get. The clothing was the crudest attempt at a uniform that we had ever seen—even in Turkey. It was made of coarse hessian, dyed green, and comprised a shapeless tunic and a pair of pants of the Turkish "baggy-behind" style. The boots were of the "cardboard and pegs" variety. Apparently the clothing and boots were all of one size, so the scene that followed can be imagined. One huge youngster—known as Aintabbi, because he came from Aintab—had managed to

secure a complete outfit, the only one to do so. Stripping off
his rags he prepared to don his new "uniform." The pants
fitted fairly well except that they only reached to his knees
instead of to his ankles, and would not meet at the waist.
The length didn't matter and a piece of string soon made out
the difference round his waist. The tunic was a different
problem, and before he finally got into it he had burst every
seam. Even that did not worry him, for he got a pal to lace
up the seams with a length of string. Micky and I were
convulsed with laughter, and the tears rolled down our faces
as we watched Aintabbi getting dressed, and by the time he
had finished with his boots we were in positive pain from so
much laughing. He was wearing an enormous pair of heelless
slippers, and we knew that the boots that he had "won"
would never fit his great feet, but we were not prepared for
what he did with them. After several ineffectual attempts to
get his feet into them, he tore off the soles and drew the
uppers over his ankles in the manner of spats, lacing them
with string and then replacing the slippers on his feet. He got
off the platform and turned around and around and surveyed
the result, and from the look on his face he was perfectly
satisfied. All his actions had been gone through with an air of
utmost seriousness, as indeed had the actions of the remainder. Everyone who had managed to get clothing lost no time
in sewing themselves into it. They made sure that they were
not going to have it stolen, and, as they never bathed nor had
a bed to get into, there was no need to remove it in any case.
It would take a far more facile pen than mine to do justice to
that "kit issue" and the scene that followed. The recruits
were amazed at our levity and could not understand what we
saw to laugh about; that, of course, made us laugh the more.

The great day came and with it the Pasha, who, from all
accounts, was satisfied with everything he saw. I wondered
what he thought as he inspected the recruits. Still, what did
clothes and boots and suchlike luxuries mean to a Turkish

soldier anyhow? All that was required of him was that he should shoot straight and die without a mess when his time came. They were treated like dogs and looked like dogs; yet, with decent and humane treatment, they would have made the finest soldiers in the world. As it was they put up a stiff resistance on every front on which they were engaged during the Great War, and that war was fought after their country had been fighting continuously for twenty years, and they continued to fight for another six years after that war was over. They were never punished by "defaulters" or suchlike punishments as in the British Army, but if they were stupid on parade, or slow, or committed a minor offence, they were punished on the spot by an officer or N.C.O., usually by having their faces slapped. It was a pitiful sight—to the average Englishman—to see an undersized popinjay of an officer smacking the face of a huge, bearded Anatolian, but such sights were common.

Not many days after the Pasha's inspection we were taken away from Osmania without the slightest warning. One morning an elderly *askar*, equipped for the road, came in to us and said, "Haidi Ingleezi. Gitior siz." ("Come on, English. You are going.") We could hardly believe it was true, but there was no doubt about it. The only men in the room at the time were two cooks of the permanent staff, and we asked them to give our farewell greetings to the Bash Chaoush and the remainder of the staff, as well as to the recruits, then, bidding them good-bye, we marched out of the depôt that had housed us in comparative comfort and freedom for so long.

CHAPTER ELEVEN

WE JOURNEY, BY STAGES, TO ALEPPO

I HAD long since discarded the rags from my feet and could once more march barefooted without discomfort, and, beyond regrets at not seeing our room-mates before we left, had no feelings or fears for the future as we headed once more for the open road.

The *askar* carried a letter concerning us but, as it was in Arabic script, I was unable to read it. He was unable to read any sort of script. All he could tell us was that our first destination was Mamourie. We wondered what reception we should get there, though we did not worry unduly as we thought it extremely unlikely that we should be sent back to work there.

From Osmania to Mamourie is only a comparatively short march and we made it without event, stopping on the way to gorge ourselves with blackberries, which grow as large as walnuts in that district. We arrived at the *sokiet khana* about the time of evening *kurrawanna*, and the Chaoush in charge read the letter that the *askar* handed to him. He was a stupid sort of brute and, despite my violent protests, handcuffed Micky and I together before pushing us into the noisome den that was the *sokiet*.

Kurrawanna was brought in in the usual round tins, one between ten men, and we had to sit in with the remainder or go hungry. We had eaten all sorts of filth at one time or another, but that was the first time that we had been *compelled* to eat out of the common dish in company with very unsavoury natives, and we felt our position keenly. I had regularly eaten that way with Ali the Kurd, and many times when I had been invited to a meal by the élite of Adana prison, but the meals on those occasions were not mad gallopings of food by unwashed criminals. Our present mess-mates were as foul a gang of ruffians as could be found, and they were adepts at shovelling food into their mouths whilst handicapped by shackles.

Our thoughts were very bitter as we lay on the filthy platform that night, for we had no idea how long we were to remain in that *sokiet* and the manacles on our wrists, besides restricting our movements, had a most depressing effect on us after our freedom at Osmania.

Fortunately we were only kept there for three days, and on the evening of the third we were taken on to the station platform to await a train going south.

Time-tables seemed to be non-existent in Turkey, or, if there were any, no one took the slightest notice of them. Passengers used to take up a position on the station and camp there until they eventually got a train that was going in the general direction that they wished to go.

On that occasion we waited until nearly midnight before a train arrived, and then it was full to capacity. The elderly *askar* who had charge of us was useless in the search for accommodation, and had we left the matter to him we might have been there yet. We searched the passenger coaches from beginning to end until we found a tiny compartment at the end of one coach which—miracle of miracles—was empty. Delighted at our good fortune we climbed in and settled ourselves on the upholstered seats, but our stay was of short duration, for the compartment belonged to two Germans, who ordered us out in no uncertain manner. We were determined to leave Mamourie by that train and eventually found room on a load of steel rails, and a cold and uncomfortable seat it was. Our escort grumbled and said that we should do better if we waited until daylight and the next train. He was in no hurry. Neither were we, but we had no intention of returning to the *sokiet*, and handcuffs again, if we could possibly avoid it.

As the train had to pass through the now completed Amanus tunnel, it did not start before daylight, so we spent a cold and sleepless night in the open, on top of the load of rails.

Early the next morning the train moved off, without warning, and chugged its way up the steep gradient towards Iran and the tunnel mouth. At Yarbagtchi it halted for half an hour and, by great good fortune, we caught sight of one of the three English prisoners who were still working at that place. We gave him a hail but it was some time before he could identify us among the crowd of natives who shared the load of rails with us. When at last he did so, he dashed into a hut and brought out the other two and they all came over to us. We dare not leave the train as our places would have been filled immediately and we should have been unable to have got on again. One of the trio was Corporal Esterson, a shoeing-smith of my battery, and it was the first time we had met since the fall of Kut. He told us that our disappearance from Iran had created a tremendous stir and the Commandant had sent the remainder of the party to some other place on the line; where he could not say. Corporal Esterson gave us all the money he possessed together with two loaves and a small bag of raisins. We were extremely thankful for his kindness as we had had nothing to eat since we left Osmania, other than the two or three mouthfuls of *kurrawanna* that we had managed to eat in the *sokiet* at Mamourie. The next time I met the Corporal was in England in 1919.

With last handshakes and a "Good luck, boys," from the trio, we left them, standing waving, as the train slowly pulled out, to continue puffing and panting its way up the Amanus.

We passed through Bagtchi—of evil repute—and on to Iran—of unpleasant memories. With great interest we gazed up at the mountain-side that we had climbed when we ran away from Iran, and Micky said, "What about a tin of tripe, Jerry?" recalling our first unpalatable meal eaten on the summit. With a piercing whistle the train entered the Amanus tunnel, that monument to the British slaves who had died in its construction. In a very short time we were choking and gasping for breath as the smoke and fumes from the engine were forced back upon us. We covered our heads with our shirts but were close to suffocation by the time we reached the open air again.

The train stopped for a few minutes at Entilli, but we could see nothing of the friends who had sheltered us there. At Islahie we were told by our escort that we had to get off, as he had orders to report there. I asked him what we were to do at Islahie but he would only repeat, "Haidi, haidi," to all my questions. We followed him to where a soldier stood on guard outside a small, low-pitched, goat's-hair tent. Our *askar* handed us over to that soldier and we were pushed inside the tent, which was already well filled.

The tent was too low to admit of standing upright and one end was blocked up with a mud wall. Sitting with his back to the wall, inside the tent, was another sentry, with his rifle across his knees.

Sitting as near to the open end as we could, Micky and I surveyed our fellow-prisoners, about sixteen in all. Nearest to us were three young Kurds, chained together at the wrists and ankles. They did not look very desperate characters and I wondered what their particular offence was, avoiding military service I conjectured. Three or four others were in ragged uniforms and we guessed that they were deserters. The rest were a nondescript crowd of Turks and Arabs.

Our escort returned with two small loaves for us, and departed again without a word.

The heat inside the tent became stifling during the afternoon, and a dust-storm that blew up did nothing to improve matters. There was an old and battered kerosene oil tin in use for drinking-water and it was only filled up once. On that occasion there was a wild scramble to get a drink, and I

scrambled with the rest of them and managed to get about
half a pint between the two of us.

At sunset we got a ration of very thin *kurrawanna*, which
had olive oil for flavouring instead of meat. After that meal
we were all marched out for the usual purpose before being
shut up for the night. On our return to the tent, Micky
and I pushed our way farther inside so that we should not
suffer so much from the bitterly cold night air. The tent was
closed for the night, with one sentry inside and one out.

As Micky and I lay chatting, the prisoner on my side
kept nudging me and whispering "Ingleezi." He was one of
the "towny" type and had had plenty to say about us during
the afternoon, and I had no wish to talk to him. When his
nudges became more insistent I told him to keep his elbow
to himself and his mouth shut. Undeterred, he whispered,
"I am a Bulgarian." I took no notice so he again told me that
he was a Bulgarian, and added that he was a friend of the
English and had deserted from the Turkish Army. I asked
him why he was not in the Bulgarian Army and he told me
that he had deserted from there during the last Balkan War
and had remained in Turkey, being conscripted when the
Great War broke out. I told him that the Bulgarians were our
enemies even as the Turks were but of the two I preferred
the Turks. That did not please him so he tried to draw me
by loudly proclaiming the Turkish victories of Kut and the
Dardanelles. I took no notice of him but continued to talk to
Micky, so he began to sing the victory song of the Dardanelles—"Chanakula"—in a piercing, raucous voice. We had
heard the tune hundreds of times and it didn't improve by
repetition. The deserting Bulgar was really singing *at* me,
for he had his mouth within three inches of my ear. I told
him to shut up but he screamed the louder, no doubt pleased
that he had found a means of annoying me. Unable to stand
his din any longer, I turned over and hit him on the mouth
with my clenched fist as hard as I could. He was true to type

and made no attempt to retaliate, but yelled out to the sentry that I was assaulting him. The sentry must have known him for he replied, "Sus, eshek!" ("Silence, donkey!") and threatened to tie him up if he caused any further trouble. After that we were left in peace.

We spent three days in that tent before we were all taken out and marched off to Aleppo, and we managed to become thoroughly lousy in that time.

Our escort on the road were four ragged *askars*, whose first job was to rope all the natives together. Had it not been for my violent protests, Micky and I would have been roped to the remainder. Our *askar* from Osmania heard the hubbub I caused and came to our rescue, telling the new escort that we were Ingleezi and would not run away.

The journey was quite a leisurely affair and the escort seemed to be in no hurry to get to Aleppo, making frequent and lengthy halts. Rolling-stock was so scarce in Turkey that most of the troops had to march to the various battle-fronts, so that at fairly frequent intervals along the road were police posts and ration dumps. At each of those places were built shelters of branches and reeds, etc., to accommodate the troops if they were to stay the night. We reached one of those posts during the afternoon of the second day out from Islahie, and had hardly got settled into one corner of a shelter when a large party of troops arrived, on their way to the Palestine front. All the available space in our shelter was taken up by the overflow from the others and I took the opportunity of chatting with those unfortunate soldiers. They were treated exactly like prisoners and were not permitted to leave the shelter—even to fill their water-bottles at a nearby stream—unless a party wished to go out, in which case they were marched to wherever they wished to go under the watchful eye of armed police. Even the N.C.O.s were subjected to the same treatment and I wondered at the stoic manner in which they all suffered such indignities. I

Other Ranks of Kut   R

was well aware that desertions on a large scale would have taken place had they not have been so watched, so readers can imagine what the conditions were like in the army of the Sultan.

At another police post, the last before Aleppo, we were forced to be inoculated. On the plain in front of the shelters a Red Crescent marquee had been set up, and into that straggled a long line of Turkish soldiers. To our surprise we were marched to the end of the queue and told that we were to be inoculated the same as the soldiers. Micky and I were greatly amused to see several of the soldiers faint as they left the tent, and two who fainted with the thoughts of the operation before they went in. There was no chance of dodging that parade, so we decided to go to the head of the queue, rather than wait until three or four hundred soldiers had been done. I told our escorting *askar* what we intended to do and left him before he could make up his mind to say "Yessok." We walked inside the tent and saw, for the first time, medical orderlies in white smocks, and iodine being used on the flesh where the puncture was to be made. The medical officer—a smart young fellow—was rapidly becoming exasperated by the cringing attitude of the soldiers, and he slapped the faces of those who pulled away or flinched when he jabbed in the needle. I considered that we had better get our dose before the needle became too blunt, so, nudging Micky to follow, I stepped into the line close to the Medical Officer. The soldiers gingerly exposed about four square inches of their chests but we pulled off our shirts before we got to the doctor. My turn came and I stepped forward. The Medical Officer was so surprised when he saw my naked torso that he looked into my face. "Who are you?" he asked. "Ingleezi," I replied, "both of us."

The Medical Officer turned to his assistants and said, "Bok siz! Bu Ingleezilar ich corkmior. Wa' allah! bir inji askarlar, Ingleezi." ("Look you! these Englishmen are not a bit afraid. By God! first-class soldiers are the English.")

As the orderly dabbed iodine on my chest the Medical Officer picked up a fresh syringe and said, "A new needle for you two." We each received a pat on the shoulder and a "Bravo!" as we passed out of the tent. As we passed down the line of waiting soldiers we were amused at the looks of wonderment that met us. No doubt the soldiers were thinking that here were two men who were so unafraid of inoculation that they hastened to receive it. Perhaps we should not have been so amused had we been operated on with a blunt needle, and I imagine that a needle quickly became blunt after being jabbed into the tough and dirty hides of some of those soldiers.

We reached Aleppo at sunset of the same day, and were surprised to find it built of stone and containing real roads and pavements.

The sight of two ragged and hatless objects, strolling unconcernedly behind a party of roped prisoners, quickly attracted the attention of the inevitable small boys, and we soon had a following of inquisitive Arabs and other towns-folk, who informed any new-comers that we were Ingleezi.

We were marched into the town jail and handed over to Gendarmes there, who wore crescent-shaped brass plates dangling under their chins on their tunic-fronts. The Chaoush in charge was a giant of a man with huge moustachios, and he wore his black and white astrakhan fez at a rakish angle. He took our party to a wide steel door of the roller type, which was lifted by four other Gendarmes, to reveal a room that rivalled the "Black Hole of Calcutta." As far as I could see, it was chock-full of prisoners and a wave of hot fetid air rolled out as the door was raised. The inmates set up a great howling and cat-calling when they saw the Chaoush. That giant ordered us to get inside, and the other Gendarmes made room by knocking back those already inside with the butts of their rifles. The prospect was truly alarming for Micky and me, and I grabbed the arm of the Chaoush and shouted, "Yessok, yessok, Ingleezilar ichun" ("Forbidden, forbidden, for Englishmen"), meaning that we were not criminals and should not be put into that foul den. The Chaoush looked closer at me and said, in a tone of wonder, "Sen Ingleezi?" ("Are you English?") As rapidly as I could I explained who and what we were and that we had already served our term of imprisonment at Osmania. The attitude of the Chaoush belied his looks—at least, so far as we were concerned—and he told us to wait on one side until he had disposed of the rest of our party. When he was ready he called to one of the Gendarmes to come along with us, and strode out into the street. We followed him, up one street and down another, until we came to an open part of the town, in the centre of which was an ornamental drinking-fountain. Outside a large building facing the open space we halted, and were told to remain where we were until the Chaoush came back. He mounted a flight of steps that led from a side door of the building.

We sat on the edge of the pavement and watched the scene of many people hurrying to and fro. There were a good many unveiled but well-dressed and good-looking girls walking up the centre of the road, and we wondered what nationality they could be. On the opposite side of the road was the entrance to a theatre, and the stall-holders outside were busily preparing their wares for the night's business.

When the Chaoush returned, he was accompanied by a young and elegantly dressed Bash Chaoush who chatted with us for a few minutes and promised to get us something to eat. He told us that he had given permission for us to remain in the building for the night and ordered the Gendarme to remain with us. We went up the stairs and into a room, equipped as an office, that overlooked the "square."

For an hour we stood at the window, waiting for the return of the Bash Chaoush with the food he had promised, but when he returned we were disappointed, for he brought only two tiny cinnamon-flavoured cakes. We were thankful for small mercies, but that did not prevent us from expressing our disgust at the meagreness of the meal—after the Bash Chaoush had gone.

Back at the window we watched the crowds entering the theatre and listened to the cries of the sweetmeat vendors. There was a constant and terrific din, and above it all could be heard the sherbet seller as he clashed together his brass cups and yelled "Sherrr-berrrt." Wearying of the scene, we stretched ourselves out on the bare floor and endeavoured to sleep, but sleep does not come easily to starving men, however tired physically they may be, and it was a long time before it came to us.

Morning came, and we were taken out of the office and into a tiny ante-room near the head of the stairs, and left to ourselves. We were not locked in, and when I looked out of the door I could see neither Gendarme nor *askar* set to watch us. There was a constant stream of civilians going up and down the stairs, and we came to the conclusion that we were in some sort of Law Courts or other administrative building.

Hour after hour passed slowly by and our hunger increased. No one seemed to bother about us, and we began to think that we had been forgotten. Two well-dressed Arabs waited in the ante-room for about ten minutes before they were called away, and they gave us each a cigarette which helped to ease the gnawing pangs of hunger a little. During our wait we had concocted a plan to call attention to our need of sustenance to whatever official should eventually interview us. It was arranged that as soon as we got in front of the official Micky was to collapse and lie feebly groaning. I was to kneel beside him and complain bitterly that lack of food had brought him to that state, and say that if we did not get food very quickly we should both die of starvation. We had it all very nicely planned out, but things did not turn out quite as we expected.

In the early afternoon, when we had given up all hopes of being sent for that day, I stepped out on to the landing determined to accost the next person that came up the stairs and beg for food. At that moment an officer of high rank came up, his sword clanking noisily at every step. He stared haughtily at me and passed into a room facing the ante-room, and I did not accost him. A few minutes later a bell rang in that room and a clerk entered, to return very shortly to tell us we were wanted. We entered the room and the clerk left and closed the door behind him.

At the far end of the room sat he of the clanking sword, and, in English, he greeted us, "Good morning, Englishmen."

"Good morning, sir," I replied. "Do you speak English?"

"Why, of course. Come closer," he said, so I whispered to Micky, "No stunts," referring to our little plot.

The officer looked hard at us both and then picked up a letter from his table.

"Well, well," he said, "I have a letter here from the Commandant of Osmania, and he tells me that you have been punished for attempting to escape. He speaks very well of you. Why were you so foolish as to think that you could escape? If you had remained quietly at your work you would be well clothed now, instead of being in rags, and you would have been happy and comfortable."

We listened to him in amazement, and, when he paused, I blurted out, "You have a poor idea of comfort, Effendi. Do you know what sort of life we lead as prisoners of war in your prison camps? Are you aware that we haven't eaten for three days?

"That is a lie," he retorted, "I sent you a cake each only last night."

"It is true that we had that small amount, but that is all we have had since leaving Islahie," I answered.

"You have only yourselves to blame for whatever hardships you suffer," was the rejoinder, which, in a way, was true enough.

"We are soldiers, Effendi," I said next, "and as such we should attempt to escape even if our treatment were of the best—which it most certainly is not."

"Well, I don't want to argue with you. Tell me where you would like to go now," the officer said.

"Do you mean that you will send us anywhere where we wish to go?" I asked, in amazement.

"That depends on where you want to go," was the answer.

I went into a whispered conference with Micky, and we agreed that, as British prisoners were now working at or near Nisibin, we would ask to be sent to that place, as it offered possibilities of escape towards Baghdad. So I asked the officer to send us into Syria, where there were others of our race working for the "Company."

"So," he replied, "then to-morrow you will be sent to Nisibin. When you get there, give my regards to Mr. Leach and tell him that I, Reshid Pasha, will be pleased to see him again."

Mr. Leach was the Regimental Sergeant-Major of the 1st/4th Hants Regiment, and a member of the Kut Garrison. When we met him, subsequently, he told us that, as senior prisoner of war at Nisibin and district, he kept all the records of the British prisoners and was responsible for their administration and the distribution of letters, parcels and clothing, etc. He had been to Aleppo several times to arrange for the dispatch of boots and clothing to the prisoners, from one or other of the foreign consuls acting on our behalf. It was on those occasions that he had met the Pasha.

Reshid Pasha stood up and said that we should remain in that building until we were sent away the following morning, meanwhile we were free to leave him. I asked that we be taken to the Swiss Consul so that we could get some money.

"Money!" he said, in surprise. "And why do you want money?"

It did not take me long to tell him why, indeed. When I had finished he said:

"Well, if it is money you want, I can give you that. Just sign your names here."

We signed some sort of document and received a lira note each.

"But, Pasha Effendi," I protested, "we need more than this, as Turkish paper money is almost worthless."

"Oh, is it," he snapped. "Turkish money is very good money and that is all you will get, and now you may go."

There was no more to be said—though I thought plenty— and we left the Pasha. I have often wondered how much the Pasha collected, eventually, from the Swiss Consul in exchange for that document we signed.

Outside the door was an *askar* waiting to take charge of us. I asked him to take us on the roof where we could get a view of Aleppo, and also got him to send out for food and tobacco. He told us that foodstuff was very scarce in Aleppo, but, despite that, we managed to make a good meal of bread and hard-boiled eggs and dried figs.

With full stomachs we were once more content and sat lazily puffing at our cigarettes as we gazed at the panorama of Aleppo with its—to us—wonderful stone-built houses. We were so accustomed to the wattle and daub and stick and rag buildings that the sight of anything so substantial as a stone edifice gave us cause for wonderment.

That night we discussed the possibility of escaping from Nisibin. To settle down to a life of slavery was the last thing we thought of doing, and the end of the war was so remote from us that we did not even contemplate it. Our greatest concern was that we might be in some prison when news of

MASS HANGING IN ALEPPO. ZAPTIEHS (GENDARMES) WEARING BRASS PLATES ROUND THEIR
NECKS, AS DESCRIBED ON PAGE 259, CAN BE SEEN AT THE BACK OF THE SCAFFOLD BETWEEN THE
FIRST TWO HANGING FIGURES

[See p. 259

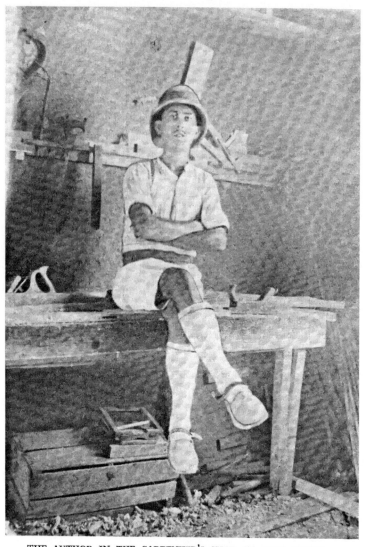

THE AUTHOR IN THE CARPENTER'S SHOP AT GHIR GHIRO

[See p. 263

a Turkish defeat came through. Then, we thought, the Turks might do to us as they had done to the Bulgarian prisoners of war at Afion-Kara-Hissar. That was one of the risks we had to run, but we treated it very lightly. We hoped that as we were to be on more familiar ground at Nisibin, we should be able to get clear of the country altogether. Little did we dream that it would be many weeks before we made another attempt to get away; weeks that were to be chock-full of incident and adventure—of a sort.

Early the following morning we were taken out of the building and attached to a party of scallywags who were going to various working camps on the line. We were marched to the station and, as usual, had to wait for hours until a train came along that had room for us. It was well after dark when we boarded a goods train and were locked into the inevitable wagon.

CHAPTER TWELVE

WE JOURNEY BACK TO NISIBIN

AFTER being bumped about all night, in an indescribable atmosphere, we were taken out of our prison van and put into an open truck at the front of the train. We thought that that was a change for the better, as we were in the open air and could look at the country we passed through, but we soon thought differently. The engines in that part of the country were fired with wood, and every time fresh logs were put on the fire, or the fire was stoked, we were deluged with a rain of red-hot cinders. Then we were kept busy knocking cinders off our bare arms or necks and putting out our smouldering clothes. The experience was similar to the one we had behind the engine from Mamourie to Iran, except that this time we were behind a full-sized engine, which meant more cinders.

During the day we passed through a region inhabited by Kurds and noticed with interest the peculiar architecture of their houses. They were like sugar-loaves or narrow, conical, bee-hives, and presented a singular appearance, very much like clusters of a certain type of toadstool.

The railhead had advanced about twenty miles beyond Ras-el-Ain, though the actual track had been completed as far as Nisibin. The "Company" were only able to obtain rails by pulling up older sections of the line. The rails on the track between Tarsus and Mersina had been removed and sent down to Syria, and, later on, other rails came from the line in Lebanon.

At the rail-head we were taken to a cluster of bell-tents erected on some rising ground. Over one of the tents flew the Turkish flag, so we guessed that it housed the Camp Commandant. We were herded into one of the tents some twenty paces from the Commandant's, and one of the local sentries mounted guard over us.

We had long since eaten the food we had bought at Aleppo and were once more very hungry. I ventured to open the flap of the tent and ask the sentry whether we were to be fed. "Yok" ("No") he answered, and pushed me back with the butt of his rifle. I persisted.

"Let me see the Commandant then."

"Yok. Yessok" ("No. It is forbidden"), he replied, and threatened me with his bayonet.

"He has only to say *yaron* (to-morrow) and then we shall have the three Y's of Turkey," commented Micky.

All prisoners of war in Turkey were only too familiar with the *yok, yessok, yaron,* that made up the three Y's. If any of us asked for anything it was *yok* that we generally got for an answer. If we wanted to go anywhere it was *yessok*, and all queries as to "when" were answered by *yaron.*

I sat down and discussed the situation with Micky. It was nearly dark, and I had no intention of going without food all night, if it were possible to beg or buy any. Eventually, I decided to risk an interview with the Commandant. I knew that it might mean a severe beating and probably result in my being tied up all night, according to what sort of man the Commandant was. Still, nothing venture nothing win, so I told Micky to hold the attention of the sentry whilst I crawled under the tent wall. With very little bother, and helped by one of the natives, I scrambled out and sprinted for the Commandant's tent. The sentry saw me and immediately gave chase, yelling at the top of his voice to attract the attention of other *askars*. I reached the Commandant's tent first and rushed inside. The great man was lying on his bed, and when I shouted, "Zabout Effendi," he jumped up in alarm. His alarm turned to surprise when he saw who it was that had shouted, and I was surprised too when I saw his face, for it was my old friend the Bimbashi of the American hospital in Adana. He recognized me at once, and the soldiers who crowded the entrance of the tent were presented with the spectacle of their Commandant shaking hands effusively with a ragged, unkempt prisoner. The Bimbashi waved them away, saying, "It is all right, this is my very good friend."

I asked that Micky be brought over, and then I told the Bimbashi, very briefly, my adventures since I had seen him last. In return he told me that he had only left Adana a few weeks previously and that Susie was keeping very well. He had, he said, managed to give her presents of fruit and sugar from time to time. "Aha! Susie. Chok tatli guz" ("very sweet girl"), he said, reminiscently. The old chap had been very fond of Susie, in a fatherly way, and had often deprecated the treatment of the Armenians by the Turks. I told him that we had been given no food that day and that we wished to buy some. He said that food was very scarce and that he received none for issue to the various parties who alighted there on their way to Nisibin or other working camps. "Of course, I can get some for you, for you are my friends. But there are other Englishmen here and perhaps you would like to go and visit them," he said.

We had no idea that any Englishmen were in that isolated spot and jumped at the chance to visit them. The good Bimbashi gave us permission to remain with them during the night, providing that we reported back early the following morning, and sent an *askar* with us to show us the way.

The *askar* led us in the direction of some large, square-rigged, goat's-hair tents, and long before we got to them we heard the lurid language of an unmistakably Cockney voice, and our hearts leapt with joy at the sound of it. We stepped inside the tent from whence came the voice, and saw six or seven Englishmen—strangely garbed—sitting down to a meal of steaming stew. The Cockney was emphasizing some remark he was making by brandishing his spoon, and when Micky said "Hullo there," he presented an amusing sight as he sat for a few seconds with his mouth open and his spoon poised in mid-air. The others were equally surprised but came to earth when the Cockney ejaculated, "Gawd blimey! If it ain't Micky Dade." He happened to be a man of Micky's regiment, the Royal West Kents.

Several of the others were known to us, and in a very few minutes we were busily engaged in eating and trying to answer questions at the same time. That was a grand meal; real soldiers' stew, with plenty of meat and—wonder of wonders—potatoes, as well as other vegetables. After we had disposed of several helpings of stew, we tasted, for the first time for years, some real tea; real "Sergeant-Major's." The senior man of that little party was a Sergeant of the Worcestershire Regiment, and he was practically in charge of the whole camp, or, at least, the employees of the Company. All the others had overseers' jobs of one sort or another, mostly to do with the receipt and dispatch of stores, munitions, etc. Some time previously, they told us, the camp had been attacked by tribesmen, and the Sergeant had organized the defence, himself working a machine-gun from the roof of the station.

It may be as well to mention here that the only permanent building on that camp was the station, built—as were all the desert stations—like a blockhouse. Those stations were obviously built to withstand attacks by desert marauders: of solid concrete with loop-holed walls and a castellated roof, from the flat top of which an excellent look-out could be kept, besides affording an advantageous position for the defenders. A central door was the only entrance and led under an archway to a small courtyard. A water-tank on the roof supplied the station staff—who were all soldiers. By closing the central door the station became practically impregnable against the rifles of the tribesmen.

On the occasion of the last attack, even the Turkish soldiers had looked to the British Sergeant as the leader of the defence. The Turkish authorities had awarded him a medal for the part he played, but the man himself pooh-poohed the whole affair, saying that he had merely protected himself, helped by the other Englishmen.

Our hosts decided that the occasion of our visit called for a celebration, so bottles of "Raki"—the Arab arack, or the Greek mastic—were produced and we proceeded to make merry. As the potent spirit loosened our tongues we began to roar out choruses that were familiar in all the army canteens of pre-war days. Arab and Turkish friends of our hosts, attracted by the noise, came trooping in and joined in the fun. I taught the other Englishmen my version of a Turkish song the tune of which was familiar to everyone in Turkey those days. The words of the refrain were in Turkish, and were, for the most part, familiar to all. I give the doggerel below, with a broad translation.

> Ek mek ek mek, kurrawanna su,
> Para yokma, ne yapporum?
> Nairdair gitior bis bilmirum,
> Ne oppollum ne yapajek.
> Bis ysirlar, zara yokma,
> Sa'ulf gelior Blighty gitajek.
>
> Bread, bread, soup and water,
> Money we have none,
> What shall we do?
> Where are we going? we do not know.
> What shall we do, what can we do?
> We are prisoners but we don't care,
> Peace will come and to England we shall go.

The given translation was immediately understood and appreciated by those present, epitomizing, as it did, the conditions we lived under and the mental outlook of the majority of British prisoners of the "Other Ranks." Our rations invariably consisted of bread, soup, and water—at least, when we were with the Turks, as apart from being with the gangs working with the German Company. We were constantly being moved about the country, and no one knew our next destination until we arrived there. We rarely had money, and we constantly debated what could, or should, be done about things in general. Finally, we retained always the unfailing optimism—or devil-may-care-ness—of the British Tommy, and knew that as soon as the war ended those of us who still survived would eventually get back to England.

The party waxed fast and furious, and the natives entertained us by singing ballads in their own tongue. One Turkish employee gave a rendering of a Turkish love-song that was very popular in those days, all about a beautiful girl with hands as white as cotton-wool, etc. At the end of each verse—of which there were dozens—we roared out the chorus, "Aman Allah! Chok sevirum!" ("Oh God! How I love you!")

About midnight we fortified the inner man with platefuls of fried eggs and tomatoes, cooked by an Arab employed by the Company as cook to the English. After that the carousal went on for another two or three hours, before we decided that we had better get an hour or two of sleep.

It must not be supposed for one moment that those particular prisoners were "on velvet" or that their life was one round of "raki and fried eggs." Far from it. They were most probably "broke" for weeks after we had gone—and after they had paid the reckoning. Compared with rations that other parties got, theirs may have been good at that particular period, eked out, as they were, by the food parcels from home that they all too rarely received. They had to work long and hard in all weathers, and were without a single amenity that they had been used to; not even a book or a paper to feed their starved minds. They slept rough and wore whatever odds-and-ends of clothing came their way, whether Western or Eastern. Add to this the fact that they were isolated from their fellow comrades in a vast expanse of desolate waste, and with the ever-present knowledge that at any time the Turks might decide to take them into their tender [sic] care again, and the picture loses its rosy hue.

We were roused from our drunken sleep by being violently shaken by an askar, who had been sent by the Commandant to fetch us. With splitting heads, and still half stupefied, we staggered to our feet, and, after bidding good-bye to our friends, reeled out of the tent and rejoined our party of scallywags. The old Bimbashi was waiting for us, and he smiled broadly as we came up to him.

"You are drunk," he said. "I heard you singing and making merry last night. Well, never mind, you did no harm and here you are again. Now you must be off on the road to Nisibin." With that he shook us warmly by the hand and waved us away.

It was not long before we shook off the effects of our carousal, but it was long before we could slake our raging thirst. Water was very scarce on that long and dusty march, and perhaps it was just as well, for to drink water after a "binge" on raki is to become drunk again. Our friends had provided us with a bag of raisins and a loaf of bread for the road, otherwise we should have been hungry as well as thirsty. We shuddered to think of our condition had we not fallen in with those Englishmen, for, it will be remembered, we had received nothing at all in the way of food—beyond the small cake from the Pasha—since the last police post before we arrived in Aleppo. True, we had bought food with the money we had got from the Pasha, but it was pure chance that we had received that money, and even had we not had it we should have received no rations. The natives with us had had none, though they all had *chupatties* in their bundles, purchased before they left Aleppo.

That day's march was just a repetition of many similar ones; pad, pad, pad in the dust of the desert track. Hour after hour with nothing to break the monotony of the bleak horizon, and with nothing to look forward to once the march was over, except the possibility of a few hours' sleep and perhaps a bowl of the eternal *kurrawanna*. It was nearly dark by the time we reached the place where we were to stop the night—Serchikhan. There was an encampment of soldiers there and, we were told, a prisoners of war camp near the railway station. We were not allowed to visit the camp, and we thought we were lucky to avoid being roped together, as were the others immediately on our arrival.

We received a small quantity of *kurrawanna* and one loaf between us, though the others of our party received a loaf each. I pointed that out to the *askar* who had brought the rations to us, and he said that there was no more bread left. I accused him of stealing our rations and was going on to abuse him when he silenced me with a blow from his clubbed rifle.

Early the next morning we were off again, and in a few hours entered the ancient town—now a desert village—of Nisibin. We were taken to the office of the Kaimakam, where we sat in the dust of the roadway awaiting his pleasure. When at last he arrived he was reading the letter our escort had delivered to him, and the contents did not seem to please him. He went among the natives, smacking the face of one, spitting in the face of another and stamping on the bare toes of others. "Nice fellow this," I thought. "One of the good old sort."

He finished his rounds and waved them away with a curt "*Moppus*" ("Prison") to the Onbashi of the escort. Turning to us, he eyed us up and down and then spat violently on the

ground and called us unprintable Ingleezi, before ordering a
waiting *askar* to take us to the *Compania*.

At the offices of the Company we waited for several hours
before we were interviewed by one of the German engineers
—Herr Vinger. He asked us whether we were tradesmen,
and when we told him that we were carpenters seemed very
pleased and said that he had just the job for us, helping to
build a bridge over the Jag-Jag River. He sent for a guide
to take us to the site of our job. There we were handed over
to an Armenian who was the head timekeeper of that particular section of the line.

Tich the Timekeeper—as we promptly nicknamed him,
owing to his small stature—was a good-natured little chap,
full of energy and bursting with importance. He gave us a
small bell-tent, that was already pitched beside a shelter that
was the carpenters' shop, and a meal of bread and cold
pilaff, the remains of his own meal. He arranged to give us
rations the following day and said he would get his wife to
cook us something to eat for that night, promising to get us a
cooking-pot and what else he could when he next visited the
Company's store.

He was as good as his word, and that night, as we sat at
the evening meal in his tent, he told us all about our job and
the conditions of service there. We were to draw rations
daily, consisting of so many grams of mutton, potatoes, peas
or beans, and a loaf of bread each. For pay we should get
twenty-five piastres a day, payable monthly, and, as carpenters, we should be regarded as *employees*—as distinct
from *arbeiters*—and draw one day's pay per month in *sert
para* (coin), the rest would be paper, and worth whatever
we were lucky enough to get for it.

At the place where the bridge was to be built were two
streams—the main river and a fifty-feet wide canal, and about
a hundred yards separated the two. A quarter of a mile
farther along the track, towards Mosul, was a much smaller

stream, drawn off from the main river near the foothills and near the rail-track at thirty feet higher level. Immediately beyond that was Nisibin station, one of the most important stations that side of Aleppo. Months before the actual rails reached there it was the clearing house for all stores, munitions, etc., destined for Mosul and beyond. A fleet of German motor-lorries—driven by German soldiers—conveyed all the stores, etc., required by the military from Nisibin to Mosul. Practically all the work done at the station was performed by British and Indian prisoners of war, even the distribution and recording of stocks, etc. British N.C.O.s had positions of authority and held jobs of no little importance.

About five miles up stream, in the foothills of the Anti-Amanus Mountains, was the headquarters of the Railroad Construction Company, and many British and Indian prisoners were employed there.

The administrative offices, ration and hardware stores of the Company were at Nisibin, as also were the quarters of the German engineers and officials. Close to those offices stood a tented camp occupied by the Turkish Commandant and his Staff.

Although Nisibin was only a village, it had assumed at that time a great importance, and there were always great activities going on in and around it, consequent on the large bodies of troops that passed through and the work of the railway being directed from there.

The particular camp where Micky and I were to spend the next few weeks contained no other Englishmen. Our tent was one of a line of half a dozen situated on the river-bank facing the river. At one end of the line was the railroad embankment, in course of construction, and at the other end was another line of tents running down nearly to the water's edge; the river itself completed the "square," which we dubbed the "compound." In the centre of the compound was the best tent of all, occupied by an Italian overseer and his

Armenian "wife." Three other Italians occupied the tent nearest the river. Our tent was at the end of the line nearest the embankment, and our immediate neighbours were an Armenian detective—though what he "detected" I could never find out—and his alleged wife. All the occupants of the compound were employees of some importance and formed a community apart. The coolies and labourers occupied a large encampment immediately behind the compound. By far the largest community in that encampment was that of the Kurdish refugees, people who had fled from the butcheries of the Russians on the Erzerum front. Their own chiefs and headmen acted as charge-hands, and practically all the Kurds were employed; men, women and children, even little toddlers if they were able to carry a small basket of earth, to help build the embankment. Children received half rations. Even full rations only served to keep body and soul together and had to be shared among those too old, or too young, to work and the sick. There were many deaths in that community. Russian and Rumanian prisoners of war formed other sections of the encampment.

After we had surveyed the camp and had got our bearings, Micky and I sat on the bare floor of our tent and laughed at the position we found ourselves in. We were in rags of the raggedest; our shirts were more holes than shirt, and our nether wear was not decent. I was barefooted and Micky might just as well have been for all the use the old bits of leather were that he still called boots. We had neither bed nor bedding, and our only worldly goods were two empty packs—made from old kit-bags—two metal spoons and an ancient safety-razor. We were tanned as black as natives, and our bodies were as hard as boards, whilst our hair hung in a tangled mass. Without doubt, we were blessed with magnificent constitutions at that time, otherwise we should have been carrion long before. We decided that before very long we should either make ourselves comfortable or make a move elsewhere, then we discussed all that the Armenian, "Tich," had told us.

Every one of the Armenians in the compound had escaped from massacre or exile in more or less miraculous circumstances. The wife of "Tich" had been left for dead in a cave full of butchered women, whilst he had escaped after being wounded in several places; the scars of his wounds being still unhealed. We had told him what we had seen of the results of the massacres in Cilicia, and, from what he told us, things were just as bad throughout Turkey.

At six the next morning we were roused by the clanging of a piece of suspended rail, the signal that announced the commencement of work. We rose to our feet, stiff and cold and not at all inclined for work. However, we went over to the carpenters' shop—which was really a shelter of goat's-hair tenting—to see what had to be done. The other carpenters were already there—two Arabs and an Indian—but they were unable to tell us what we had to do. We looked over the tools and were not greatly impressed, as, for the most part, they were of Asiatic type; saws that cut on the up-stroke and drills worked on the bow-string principle. After hanging about for an hour without anyone coming to start us to work, we went in search of the Italian overseer. We found him cursing and swearing at a gang of coolies in a mixture of Arabic, Turkish, and Italian; *Sacramento* being easily the word most often used. From then on we referred to him as "Sacramento." He was a big, burly chap; at times very genial, at times brutish and obscene. I asked him what work we had to do, and he said that all he knew was that trestle bridges were to span both streams, and that the work was not in his province but came under a German overseer. His job, he said, was mostly "cemento," though he was also putting the piles in the river-bed and building the embankments, as well as the huge concrete "pads" on either bank, which would receive the iron girders that would eventually carry the actual rail track over the bridges. He suggested that we wait until the bridge engineer came over to start us, after breakfast, so we wandered back to the carpenters' shop to "scrounge" material for bedsteads. Those eventually consisted of rough boards nailed to low trestles, with three-inch high wooden "pillows," and, though they were hard and rough, served to keep us off the ground at nights and were useful as seats at other times.

Breakfast-time passed—with no breakfast for us, as we had not yet been issued with rations—and Herr Vinger—the bridge engineer—arrived. He could not speak English but he knew a fair amount of Turkish, so our conversation was carried on in that language. He told us that, starting on the morrow, we should work with two German carpenters in preparing the timbers for the bridges, etc., meanwhile we could assist the Arab carpenters. I pointed out to him that we could not work with Arab tools, and, even if we could, we had no desire to work with Arabs, so suggested that we spend the day trying to get clothing and bedding. After a lot of humming and ha-ing he agreed, warning us to be ready to start early in the morning.

"Tich" had returned with the rations, so we drew what we had to come and had our breakfast—dry bread and water. Rations consisted, normally, of a few ounces of meat, dried peas or beans, salt and bread—as I have already stated—so that we were only able to have one meal a day, cooked after we had ceased work. Tying up our tent flap, we asked "Tich" to keep his eye on our belongings and set off for Nisibin, and to find Sergeant-Major Leach.

At the top end of the village, in a small caravanserai, we found Leach and his helpers—three other Englishmen. A Eurasian Captain of the Indian Medical Service was nominally in charge, but Leach was the virtual chief. A Sikh Havildar (Sergeant) and several sepoys worked under him in the interests of the Indian prisoners. Leach was a very efficient man and universally popular, not only with the prisoners but with the Germans and Turks with whom he came into contact. Unfortunately he could do nothing for us in the way of clothing or bedding, except to promise to give us what he could from the first batch of clothing that he received from the Swiss Consul in Aleppo. Although it was the latter end of 1917, no clothing had yet reached Nisibin for the prisoners, and most of them were in the rags of uniform in which they had been taken prisoners in April of 1916; uniform which had seen much service long before that time. Our hopes were dashed, as we had hoped to get something, if only old clothing. We cheered up considerably when Leach gave us a food parcel addressed to a man long since dead, especially when we found that it contained a half-pound packet of tea, among other things.

"Dead men's parcels"—as such were always called—were opened and the contents shared among those who were unfortunate enough not to receive parcels of their own—and there were many of us in that party. There were intervals of many months between each arrival of letters and parcels for the prisoners of war in Nisibin, and even then only a very small quantity would arrive. That action of delaying or obstructing the delivery of mails was one of the worst features of the treatment of "other ranks" prisoners by the Turks. All the letters and parcels were sent, in the first place, to Afion-Kara-Hissar from Constantinople, where the Commandant and his thieving staff helped themselves before handing them over to the Senior N.C.O. of the prisoners for eventual distribution. After they had been sorted, those parcels addressed to men known to be dead were shared by the prisoners at Afion-Kara-Hissar. Those addressed to men whose fate was dubious were retained at Afion-Kara-Hissar, pending further news, the remainder were handed back to the Turks for dispatch to camps down the line. It might be days or weeks before they left Afion-Kara-Hissar, dependent on the attitude of the authorities, and it was the same at all the other camps, with the result that many months elapsed between deliveries at Nisibin. During the period that I was a captive—nearly three years—I received only three letters and no parcels at all. The letters I received at Nisibin, in one issue, and they had arrived purely by chance. That was due, in part, to my own fault. At Afion-Kara-Hissar, Micky and I had become almost legendary, as stories trickled through from various parts of the country that we were variously in Constantinople, Damascus, Aleppo, Van, and a score of other places, and that we had variously been shot, tortured to death, captured by Arabs, or escaped. So that all the parcels that arrived for us there were stored until definite news of our addresses could be obtained, with the result that we did not receive any of them, and at the end of the war there were over two hundred parcels there for me alone. A good deal of money was sent to me by the Royal Artillery and other prisoner of war funds, but I got none of it. Regimental and other societies regularly sent money and parcels to the English prisoners in Turkey, and it is a bitter memory to think that the greater part of what was sent did not reach those to whom it was sent.

CHAPTER THIRTEEN

HARD WORK AND DANGEROUS PLAY AT NISIBIN

WONDERING what we were going to do when our rags finally dropped off us, we made our way slowly back to our tent by the Jag-Jag River. Before we arrived back I had thought of a possible way to replenish our wardrobe. After putting our parcel in the tent I went over to where "Sacramento" was busy and asked him for a couple of cement sacks. He protested that they were a valuable commodity and that he was held responsible for the return of them, but he ended by giving me two of them. Then I borrowed a needle and some thread from Mrs. "Tich" and returned to our tent and Micky. Between us we fashioned shirts from those sacks, and, when we put them on, no Piccadilly elegant ever got so much satisfaction from his clothing as we did from ours that day. It says much for the state of our skins at that time when I state that we didn't even notice how rough the material was. Those cement-sack shirt-cum-tunics served us well for many a long day. With what remained of our ragged shirts we repaired our nether garments—in my case shorts, and in Micky's drill trousers.

"Tich" had procured for us a two-gallon iron cooking-pot, so, after we had finished tailoring, we built a fireplace and prepared our evening meal. That meal was the first really satisfying meal that we had had for a very long time. We put everything we had into the pot and made nearly a gallon of stew. When it was ready we sat with the pot between us—having no plates—and did not get up until it was all gone. Being carpenters we had access to the wood pile so we were able to build a big fire and thoroughly warm ourselves before going to bed that night.

The next morning the German carpenters arrived and we were set to work adzing logs of Turkish pine into shape, ready to be worked for the bridge trestles. Not many of those logs had arrived when we first started, so, to keep us fully employed, the three other carpenters were sent elsewhere and we filled in our time, whilst waiting for the arrival of more logs, by doing a hundred and one jobs of joinery that were required. A chest of tools had been sent over from the store for our use. We speedily discovered that, as *employees*, we ranked much higher than mere *arbeiters* and had a certain amount of authority, which we used to our own advantage on every possible occasion. As a *terjiman* I soon became regarded as an overseer, and, although I was not officially recognized as such, I assumed that status and played the rôle for all it was worth.

The river was at its lowest level, and as soon as the pile-driving apparatus arrived one of the Italian *cementajis* (cement workers) took charge of it and prepared to drive the piles into the river bed. The piles were logs of timber about two feet six inches in diameter by ten feet long, pointed and shod with steel "toes." The driving end was reinforced with steel bands to prevent splitting during the driving process. We had never seen a job of work of that kind and we were interested spectators when the job commenced. The pile to be driven was pushed into the water and up-ended into position by a horde of Kurds, floundering about waist-deep in the river. When the pile had been manœuvred into position a thirty-five feet long skid was raised alongside. The "skid" was fitted with steel guides and runners to take a huge iron weight that was the "driver." A rope was secured to a ring at the top of the weight and passed over a pulley at the top of the skid, and from there out to the river-bank. Several hours of struggling, duckings for the coolies, cursing on part of the Italian in charge—a thin, bearded, and unsmiling man, whom we dubbed "Spagoni"—and much strenuous labour passed before the actual driving commenced. When all was ready a gang of about fifty was detailed to stand by the rope, after receiving explicit instructions as to what was required of them. The instructions were given first to an Armenian by the Italian, in French, who interpreted them for the Kurds. At a given signal the coolies were to haul on the rope and pull the weight to the top of the skid. At a second signal they were all to leave go of the rope simultaneously, thus letting the weight drop on to the pile, which was supported meanwhile by the Kurds in the river. The first signal was given and the weight hauled slowly to the top of the skid, whilst the Kurds supporting the pile gazed up at it apprehensively. The long line of Kurds hauling on the rope watched "Spagoni" drop his uplifted hand and then let go of the rope. "Whee-ee-ee-thud." The weight screamed down the runners and crashed on to the top of the pile. On the bank was pandemonium. Entirely unused to work of that nature, the Kurds had not acted in unison when the signal to "let go" had been given. Several who had been tardy in letting go the rope had the skin taken clean off the palms of their hands; others had been lashed on the legs as the rope flew along the ground, whilst one man had his arm pulled out of its socket. Those who had not been hurt laughed at their less fortunate fellows and considered themselves to be very smart fellows. A Kurdish overseer was put in charge and the signals shouted, so that the coolies had no need to take their eyes off the job. Casualties were replaced and the performance repeated until, before very long, the work went along smoothly and the pile-driving went on apace.

We had begun to cut the huge mortices and tenons in the baulks of pine, ready to assemble into trestles, and were warned by Herr Vinger not to spoil any of them, as there was no extra timber of that size available in the country. That was an interesting point, and after the German had gone we discussed it at length. It seemed as though a grand opportu-

nity for delaying the completion of the bridge, and therefore
the railway, had come our way. To delay the railway meant
delaying the rapid transit of war material to the Mesopotamian front, and might greatly assist our comrades on the
English side. After work that night, as we sipped our hot
but very weak tea—we had to make it last a long time—we
discussed ways and means of how to utilize our knowledge of
that shortage of timber. Eventually we decided that little
could be done whilst the two German carpenters were still
on the job, but that we would keep our eyes open for some
way of spoiling the timber without drawing the blame on to
ourselves. We knew that if we did anything of the kind, and
were found out, we should be shot without mercy; probably
tortured beforehand by the Turks. Our opportunity was to
come, but not just then.

On our first Sunday off we visited the English prisoners
at Nisibin station. They were living in goat's-hair tents and
we found many old friends of ours among them. Not all of
them were of the Kut Garrison; some were of the Relief
Force, some from the Palestine front. For hours we sat and
chatted and exchanged news. They told us of the many
schemes they carried out in order to supplement their
meagre rations. Most of them worked in the store-houses, and
it was a standing joke among the native workmen that the
Ingleezi always went to work in cloaks or overcoats, no matter
how hot it was. There was a very good reason for that queer
custom. Before leaving work for the day, nearly every one of
the party managed to conceal something or other on his person
—pilfered from the stores—and the overcoats helped to
conceal them. Among other things, such items as strings of
figs—wound round the body—or sticks of solder—stuck into
trouser bands or belts—were part of the daily haul. Solder
and such-like material was unprocurable at that time by the
village workmen, and much secret bargaining was carried on
in the bazaars of Nisibin with the British prisoners. Several

of the men who did not possess overcoats used to balance a coiled string of figs on their heads under their helmets. One youngster of the Manchester Regiment—he was not more than eighteen or nineteen—played a very risky game for a long period. When a consignment of rifles came in they were usually uncased and stored loose until they were dispatched to Mosul. That was to save excess weight being carried by the lorries. The boy of the Manchesters was employed in the rifle store—a special building with a tiny barred window —and he often contrived to get himself locked in for the night. Working silently all night, that unsung hero of the Great War used to extract the striking pins from the bolts, or render them unserviceable in other ways, in such a manner as not to be detected until they came to be used. The hazard was very great, because a Turkish soldier was always on duty outside the rifle store during the night, and he would have raised an alarm had he heard the slightest noise coming from inside. I have often wondered what happened when those rifles came to be used hundreds of miles farther down the country. Other acts of sabotage were regularly performed by British prisoners at different parts of the country on the railway. At Dorak, on the northern side of the Taurus Mountains, a Sergeant and two or three trusty pals managed to damage most of the aircraft that was destined for the Palestine front by sawing through the longerons, etc., with hack-saw blades. Another man of the Manchester Regiment, working in the Taurus tunnel, had stolen some dynamite, used for blasting operations, and had prepared to blow up the tunnel. He was discovered in time by a Petty Officer of our Navy, in the act of laying a gunpowder "slow match" to the tunnel mouth. He had got the gunpowder by extracting the bullets from cartridges he had stolen. The Petty Officer would not let him carry out his plot, knowing that the prisoners of war working on the tunnel would be suspect and suffer awful punishment—most probably death.

The lad at Nisibin occasionally pushed a rifle through the bars of the tiny window to a waiting confederate, and disposed of it later at a nearby Kurdish village. In that way he too augmented his rations. We were told an amusing tale of how the Britishers both at Nisibin and the Headquarters Camp had first come to work at their various jobs. When they had been first drafted from Afion-Kara-Hissar they had been put to work as coolies, building the track between Ras-el-Ain and Serchikhan. They worked in parties of six and had to complete a certain portion of the track each day, and Arab overseers saw that they did so. It meant hours of slaving under a scorching sun to complete the portion allotted by "cease work," so they had contrived to make things easier. They dug clods of sun-baked earth and so arranged them that, by shovelling loose earth on the top, they gave the appearance of a solid track, when in reality it was a mere shell. That was the reason, early in 1918, when the rails had been laid and the train came along, that whole stretches of the track had to be rebuilt. Once a week a German engineer used to visit them, and to him they sold, for a few *para* (farthings), many ancient coins that they used to unearth when digging material for the track. One day that German was struck with a brilliant idea. The Company were extremely short of skilled men and they were wanting large numbers for the building of Nisibin station and the headquarters, etc. It dawned on that German that those English coolies might be intelligent enough to be skilled in other ways besides digging and track building, so they were ordered to give their names and trades to the Armenian clerk. Suspecting some sort of trick, those irrepressible Britons gave the Armenian an extraordinary list of "trades": pavement artist, goalkeeper, hot-cross bun stamper, Coronation programme seller, and milestone inspector were some of them. The list was given to the clerk, who gave it to the German on his next visit, and he, being unable to read English and suspecting nothing, took it into the Company's headquarters at Nisibin, where it was duly translated. The following day the German came back in a towering rage and called the "pig-dog" Englishmen all the nice names he could think of, one being a name the Germans in Turkey had coined for contemptuous reference to all natives—*Benhauzer*. The upshot of it all was that the English prisoners were sent into Nisibin and sent to the various places where skilled men were required. There they were detailed off as joiners, blacksmiths, bricklayers, etc., regardless of whether they knew anything of those trades or not. The Chief Engineer—who had given orders for that to be done—was a very astute man, for in a few days the men themselves had changed jobs one with the other until they were all working at something with which they were familiar.

Micky and I greatly enjoyed hearing all those things, and we felt that it was good to make contact again with our own comrades, who were causing their captors annoyance and inconvenience in their own particular way even as we were in ours. We returned to our camp in the compound fully determined to scrounge and wangle all and as often as we could.

The days passed in quick succession as we worked either at the bench or on the bridge timbers; days that were full of incidents that served to amuse or annoy us. It would take a large volume to describe in detail all that happened during the months that we worked at Nisibin, so I shall confine my descriptions to those incidents that were outstanding, or those that will help my readers to form a mental picture of the many and varying conditions there.

Among the coolies in our encampment fuel was extremely hard to come by, consequently the chips and shavings from our shop were in great demand when it was discovered that we were only too pleased to get rid of them. What had happened to the shop refuse before we had taken over we could only guess, as the Kurdish women—who normally collected fuel for their own fires—gave our shop a wide berth during the first few days of our occupation. Then one or two young girls came along and shyly begged for shavings. We had fellow feelings for those Kurds and smilingly told the girls to take what they wanted and send others along for the remainder. The crowd that arrived at "cease work" the next day was so great that we were forced to limit the distribution to some half a dozen girls, who used to clean and tidy the shop in exchange for the refuse. One of those Kurdish girls was a very beautiful creature; blue eyed, fair skinned, and possessing a superb figure. We named her Susie, as her own name was too much of a mouthful, and she speedily answered to that name as her shyness wore off and when she found that our smiles and friendly gestures concealed no ulterior motives. Susie was to have an unpleasant experience. A Turkish Onbashi had been posted to our section as a "ganger" over a party of women and children working on the embankment. "Tich" had told us that he was looking for a wife, as he had been discharged from the army— supposedly disabled, though we could never discern any disablement—and would not be returning to military service. We were greatly surprised when, one morning, we saw Susie sweeping out his tent, and, not unnaturally, we concluded that he had taken her to wife. We were vaguely disappointed, as we had no liking for the Onbashi, who was a raucous-voiced individual and far too free with his whip, and we thought that Susie could have done much better for herself among the Kurdish males. A week later Susie had vanished and her place had been taken by a girl about fourteen years of age. She had been there for a couple of weeks when, after work one night, there was an unexpected merrymaking outside our tent. We were eating our evening meal at this time and wondered at the sudden demonstration, so went outside to investigate. Holding hands in a circle of dancing men and women stood the girl and the Onbashi.

We sat and watched as the dancing became more furious and the onlookers began to clap and sing. The proceedings were kept up for several hours, and I was at a loss to know what it was all about. The next morning "Tich" told me, in answer to my queries, that the girl and the Onbashi had become betrothed. I pointed out that he had lived with her for a fortnight and with Susie for a week previous to that, and, so far as my knowledge of Kurdish customs went, that was very unusual. He agreed and then told me that those Kurds were so poverty-stricken and their outlook so hopeless that many things happened among them that were not customary but were born of necessity. The Onbashi had had Susie on trial, and as she didn't suit him both she and her family had been sent to a different section of the line, whilst he took on another "sample." The second girl was, apparently, more to his liking, and she continued to live with him until they were married, a few weeks later. Micky and I were invited to the wedding feast and stayed there until the *raki* got the better of most of the males and the party got rough, when we took our departure. The day after the wedding the girl's mother took up residence with the newly married couple, presumably to teach her the domestic virtues. There was a sequel to her coming some weeks later. I was busy working on the bridge one afternoon when I heard screams and shouting coming from the direction of the compound. Looking over in that direction I was amazed to see the Onbashi beating his mother-in-law with the butt-end of his rifle. She was on the ground and the blows that fell upon her were plainly audible to me. Used as I was to acts of appalling brutality, I could not be an idle spectator of the scene. Calling to Micky to follow me, I rushed over to the compound and wrenched the rifle out of the Onbashi's hands, demanding to know why he was treating the woman in that manner. He made as though to attack me but I threatened to club him with his own rifle if he dared to touch me. He quickly calmed down when he saw that he had neither a scared woman nor a cringing native to deal with, especially as Micky was now at my elbow. He explained that the woman had stolen his money from his clothes-box. I asked him how he knew that she had taken the money, and he replied that it was gone and, as she was his mother-in-law, she was the most likely person to have taken it. After a good deal of argument he accompanied Micky and I to his tent and we conducted a thorough search. Somehow I was convinced that he had not lost his money but was using that tale of theft in order to get rid of the woman. I formed that opinion by the great reluctance he showed to having his tent searched. Sure enough, we found the money, wrapped in a shirt and hidden in the bedding—not in his box as he had averred. He had resorted to a typical Turkish method of "framing" the poor woman. She—poor creature—never returned to the camp and the Onbashi and his girl-wife continued to live happily together.

Many weeks later I saw Susie working in a different gang, half naked and very thin; a different girl from the blue-eyed lass we had known.

Work was steadily progressing on the bridge. Practically all the timbers had been prepared and numbered and were ready for assembly and erection. The two German carpenters had been taken off the job, and I was placed in charge. That was just the opportunity that we had been waiting for. We sawed half-way through the tenons of most of the bracing struts—where they would not easily be detected—and mutilated other pieces. The struts and cross-pieces were secured to the main timbers with iron "dogs," and those we hacksawed half through at the angle, in as many cases as we dared, filling up the cuts with a mixture of black ash and water. We calculated that the structure would be sufficiently strong to allow of the completion of the track over it, but that it would not withstand the weight and vibration of the train passing over it. The trestles in both streams were erected and completed less the top cross-beams, the timber for which had not arrived. During the period of waiting for that timber we did a lot of work in the shop, making cupboards, etc., for the German engineer. The concrete "pads" on either bank were finished, and the embankment was growing apace. To speed up the work on the embankment, a set of steel trucks had been sent for and a light railway line laid to accommodate them. The Russian prisoners were put on to work them, and, as the embankment became higher, it was necessary to support the track on trestles from the diggings to the tip. Those trestles were made by us out of material that we considered far too light—there being no heavier stuff available—but which the Italian, "Sacramento," insisted were good enough. Hitherto, the material for the embankment had been carried in hand-baskets by women and children, but they had been taken off to commence the embankment between the two streams, leaving the Russians to complete the main one with the aid of the trucks. Every time we saw the string of empty trucks hurtling down from the top of the embankment we predicted an accident, as we knew that the trestles we had made would not stand the strain for long. Our predictions came true, for on one occasion one of the trestles collapsed and precipitated the train of light trucks from a height of about twelve feet. Someone screamed, and we dashed over to see if anyone was injured. We found one of the Russians, who had been riding the train, lying beneath a truck with blood pouring from his mouth. The truck was pulled clear, but it was plain to see that he was beyond human aid. Another Russian pushed his way through the small crowd that had collected, gave one look at the dying man and then rolled him over and commenced to search his clothing, finding what, apparently, he had been seeking—a thin roll of Turkish lira notes. I was told that the man was his brother. During the search, the dying man's face had been buried in a morass of blood and mud. I had never witnessed anything quite so callous in my life. When the man was dead he was carried into the tent of the Russians and immediately prepared for burial.

Life went on as usual.

In order to cross the streams dry-shod we had built over them narrow foot-bridges of a double thickness of boards—planks being non-available. Where one end of the foot-bridge over the main stream passed on to the bank, a woman was in the habit of stowing her bundle and cloak during the time she was at work on the nearby embankment. Becoming short of boards we had gradually used the top layer from that bridge, so that it was scarcely safe for a heavy man to walk on. One morning Herr Vinger came along on his horse, and, as was his wont, made to ride over the bridge. I shouted to him that it was not safe, but he either did not hear or did not understand me and rode on. To my surprise he reached the other side without mishap until he came to the last lap—the bit over the bank—when the hind feet of his mount smashed through the boards. The horse kicked free and cantered up the bank. Several women had observed the incident, and they shouted out something in Kurdish to the woman who owned the bundle, which was under the smashed boards. She ran up to the place and rapidly pulled her bundle clear and unrolled it, disclosing—to our great horror—a few-months-old baby. Its head had been crushed like an egg by the hoofs of the plunging horse. The woman regarded the tiny corpse for a moment or two and then flung it into the river and went back to work. No doubt it was an economic problem unexpectedly solved for her, but it was a horrible thing to witness.

As I seem to have wandered on to a page of horrors I will describe just two more dissimilar ones which will suffice to illustrate the awful disregard for human life that was apparent around us.

One pouring wet night I had occasion to go into Nisibin after dark, and, as I was passing an encampment of Turkish soldiers, I heard someone groaning inside one of the ground-sheet bivouacs. Whoever it was seemed to be very unpopular, as others were telling him, in no uncertain manner, to keep quiet. All at once I heard the sound of blows being struck and a man was flung out of the bivouac on to the road. I hurried on. My business completed, I returned by the way I had come, and found, stretched by the side of the road, the body of a Turkish soldier—the man who had been flung out. I shouted out, "Oh, Askarlar!" Someone answered, "Ne var?" ("What is it?") "Bir askar var, erlmish" ("There is a dead soldier"), I replied, "Zara yok, git sen" ("Never mind, you go away") was the astonishing response. Needless to say, I went away.

The other incident happened in our compound. I had known for long that the "wife" of the Italian overseer—"Sacramento"—was an expectant mother, and that she was sorely troubled at the prospect of having a half-caste baby to look after, knowing that if the Italian was moved up country she would be lucky if he took her along with him. There was nothing that she could do about it, though such a happening among the unfortunate Armenian women who had become mistresses of either German or Turkish officials of the Company was rarely permitted to occur. Micky and I were sitting outside our tent on the Sunday afternoon that the baby was born, and we heard its first puling cry. "Sacramento's" tent had a low concrete wall built around it, and, within a few minutes of the baby being born, he strode out of the tent with it and, holding it by the ankles, dashed its head against that wall. He flung the corpse into the river and returned to his tent as though nothing out of the ordinary had happened. I like to think now—as I thought at the time—that it was the best thing that could have happened for everybody concerned, though the manner of the killing was inexcusable. We had become so inured to such horrible sights that, beyond a momentary desire to vomit, we experienced very little feeling about the matter.

Christmas came and passed almost unnoticed. We were pleased because we knew that spring and warmer weather were the nearer. Our cement-sack shirts were our only covering by day and night through the winter of 1917–18.

At the beginning of March we were sent for by Sergeant-Major Leach, who, to our great joy, gave us boots and clothing from a consignment—the first—that he had just received. One suit was made of navy-blue serge with yellow braid facings and semi-military cut—after the style of those worn by the old Militia. The other one was civilian pattern, made to a design fashionable a hundred years before. The boots were real English military ones and, to us, jewels without price. Overcoats of navy blue, with a red armlet inlet into one sleeve, completed the first issue of clothing we had for over two years. I had the suit of near-military cut. We decided to keep the clothes for non-working days in order not to wear them out too quickly. Shortly after that red-letter day there occurred an episode in our lives that is one of my most pleasant memories of those Nisibin days.

We were busy one day in the shop making deck-chairs for two German nurses who had recently arrived at the Company's headquarters, when in walked a Turkish Yuzbashi (Captain) and a civilian. Not being in love with anyone or anything Turkish at that time, we ignored them and continued with our work. After a few minutes the civilian said in English, "Are you English?" Micky and I looked at each other and I said, "Are we, Micky?" and continued to work as before. Again the civilian spoke, this time to ask, "Are you carpenters?" A most fatuous question that caused us to blink and ask each other again, "Are we?" A few minutes' silence and then," I am speaking to you," from the civilian. I turned to him and said, "Oh! And who the blazes might you be?" He replied, "I am an Egyptian, and my officer wishes for you to make him a chair like that," pointing to one of the deck-chairs we were busy making. "If you are an Egyptian, why aren't you in Egypt?" I inquired, and, without waiting for a reply, said, "You can tell your officer that we have neither the time nor the inclination to make him anything." Then I turned back to my bench. The Egyptian was furious and said, "How dare you speak like that? You are prisoners and my officer is a Captain and will have you punished." He was quite unprepared for the outburst that followed—most of which is unprintable. I had become an adept at the Turkish way of showing contempt—by spitting violently on the ground and naming the object of contempt—and gave him a demonstration of my prowess, naming the Turks and all things Turkish. White with rage, he repeated all I had said to the Yuzbashi, not knowing that I understood Turkish. To my surprise the officer calmly said, "But isn't it true what he says?" I quickly turned to him and said, in Turkish, "Excuse me, Effendi, but do I understand you to say that you agree with me?" He was surprised to hear me speak in Turkish and said, "Now I must be careful what I say," and laughed. I asked him to send the Egyptian away, as he annoyed me, and then followed a most interesting and enlightening conversation. He told me that he hated the very idea of Turkey being in the war at all, especially on the side of the Germans. He gave it as his opinion that Turkey had lost a valuable opportunity to enrich herself by not remaining neutral. According to him, the Germans held the Turks in contempt and did not offer to conceal it on most occasions. He called them by a vile name. He explained, as a reason for his being in our shop, that he was an Engineer Officer and had been sent, with a company of sappers, to assist on the construction of the bridge and embankments. That was news indeed— particularly in view of what we had done to the bridge timbers. I told him that we were working for the Company and under no circumstances would we work for or under the Turks. He was not at all put out by that, but told us that he had no jurisdiction over us and was only to carry out the requirements of the Bridge Engineer. As we were talking the gong sounded for midday break, so we all went over to our tent to smoke and continue our chat. The Yuzbashi proved to be a very charming man, and before he left he insisted that we visit him and have dinner with him on the Sunday— our day off. Just as he was about to leave he excused himself and then asked whether we slept on the hard beds that we had been sitting on. I told him that we did, and that we had neither bedding nor blankets. He sympathized with us and said that he could not help us in the matter of blankets but would try and find us something to take the hardness of the bare boards. With a smart salute he left us and we returned to work. Less than an hour later a Turkish soldier came into our shop, and, saluting, said, "My Captain has sent these to you with his greetings," and handed to us two large goatskin rugs. The Yuzbashi was certainly a man of his word, unlike most Turkish officers of that period.

There were still three days to go before Sunday, when we were to have dinner with the Yuzbashi, but all our conversation during that time was about the projected visit. Meanwhile, the Sapper company had commenced work on the embankment, helping the women on their section. The Yuzbashi spent a good deal of his time in our shop during those three days, and always saw that we were well supplied with cigarettes, of the Turkish Regie variety—a brand well beyond our reach. We made him a deck-chair, to his great delight. Sunday came and we prepared for the great event. We bathed in the river and carefully shaved with our antique razor before getting dressed in our best clothes. Unfortunately we had neither hats nor caps. We had tried making caps but those that we had made—after a terrific struggle—were only fit to keep off the sun whilst we were at work and were horrible-looking things. Cap making is one of the most exasperating jobs that I have ever tackled, and I have tackled not a few. We had tried making the "pork pie" variety, the "Brodrick," and the ordinary cap, but none of them was a conspicuous success. When we were all ready we set off for the Yuzbashi's tent, situated near a flour mill on the smaller stream, a quarter of a mile from our compound. The Yuzbashi was on the look-out for us and came to meet us, showing obvious pleasure at our arrival. Two other officers were with him, and we all shook hands before entering the tent, which had been prepared for our arrival. After a light luncheon of fruit, honey, and bread, we spent the afternoon looking at the Yuzbashi's collection of photographs and chatting on a multitude of subjects. After sunset dinner was served, a wonderful repast of which the *pièce de résistance* was a chicken *pilaff*. *Raki* was produced and after a few "pegs" the party became very lively. The Yuzbashi was keen to learn English phrases, mostly concerning the fair sex, such as "You are a beautiful girl," "Allow me to kiss your hand," etc. Micky drew lifelike sketches of the company, which the Yuzbashi claimed for his own as mementoes of the occasion. It was after midnight before we left, and after we had solemnly promised to pay another visit the following Sunday. We were provided with an armed escort for our protection and returned happily to our comfortless tent. Early the following Sunday we again presented ourselves at the Yuzbashi's tent, and, after a glass of sherbet and a cigarette, he took us into Nisibin to a house where we met other friends of his. There we met a Bimbashi of the Medical Corps, a man who held similar opinions politically to those of our friend the Yuzbashi. During the morning we were all photographed, and Micky and I had to pose shaking hands with the Bimbashi and Yuzbashi. Mint-flavoured coffee was served, and after a light luncheon we returned to the tent of the Yuzbashi, where the rest of the day was spent as on the first occasion. We had arrived at the stage where we addressed each other by our first names; the Yuzbashi as Hassan Yuzbashi, and he us as Jerry Effendi and Micky Effendi. Hassan told us that he was arranging picnics and various other entertainments for every Sunday, and that we were to be guests of honour. On the following Sunday, he told us, an important German officer was passing through Nisibin on his way to Mosul, and there was to be a reception in a restaurant in the village to which all the Turkish officers in the locality had been invited. He said that we must accompany him and his friends. That promised to be something very much out of the ordinary for us, so all during the preceding week we struggled and contrived to make some sort of presentable headwear. Eventually, Micky evolved a primitive type of college cap, whilst I—to match my near-military suit—contrived to make something that resembled a cross between a pudding-bag and a shako.

Sunday came along, and we met Hassan at his tent before accompanying him to a tea garden on the right bank of the River Jag-Jag, just below Nisibin. Hassan said that he had arranged to meet a party of his friends there, and at noon we would all proceed to the reception. We sat sipping glasses of tea for about half an hour before his party arrived, riding in from the direction of Mosul. One of the party was a Colonel of Artillery and I was presented to him as an Artillery Lieutenant, whilst Micky was given the rank of Lieutenant of Infantry. Micky was greatly amused when I interpreted our sudden rise to commissioned rank. The Colonel was a big man, tanned as brown as a berry and with a face like a hawk. He was inclined to be taciturn and never once smiled. I formed the opinion that he was a most efficient but very cruel officer. The rest of the party—two Yuzbashis and three Awl Thanis—were jovial types and very pleasant to us. At noon, as we rose to go on to the reception, the Colonel said that he would pay a visit to the Kaimakhan and then return to his unit, as he had no wish to meet the German. When we arrived at the restaurant—the only one the village possessed —a Turkish band was attempting to play European music outside. One of the tunes they played subsequently sounded like a pot-pouri of *Colonel Bogey, God Save the King,* and the *Marseillaise.* We all trooped into the place and found it already crowded with German and Turkish officers, and— to our surprise—several highly painted ladies, who were sitting with the German Staff of the "Big Noise." There were no vacant seats at the tables so we all sat in a row along the wall near the door. Micky and I were subjected to hostile stares from the Germans, and before many minutes had passed the Greek proprietor of the restaurant came up to Hassan Yuzbashi and said, "Excuse me, Yuzbashi Effendi, I am to tell you that the Germans object to the presence of Englishmen in the room, and request that, if they are your friends, you will ask them to leave." Hassan jumped to his feet and asked the Greek whether he had another room. The Greek replied that that part of the main room that was screened off was vacant. Hassan turned to us and said, "Gel Effendilar" ("Come, gentlemen"), and strode across the room to the doorway in the screen, closely followed by Micky and myself, the Turkish officers of our party and half a dozen other Turkish officers who had listened to the conversation. I was rather dubious of the result of that sudden exodus from the main room, as we were indirectly responsible for it, and said as much to Hassan. He told me not to worry as all the Turks present were his personal friends. Thinking of possible reprisals from the Kaimakhan I mentioned that also, but Hassan said that he *dared* not interfere. I came to the conclusion that Hassan and his friends belonged to a secret society, of which I knew there were several among the military caste during those days. However, we were reassured and entered fully into the spirit of the party that followed. *Raki* and wine flowed like water, and we began to sing, when, the Turkish officers in the next room getting bored with the formal affair, our party was increased four-fold. Micky and I became the centre of attraction and everyone tried to make us understand that their friendship was sincere. One young spark gave me a petrol-lighter that was made in the shape of a hand-grenade, which he said he had taken from a Russian officer prisoner. After sunset, a meal of many dishes was served, and then the party continued, eventually developing into an orgy. At midnight those of us who were able reeled through Nisibin on our way to Hassan's tent, singing and bawling at the top of our voices. Two of the party fell into the stream outside the tent, so we all waded in to their assistance, getting very wet in the process. After more drinks and another meal with Hassan we staggered away to our own tent, assisted by our usual escort of *askars*. It had been a grand party, but we did not feel inclined for work the following day.

The next Sunday was to have been the occasion of a fishing picnic, but, alas! it was not to be. Hassan came to us during the week and said that he and his Sappers were being sent to Aleppo on the Saturday, *en route* for the Palestine front. He offered to disguise us as Turkish soldiers and help us to get away, if we cared to take the risk. I, he suggested, could act as his batman, and Micky could help his cook, so that we should always be near him until we got to the front. It was an alluring suggestion, and had Micky been able to speak even a little Turkish we should have taken the risk. As it was, I had no intention of leaving him behind, so had to say good-bye to our friend Hassan Yuzbashi.

During the time we had been working at Nisibin we had gradually collected various odds and ends to make ourselves more comfortable, and had even been able to dispense with our cement-sack shirts in favour of some of cowboy plaid issued to us by Sergeant-Major Leach. Our status had considerably improved, and we thought that it was time that we came into line with the rest of the inhabitants in the compound and had a servant. I saw "Tich" on the subject and he readily agreed to help us, recommending an Armenian girl to us who had recently escaped from the Arabs. He provided us with a large goat's-hair tent, which we fitted to a square-rigged framework of poles to form a fair-sized hut. Into that we moved all our belongings and made over our tent to the girl. She was a pleasant little creature of about thirteen years of age, named Gulingia. We called her Nellie, which was easier. Her duties were very light: cooking our one hot meal of the day, making tea for breakfast—which we took without sugar or milk, and which, together with a small piece of bread, was all we could afford for that meal. We had acquired a charcoal brazier for heating our hair-covered hut, and one of Gulingia's duties was to get it going by the time we ceased work at nights. Then, after we had eaten our meal, she would sit for an hour or two and tell us of her adventures. That poor child had had an amazing experience of life in her few years, an experience that, awful though it had been, had failed to kill her spirit or quench the gay laughter that came readily from her lips. She had been in the same party of women and girls as "Tich's" wife, that had been butchered in a cave or pit. Her mother had been of the party, and her last act had been—as she was bayoneted—to fall across her daughter, covering her with her life's blood and hoodwinking the Turks into thinking that she too was dead. Gulingia remained under her mother's body for hours, until the last soldier had left the scene of carnage. She had commenced to wriggle free when several of the ghouls returned, and she saw them opening up the stomachs of some of the dead women in their search for gold coins which they believed the women had swallowed. The practice of swallowing coins, in order to conceal them, was actually carried out by some of the Armenian women, and, when it was discovered by the

Turks, resulted in the most appalling atrocities being committed. Gulingia had managed to escape from the shambles but had fallen into the hands of Arabs—like many others of her unfortunate race—and had lived a life of virtual slavery until the tribe neared Nisibin, on its grazing circuit, when she contrived to escape from them and reach other Armenians who were working for the Company. Inquiries among them had resulted in her finding "Tich's" wife, the only other survivor of the party from her village. She was a very hard-working and domesticated little girl and we were as kind to her as we knew how. We were very sorry when "Tich" was moved to another section of the line and took Gulingia with him, to become a member of his family.

We were loath to lose the privilege of having a servant, paid by the Company, so we looked around for someone else who might fill the post satisfactorily. We chose a local girl—a Jewess from Nisibin—but she was hopeless from the start. She could, or would, not understand the need for strict economy in the use of all our foodstuffs, but seemed to think that we possessed the means of getting anything we wanted, and in unlimited quantities. She was taught to brew tea by using as few leaves as possible and until no more colour could be got from them, but when left to make it herself always made it as black as ink and threw away the leaves after only one brew. We very soon discharged her and signed on a Kurdish boy. He was a keen and willing lad and spent hours by the riverside trying to raise a shine on our old iron cooking-pot. Unfortunately, he only spoke a wild dialect of Kurdish, and we found it impossible to make him understand what we wanted unless we used an interpreter— obviously a hopeless proceeding. As compensation when we dismissed him, Micky gave him his ragged trousers—the boy only possessed a shirt—and he was quite happy to return to his gang. He caused us no little embarrassment by kissing our hands before he left us.

Before that winter was over, we found it increasingly difficult to use the paper money paid to us by the Company. The shopkeepers in the local bazaar would not take it at any price, excepting one who used to sell *raki* in a little room behind his shop to those whom he could trust not to inform against him—as it was illegal to sell *raki* to prisoners, or for prisoners to buy it. Occasionally, Micky and I would get rid of our surplus paper money in that "glory hole" in the bazaar, and drink the fiery spirit until we were in a state of happy insensibility to our condition of life. The only other place we could spend the well-nigh valueless paper money was at a shop near the station, run, on behalf of the Company, by an English Sergeant. Before purchases could be made from the shop a list of what one required had first to be approved and signed by the German in charge at the station. Even then it rested with the Sergeant as to what quantities could be bought of any particular commodity. Naturally, prisoners got whatever they wanted, providing such things were in stock; usually dried figs, dried apricots, cereals, cigarette tobacco and the like. Others were not so lucky, particularly Turkish officers, regardless of the list being signed, as the Sergeant's word was law in the running of the shop.

Shortly after Christmas we had learned that a friend of Micky's—a man of his regiment—was working at Serchikhan, and I eventually succeeded in persuading Herr Vinger to get him transferred to our section, in order to work with us, saying that he was a good carpenter. Actually he was nothing of the sort, but he had quick enough wit to learn sufficient of the trade to pass muster whenever the German was around. He was Lance-Corporal Richard Hicks, of the Royal West Kents, and proved a welcome addition to our company.

Winter was passing into spring when there occurred an unexpected happening that was to have far-reaching results for Micky and me. Hicks and we two were sitting in our hut one night after dark, discussing the pros and cons of a projected attempt to escape, as Micky and I had considered for long that we had remained in one place long enough. Suddenly we were startled by a vivid flash of lightning, followed by a terrific downpour of rain. It was entirely unexpected as there had been no sign of a storm at sunset. The rain fell in torrents and threatened to beat our little hut to the ground. Lightning played continuously, and we were almost deafened by peal after peal of awe-inspiring thunder. Soon the water began to swirl around our feet and we hastily piled all our belongings on to our beds and sat on the top of them. We thought that it was merely surface water that would seep away as soon as the rain stopped. We heard the Russians shouting excitedly, and, as we knew that they slept on the floor of their tents, thought that they were only making a fuss about getting flooded out. Little dreaming of the true state of affairs, we continued to chat, until we noticed that the water in our tent was rising rapidly, then we became alarmed. I stood on my bed and looked through the gap at the top of the door to see what was happening. The next vivid flash of lightning revealed a vast sheet of water as far as I could see, and, a few yards from our hut, a huge log of timber just beginning to float. The sight of that floating timber did more than anything else to make me realize our danger. We forced open the door and went outside to see what the rest of the camp were doing. To our amazement, we found that nearly all the tents in the compound had vanished. Dashing back into our hut we made a pile of the three beds and put all the stuff we were unable to carry on top of the pile, then started off for the higher ground near the station. We were not prepared for the scene of chaos that met our eyes when we rounded the corner of our hut. The irrigation stream near the station had become so swollen that it had burst its banks, and was rushing diagonally across the coolie and prisoner encampment in a raging torrent. All the tents had been swept away and hundreds of men, women, and children were trying to pass the swirling mass of water. They were a disorganized, panic-stricken rabble, and as fast as they stepped into the stream were swept off their feet and whirled away. We joined the Russians and Rumanians and shouted to them to hold hands and cross the stream in a body. At first they were too scared to take any notice of us, but we continued to bawl at them until they got the idea. We three Britishers joined hands with them, and, when all were ready, crossed over in safety, one solid mass of struggling, slithering humanity. The Kurds saw how it was done and followed suit, though not before a good many were drowned.

At the station we found the British camp under water and the occupants, shivering in their sodden clothes, sheltering in one of the goods sheds. In a very few minutes the shed was full of prisoners and coolies; drenched to the skin, crying and talking in half a dozen tongues, bewailing their fate and creating the very devil of a bedlam. Micky and I had a very serious problem to discuss, one that must be discussed at once and in secret—not even with the third member of our party, Dick Hicks—and it was with great difficulty that we found a spot where we could talk without the likelihood of being overheard. Our problem was whether the bridge— with its weakened struts, etc., would stand the weight of water that was being hurled against it. The last glance that we had had of it showed the flood water within six feet of the top cross-beam, many feet above the flow baffle that we had built at the base and which had been built to the height of the normal high-water level. If it did not withstand the flood what would be the result when the pieces were collected and it was discovered—as it was sure to be—that the timbers and iron dogs had been tampered with? We recalled an incident that had happened several weeks earlier, when Micky had become possessed of a large sheet of white paper and had

amused himself by drawing an imaginary picture of "The
First Train Over," showing the bridge broken in the middle,
a string of carriages hanging down like a chain, passengers
falling into the river, etc. He had drawn a most decrepit
engine, covered with cobwebs and preceded by a man
carrying a red flag, and Arabs pushing in rear of the train.
The picture had taken over a week to complete, as other items
were added to it from day to day as we thought of something
else funny in connection with Turkish railways in general and
that one in particular. When it was finally completed—
because of lack of space to add any more—we hung it in the
carpenters' shop. Herr Vinger saw it and was greatly annoyed.
Apparently he did not possess a sense of humour, for he asked
us what we found in the bridge to be funny about. He took
it away with him, apparently to show his chief—who must
have seen the funny side of it, for the next time I saw it it was
hanging on a wall in the Engineers' mess. We thought now
that that picture might prove to be damaging evidence
against us if it was discovered that the bridge had been
wilfully weakened. We had intended to have remained in
Nisibin only until such time as the first train was due to cross
the bridge, and our plans for escape were not completed.
Wet clothes were forgotten as we sat and discussed our
problem. Ideas by the score were thought of, propounded,
debated, and rejected. At long last we decided that at the
first streak of daylight we must go down to the river and see
what had happened, as, until we knew for sure that the bridge
was wrecked, we were unable to bring ourselves to a point
where we should abandon everything and vanish from the
district without food or proper preparations. Although we
prisoners were given a good deal of liberty at Nisibin, it was
not because of any change of feeling on the part of the Turks,
but because the country itself was a natural prison. To the
north ran range after range of bandit-infested mountains—
the Kurdish Alps. To the south was the desert land of

Northern Mesopotamia, the stamping ground of the Shammar Arabs, a tribe that had at no time shown itself friendly to the British. All the villages between Nisibin and Mosul were frequented by pillaging Turkish soldiers, and it would have been highly dangerous to have visited them in search of food. So, unless circumstances compelled, we had no intention of going into the "blue" totally unprepared.

As dawn was breaking we called Hicks from where he had spent the night among the other Britishers, and set off back to the compound. The whole scene was now truly astonishing, and it was difficult to believe that the havoc we saw was the result of a few hours' storm. The waters had subsided from the area between the station and the Jag-Jag River, leaving behind a sea of mud that was strewn with the debris of the wrecked camp. Hundreds of dead fish were lying around and Kurds were already busy collecting them as we slithered along beside the now ruined embankment. Alone of the scores of tents that had gone to form the camp stood our hut, a tribute to British workmanship. As we drew nearer to it we saw many bodies of children half buried in the mud. Of the bridge there was no sign; it had vanished completely. The river was still swollen but had sunk to a level below the tops of the piles, on which still were fastened the bottom cross-members of the trestles. Not so much as a stick of timber was to be seen, so we decided to follow the course of the river as far as we could to see whether any parts of the bridge had been caught up on the banks. We reached the old stone bridge at Nisibin without finding anything, and, by the looks of things there, the river had swept well over the top of that bridge. Crossing the main road we continued our search for several miles, at times being almost bogged thigh-deep in the mud of the river-bank. Not a vestige of our bridge did we see, and it was with light hearts that we retraced our steps back to our hut, for our problem—for the time being—had been solved. We learned later that a posse of Gendarmes had been sent in search of the missing timbers, but they had been unsuccessful. No doubt the riverain Arabs, lower down the valley, thought that the arrival of so much potential firewood was a gift from heaven.

We set to and made things ship-shape in our hut, and, with firewood got from the station, made a fire and cooked some sort of meal. Herr Vinger and other officials of the Company came and looked at where the bridge had been, but they did not speak to us. Our projected plan of escape was once more discussed and most of the details settled. For a week we did no work, as there was nothing for us to do. The sun had soon dried up the mud, and the camp was being formed again and the coolies back at work repairing the damaged embankment. Then, one day, we were sent for to report at the Nisibin offices of the Company. There we were told that, as we should not be required near the river for some time, we were to be sent elsewhere. Hicks was to report to the Engineer at the station, whilst Micky and I were to have our kit ready to move by the following morning, when an *arabah* would be sent for us, to take us to our next job. What that job was we were not told, and we could not even conjecture, not having the faintest idea.

CHAPTER FOURTEEN

THE "HOUSE ON THE HILL"

PACKING up was an easy matter, for we had very little to pack, so we were all ready and waiting when we received a message the next morning to say that the *arabah* was waiting for us at the station. Our gear was carried for us by coolies to the waiting *arabah*, which was already loaded with planks of wood. I asked the *arabanchi* where we were being taken, and he waved his whip in the general direction of Kurdistan and said, "Illah beit ala Tell" ("To the house on the hill"). Further questioning elicited the information that the house was a new one, standing alone, that had been built for an Alliman (German).

When our kit had been loaded on to the *arabah* we set off in a north-easterly direction, passing through another large encampment of refugee Kurds. About five miles from the station we came to a one-storied house that had been built on a low mound and was surrounded by a palisade of poplar poles laced with wire. The nearest habitation to it was the last tent of the Kurdish encampment, three miles away; beyond was desolation. That was the "House on the Hill," and the place where we were to spend another month or so. It had been recently built of sun-dried mud bricks and had neither doors nor windows fitted into the openings. Whilst the *arabanchi* was unloading our kit and the timber we explored the interior. There was one fairly large room, to which access was gained from a smaller one that contained an exterior doorway, a third room that had only an exterior doorway, and a small narrow room that was only accessible from the outside. We selected the third room as our living quarters and the large room as our workshop, putting our kit into the one and the timber into the other. We had no idea what we were expected to do—nor did we care so very much—so, after the *arabanchi* had gone, we proceeded to make ourselves comfortable in our new home. We were thus busily employed when we heard someone galloping up to the gateless entrance to the palisade. Hurrying out of the room we were in time to meet our visitor as he was dismounting. He was a German— a stranger to us—and he introduced himself as Herr Vertzel, deputizing for Herr Vinger. In a queer mixture of English, German, and Turkish, he told us that the house had been built for Herr Vinger and his wife and family, and that our job was to make doors and windows—the latter complete with wooden shutters—and to fit them into the openings. We pointed out to him that we had no tools or other equipment for the purpose, neither had we nails, screws, nor any hardware. I asked him how we were to be supplied with rations, pay, etc., and was told that we should have to go down to our section to get what we required. The tools and other material, he said, he would have sent to us that very day. With a "Guten tag" he galloped off and left us. We looked at each other and laughed, we were certainly getting a variety of jobs, and that one appeared as though it might be a very easy one, as we were bound to be left alone for considerable periods. The rest of that day we spent in spying out the land in the near vicinity. Before sunset we got in a supply of water from a tiny stream that passed within a hundred yards of the house, and then boarded up the doorway and window opening of our room from the inside and lit a fire in one corner of the room. There was nothing left for us to do but cook our evening meal and after we had eaten it, go to bed.

The following morning early, another *arabah* arrived, bringing more timber, a box of tools, a couple of buckets and some ready-made doors. Herr Vertzel came along very shortly afterwards and asked us if there was anything else we required. He said that there was a quantity of nails, etc., in the tool box and that we could always get more by going to

THE KURDISH ALPS. SCENES SUCH AS THESE ARE PREVALENT IN THE AMANUS, ANTI-AMANUS, AND TAURUS RANGES THROUGH WHICH WE PASSED

[*See p.* 306

BEDOUIN CROSSING "THE BLUE"

[*See p.* 347

the Company's store in Nisibin. He promised to visit us once or twice a week to see how we were getting on. Herr Vertzel was a very pleasant type of German, whose only failing—so far as we were concerned—was his insistence in trying to talk to us in English. He knew far more Turkish than he did English, and I always spoke to him in that language, but he said that he wanted to learn English and nearly drove us crazy by his attempts to make us understand what he tried to say.

All the timber we had received was in baulk, and would have to be ripped down by hand into small stuff. Evidently it was intended that we should have no spare time on our hands. We had other ideas, as we intended to work neither hard nor long, but would content ourselves by having something fresh to show Herr Vertzel on each occasion that he visited us. It was arranged that we should draw rations twice weekly, and that would mean that one of us would have to trudge the six miles down to our section and back in all sorts of weather—not a pleasant prospect. Rations at that period were tending to become less and of poorer quality, consequent on the food shortage that was general throughout the country.

For the first few days we worked hard enough, fitting a door and shutters to our own room as a protection against robbers. We had absolutely no protection from the wandering bands of Kurdish thieves that infested that part of the country, and we meant to make ourselves secure from attack. One incident—that had an amusing sequel—will serve to show that our fears in that direction were not groundless. We were busy in the workshop one morning, when in strode three Kurds, fully armed and arrogant. For a few minutes they regarded us steadily, without saying a word, then commenced picking up our tools, opening boxes and poking around the place. I asked them in Arabic and Turkish what they wanted but only received "Ne zani" ("Don't understand") in Kurdish, in reply. We became uneasy at their manner and were afraid that they would soon begin to "collect" things, so we determined to put on a bold front and turn them out. Arming ourselves with adzes we pointed to the door and said, "Yellah, yellah." They looked at us but continued to poke around the shop, picking up first one thing and another, so we went up to them and pushed them through the doorway. They immediately commenced to jabber excitedly, and the younger of the trio made to load his rifle. He was stopped in that by the other two, who said, as far as I could understand, that the sound of a shot would bring the police to the spot. We were not aware at that time that two Gendarmes occupied a disused flour-mill a mile to the north, near the foothills. A little more jabbering among themselves and the Kurds strode off. We discussed the incident and wondered whether they would return, fearing that they might attack us during the night. Before we ceased work that day we boarded up the doorway and windows of our workshop, and at night made the door and shutters of our own room doubly secure. After supper we made our beds on the floor, as being the safest place in the event of any firing. Well into the night we lay and talked in whispers, momentarily expecting an attack, but, as it did not materialize, we fell off to sleep. Just before daylight we were awakened by a fusillade of shots, fired at close range at the house. In silence we lay waiting for we knew not what. Nothing else occurred—just that one burst of firing. Daylight was coming through the chinks of our shutters before we deemed it safe to go outside. There were footprints all around the house, and four doors, that we had left leaning up against the side of the house, had vanished, besides our two buckets that we had inadvertently left standing outside our door, full of water. We concluded that the shots had been fired as the thieves were departing, perhaps out of bravado, or perhaps in disgust at not finding as much loot as they had anticipated. As we were debating what was to be done with regard to the missing doors Herr

Vertzel rode up. I told him what had happened and wound up by saying that we must be armed if we were to remain alone in that isolated house. He sat on his horse, apparently lost in thought, and I, thinking that he had not fully understood what I had said, repeated my statement.

"Ya, ya, vait," he said. I waited, wondering what could be causing him to ruminate so deeply. Suddenly he said, "Ya, so. In de night de tief he vas gom, und de doors in de pocket he vas put, und avay he vas run mit dem." He had been spending that time in thought, trying to render into English the information I had given him. Again I pointed out the necessity for supplying us with arms, and he said that he would have rifles sent up to us on the morrow, together with new doors or timber from which we could make new ones. I insisted that we must have them—the rifles—that day, as the thieves might take it into their heads to return, so he galloped off, saying that he would see what he could do.

About three o'clock that afternoon we saw a Turkish soldier approaching carrying a rifle and bed-roll. Our plan to secure weapons had miscarried, and we were to be supplied with a guard. A guard was the last thing we wanted, even if we were to be attacked every night, as a guard meant a spy on any activities that we might wish to carry out that were not in accordance with the purpose for which we were employed. There was no telling what we might get up to if we were left alone long enough. When the *askar* came up to us I asked him what he wanted, and he replied that he had been sent to guard the place. I told him that we did not require a guard and that he had better return to Nisibin. Not unnaturally, he looked at me in amazement, and said that he had been sent and he must stop there. When he asked where he was to sleep I said that if he had come to be a guard he would have to remain awake, not sleep. Although we were annoyed at his being there, and ragged the poor chap, it was not his fault, and we told him that he could sleep in the small, narrow room at the back of the house. During the night he must have felt lonely, for we were awakened by him singing in a high-pitched tremulous voice. I tiptoed round to his room and found that he had well and truly barricaded himself in. He had made sure that *he* was safe from attack. The following morning I insisted that he return from whence he had come, and in the end he went.

It is one of the most amusing of my memories to recall how I, a prisoner of war, sent back to his unit the soldier that had been sent to guard me. It could not have happened anywhere but in the Turkey of those days.

The next day, Herr Vertzel came to us and wanted to know why we had sent the soldier back. I told him that we had asked for arms, not a sentry, particularly a sentry who had barricaded himself into a room all night. The German was greatly amused at the disparaging things I said about the valour of Turkish sentries and that one in particular, but explained that the Commandant would not agree to our being armed, so we must either have the sentry or look after ourselves as best we could. He then told us of the police post that was not far off—comparatively speaking. After he had gone we decided to pay a visit to that police post, and we set off in the direction that he had indicated. In the ruins of a very old mill we found two decrepit old soldiers who looked as though they had been there since the commencement of the war. One of them was groaning and complained tearfully that his body was full of pains. When I suggested that he should go into Nisibin and report sick he looked at me in horror. No doubt he thought that if he went into Nisibin he would lose the easy job he had; might, in fact, be sent to the front and become a real soldier. Their motto was, no doubt, "Out of sight, out of mind." We asked them whether they had heard the firing two nights previously, and they replied that they had, but, as the sound of shots was no uncommon thing, they had taken little notice of it. We left them with a feeling that we could expect little help from them in the event of an emergency, and were almost convinced that they were in league with the robbers.

The problem of obtaining adequate food was becoming daily more acute, and we could find no means of augmenting our meagre rations. One day I decided to "raise the wind" in a novel way. I went down to the Company's store and obtained a quantity of four- and six-inch nails, which I brought away in a straw basket. Instead of returning to the house I proceeded along the Mosul road for nearly a mile, and then sat down and offered the nails for sale at four for a piastre (twopence) to the Arabs that were constantly passing. Nails of that size were quite unobtainable in Nisibin and were very useful to the Arabs for a variety of purposes, so it was not long before I had got rid of my little stock. Micky was highly delighted when I returned with the money, as I had not told him of my plan. He made a trip into the bazaar and bought food and tobacco and—a great luxury—candles. When he returned I went out and bought *helva* (a sweetmeat) and raisins, and that night we had a glorious feed.

On another occasion we watched for hours a sick pony— belonging to the Kurdish refugees—that was vainly trying to find something to eat near our house, in the hopes that it would lie down and be unable to rise again. We had visions of steaks and fried liver. The Siege of Kut had taught us that most things that could be eaten were food. The poor beast did not seem at all anxious to lie down, so, wearying of watching it, we went up to it and tried to push it over. It was only a bag of bones, but it resisted our attempts to push it over. We could have thrown it in the approved manner, but we reasoned that if it were strong enough to require throwing it would be able to get up again, and neither of us felt like killing it with a hammer or chisel—the only weapons we had. We were not to get our bellies filled from that source, for the next day the owner came and led it away, and we saw it no more.

Rations from the Company had been still further reduced, and the lack of food had become a dominant factor in our lives, when we resolved on most desperate measures to ease the pangs of hunger. Running from the foothills to the Mosul road was a track coming from some far-away village, one that was not too frequently used. We determined to arm ourselves with *kessers* (handadzes) and waylay the first man that came along. Should our victim offer resistance we should have had no hesitation in attacking him. As luck would have it, a fortunate circumstance saved us from becoming bandits on the very day we had chosen to put our plan into operation. We had just left the house when we saw Herr Vertzel approaching in the distance. It was not his normal visiting day, and we wondered what he could want. He had brought us our one day's pay of hard cash—long since overdue.

Despite the very few hours a day we worked, the work we had to do in the house was coming to an end, and we wondered what else we should be required to do, and where we might be sent. We had no desire to return to our section, where we should have to work regulation hours and where we should be under constant supervision. To make the job last out longer we contrived to push down the outer wall of the small room at the back of the house. On the next occasion of Herr Vertzel's visit we showed him the damage and told him that it was caused by the rain constantly beating up against it. As the heap of bricks was now reduced to mud, he had no evidence that such was not the case. It was impossible to repair it until the end of the rainy season, so for the time being we knew that we should remain where we were.

One day Micky paid a visit to the headquarters of the Company, in the Kurdish foothills, to see friends of his there and, if possible, to get food. He returned with a quantity of horse-beans—which, he said, formed the staple diet of the prisoners there—and an order from one of the German clerks of the Company for a set of chessmen and a playing board. We set to work and cut a set of pieces from a couple of pick helves. It was laborious work, and we were very painstaking, but we were proud of the job when at last it was completed, expecting that we should get at least a lira in hard cash for it. We had no suitable wood to make the black squares on the board, so we inlaid them with bitumen. Micky set off on the eight-mile journey to deliver the goods, whilst I remained at the house preparing a list of what we would purchase with the money. It was late at night when Micky returned, footsore and wet through. For several minutes he stood and cursed all Germans and the one who had ordered the chessmen especially. When he had finished he told me that he had been offered twenty-five piastres in hard cash, or one lira in paper, for our masterpiece. That offer he had scornfully rejected, and so great was his chagrin that he had been on the point of striking the German, but was pulled away in time by one of the English prisoners who was present. An English Sergeant had bought the set for half a lira in cash, so we had some return for our labour, though my shopping list had to be reduced by half.

Shortly after that episode we acquired a pair of pariah puppies. They were born—together with others of the litter —in a hole not far from our house, and we had to wait several days before the mother of them roamed far enough away in search of food to allow us time to get them. We had no time to choose, but grabbed up two and ran back to the house, hotly purusued by the furious mother. They were like a pair of woolly lambs; both females and both pure white, they brought a new interest into our lives. Unfortunately, the one that Micky had chosen did not live more than a week or two, but mine—which I had named Winnie—thrived and showed promise of becoming a good watch-dog, though how it thrived on the food it got I never could tell. We buried the dead puppy under a cairn of stones, but a fortnight later, so scarce was food, we took the little body and skinned it and fed it to Winnie.

Spring came and the worst of the rains passed, and for hours we lay idling in the warm sunshine, plotting and scheming and wondering whether it was worth while making another attempt to get away. We amused ourselves one afternoon by building a huge pile of bones, surmounting it with a human skull, right in the centre of a camel route, and then watching to see what happened when the usual evening caravan came along. As we watched, the string of camels were brought to halt and the obstruction inspected by several Arab cameleers. There was much jabbering and waving of hands, and the caravan eventually led in a wide detour round our "monument."

Our peace was disturbed one day by the news that a party of Germans were to be billeted in our house. Herr Vertzel told us that they were tradesmen who had been invalided from the army in Flanders, and had been sent out specially to make up the shortage of skilled workers. We did not relish the idea of having Germans about the place and concluded that it would not be long before we were moved. On the day that they were due to arrive we collected a score or more of skulls from the place where the refugees were wont to bury their dead. The graves had been dug so shallow that the jackals had very soon unearthed the bodies, with the result that the whole area was strewn with bones. The skulls that we collected we placed on top of the palisade poles, on either side of the entrance. On the top of the two that were on either gatepost we put caps, fashioned out of sacking, and stuck cigarette ends in the teeth. Then we sat and waited for our unwelcome fellow-lodgers, intending to watch their reaction to our gruesome display. Near midday we saw them approaching; two of them walking in front of a loaded *arabah*, three others riding on the load. The two afoot were the first to reach the gateway, and they solemnly raised their hats to the grinning skulls on either side. At least, we thought, they had a sense of humour and might not be such bad fellows after all. When they had gone to the large room—which, until we were notified of their coming, we had used as a workshop —we sat down and waited for the visit that we anticipated would be made. However much we disliked the idea of the Germans living in the same house as ourselves, we were not churlish and had prepared a large can of very weak tea—the best we could do—in case they wanted refreshment after the five-mile journey from Nisibin. Very soon a huge fellow came in and greeted us with "Mahlzeit." We shook hands and indicated that the tea was for his party. He was very pleased and seemed anxious to be friends and, by signs, suggested that we take the can along to the other room where his pals were. We followed him and were introduced to the others, who showed their appreciation for the tea. We had neither sugar nor milk, but they had plenty, and when some had been added to the tea we all sat sipping and chatting quite friendly. For a cook they had been supplied with a Hindu from the prisoner of war camp at the station—a Hindu that had been a "sweeper" (one of the untouchables) before his capture. He knew no German and they had no Hindustani, so there was going to be some fun in their household for the first few days. As they commenced to unpack, we withdrew and returned to our own room to discuss them. An hour passed, and the big fellow—who we came to know as Adam Renner—a German Pole—came round to see us, bringing with him a package of sugar and tea and one or two other luxuries, which he unostentatiously placed on our table. He sat and chatted with us for a time, inviting us to supper that night before he left us. Adam Renner was to prove a very genuine man and a jolly good friend to us. He was by far the most friendly of the party and a real devil-may-care sort of chap. They were all very pleasant and friendly enough, but Adam was a man after our own heart. He had been wounded eleven times during his period of service on the Western front, and his body still bore half-healed evidence of his ordeals. Despite that, he was as strong as an ox. Four of them—including Adam—were masons and one an architect, and after they had been with us for a few days the architect was sent for to join the Engineers' mess in Nisibin, whilst one of the masons was sent on to Mosul. The remaining three stayed with us for several weeks, and many a gay time we had together. I very quickly learned enough German to be able to carry on a long conversation with them, so the language difficulty was disposed of. When they required meat, Adam and I would go into Nisibin on a Sunday morning and buy a live sheep, and a great time we had in getting it home. We had invariably to carry it the greater part of the way, and a filthy mess we got into doing it. Those Germans were very generous with all that they had and we were rarely very hungry after they arrived. One day Adam and I got gloriously drunk in the village restaurant, and sat and sang *God Save The King* and the *Marseillaise* at the top of our voices. The advent of the Germans at the "House on the Hill" was a very pleasant interlude, but it was not to last long.

One very unhappy incident occurred during the latter part of the time we were in that house. An English prisoner from the station camp brought us the news that Sergeant-Major Leach had died of typhus, and a request from the rest of the British that we would act as undertakers. It was not a task to our liking, but we readily consented to do so, and spent a day at Nisibin making the coffin and preparing it to receive the body. The funeral was the best conducted one that I witnessed as a prisoner of war, and several Germans attended. Sergeant-Major Leach won respect and popularity by his unfailing courtesy, willingness to help others, and hard work on behalf of the prisoners at Nisibin, from captives and captors alike. His going was a great loss to the British community at Nisibin and to all the little groups of Englishmen in isolated camps for miles around.

Not long after we had buried the Sergeant-Major we received a sudden order to report back to our section on the Jag-Jag River. With a certain amount of regret we packed our kit and bade good-bye to our German friends, and, with a last look at the "House on the Hill," trudged off towards Nisibin, with the *arabah* conveying our gear creaking and groaning behind us.

CHAPTER FIFTEEN

ANOTHER BID FOR FREEDOM

THE scene on the river bank was greatly changed from the old days, and most of our old friends had gone. The compound had not been re-formed after the flood, and the Russian and Rumanian prisoners had been sent elsewhere, as had most of the Kurdish refugees. All the concrete abutments had been completed and the embankments repaired and levelled, and preparations were in hand to build concrete piers where once had stood our trestles, using the piles in the river bed as "keys." We were not permitted to live on our own near the job, but had to join the other Englishmen in the camp at the station. Our job was to make and fix the shuttering for the piers, assisted by native carpenters. I did not get back my status as overseer, and Micky was often taken away to do odd jobs elsewhere. It was on one such occasion that he got into trouble and we were both whipped, an incident that was the deciding factor in our carrying out our oft-discussed plans for another attempt to escape.

Micky had been taken away to do a job of work near the station, and, from what he told me, the native overseer had treated him like a coolie until Micky had lost his temper and had knocked him down. He was promptly arrested and taken to the Commandant's camp. Word was speedily got to me, and I set off to see what I could do in the matter. I found Micky under guard in a tent at the Turkish headquarters and, after hearing his story, worked out his defence. The next morning he was taken in front of the Commandant for trial, and I attended as his interpreter. The German Engineer in charge of the station section was there, together with an interpreter and the overseer whom Micky had struck. The German was surprised to see that Micky had an interpreter of his own, and he protested to the Commandant that I was unnecessary to the occasion as his interpreter could speak English. I was in the fortunate position of being able to understand enough German and Turkish to be able to join in the argument that followed, and in the end I was allowed to stay. Both sides were listened to impartially by the Commandant and it ended by Micky being awarded twenty strokes—a light sentence really. The amazing part of the whole proceeding was that I too received the same punishment—for acting on behalf of the accused, presumably. We were whipped there and then, in front of the German and the Commandant and the rest of them. Micky could not sit down for a week after it, but the Chaoush that administered the punishment was lighter with his strokes when it came to my turn, and I only suffered a temporary discomfort.

That was the finishing touch, and that night we discussed our plans in real earnest and decided to commence preparations right away. Briefly, our plans were these:

We were to organize and equip a party of eight for a journey of approximately six weeks. Our route would be to Baghdad; crossing the Jebel Sinjar in a direct line from Nisibin and continuing across the desert that lay between that range of hills and the Tigris, leaving Mosul on our left. Our equipment was to consist of water-skins, compass, watch, small arms and ammunition, and a few medicines. We were to make concentrated food for the whole party, sufficient for the journey, easy to pack and of small bulk.

We had already decided on the type of rations that would serve us best, and we anticipated little trouble in getting what we wanted in that direction, but the equipment was a different matter. To get what we wanted we were prepared to "beg, borrow, or steal." By our reckoning, we considered that we could reach the Jebel Sinjar in four days, cross them in one and reach Baghdad four weeks later. From information I had received, I knew that the inhabitants of the valley between Nisibin and the hills would be a source of danger to us, and that the Yezidis in the hills might possibly be the same. On the desert we had to avoid the Bedouin Arabs, who would have begun their annual grazing circuit. We anticipated that, as the rains had scarcely ceased, we should be able to refill our water-skins fairly frequently on the first part of our journey, thus shortening the length of our hardship when we should have, eventually, to conserve our water. On the occasions when we had visited the Engineers' office in Nisibin we had both contrived to study the map of the surrounding country that hung on the wall there, but we had never had sufficient time on those occasions to make a sketch of our proposed route. To procure a map was practically impossible, and we did not waste time attempting to. The Turkish forces, we knew, would be tied to the Tigris, and it was our intention to skirt the flank of them as we neared our destination.

To recount all the schemes and "wangles" that had to be carried out before we obtained all our gear would fill several chapters, as it took us, and several trusted friends, a long fortnight of concentrated effort before we got all that we had planned to get. Water-skins were harder to buy than we had anticipated, and those we got were far from good ones. There seemed to be a great dearth of such things in Nisibin, though they were common enough articles of general use. The compass we got was a small pocket affair, stolen by one of our friends from the office of a German cashier at the Company's headquarters in the foothills north of Nisibin. The watch I stole from a shop in the bazaar. Vaseline and quinine and a small quantity of iodoform ointment were obtained for us by a prisoner working in the camp sick-quarters, and a great task he had to get them, as such medical stores were as rare and as valuable as diamonds in Turkey in those days. We managed to buy an assortment of old revolvers from different people in the village, and the ammunition to fit them came from various similar sources. Most of the ammunition was old stuff, mostly refills, and it was doubtful whether it would be of any use. It was the best we could get, and, in any case, we hoped that we should never be in a position where it would be necessary to try it out. For rations we purchased a quantity of wholemeal flour, dried figs, raisins, and rice. The rice we boiled "dry" and mixed with the flour, together with the figs and raisins, previously chopped small. After thoroughly kneading the mess we rolled it out and cut it into fair-sized biscuits of equal size and shape, which we subsequently cooked in the manner of *chupatties*. When the biscuits had been dried in the sun for two or three days, we packed them into the six packs that we had made.

The choosing of the party was considerably more of a problem than getting the gear together, though we knew that there were scores of Englishmen who would have jumped at the chance of coming with us. Eventually, we decided on four Englishmen, one Sikh and one Hindu. The two Indians we wanted to carry the water-skins, as we thought that they would be able to manage that job much better than any Englishman. Two of the Englishmen we had chosen were at Serchikhan, and we had to get word to them to find a way of getting to our camp at Nisibin when we sent word that we were ready. Another one was at the Company's headquarters, and the fourth at the station camp.

At long last all was ready, and we sent off word to all the members of the party, giving them the day and the time when they were to arrive at our camp. At the appointed hour everyone was present, greatly excited and anxious to learn our plans. Micky issued the packs and revolvers whilst I detailed to them the route we were to take, etc. We took a solemn oath that we would all abide by the decision we had made, whereby, should any member of the party fall sick *en route*, he should be given twenty-four hours in which to recover, failing which he would be left with sufficient rations to enable him to get back to Nisibin or the Turks. There was no more to do or say, so, adjusting our packs, we filed out into the darkness.

It was midnight, and we knew that we need not fear the sentries so much as our own comrades in the camp with whom we had not seen fit to discuss our plans. Only three other people outside the party knew what we had planned to do, as we had discovered, on similar occasions, that even one's own friends are apt to prove a source of danger by un-wittingly revealing one's secrets, thus focusing the attention of the rest of the prisoners upon one and raising the suspicions of the authorities. So, with stealthy steps, we glided by the tents and storehouses and headed in the opposite direction to the way we intended to take. After half an hour of marching in Indian file, we halted and listened for any signs of pursuit. There was none so we moved off again, this time making a wide detour that brought us back to our proper route by avoiding Nisibin and its environs. In complete silence we marched steadily on in a direct compass course to what we knew to be a pass in the Jebel Sinjar. The first two hours proved very easy going, but after that we walked into a belt of thistles six to ten feet high. There were disadvantages to starting our journey at the tail-end of the rainy season, and those giant thistles, and crops of rank vegetation, and swollen streams were some of them. I experienced a sense of great elation at being once more free and able to go whither I choose, though the difficulties of that first night's march were by no means encouraging. We were soaked to the skin with constantly fording streams and deep irrigation ditches, and our hands and faces and bare knees—we all wore shorts, mostly made of cut-down trousers—were like raw meat. Occasionally we heard someone shouting, as though our movements through the crops had been heard. On those occasions we halted and listened, our hearts pounding against our ribs as we sat in dead silence until we were reassured that we were not being pursued.

We were still marching at dawn, when a mist filled the valley. Suddenly, we were startled by voices that were not a dozen yards from us. We dropped flat on the ground and cast off our packs, fearful of recapture and ready for flight if need be. The voices came from a party of mounted Arabs who were taking their flocks to pasture. How they missed stumbling on to us I have never understood. Fate was kind to us, and after they had gone we continued on our way. The mist lifted and left us in a very exposed position within sight of two villages, and we had several miles to go before we could better it. To proceed in broad daylight was extremely dangerous, so there was nothing for it but to lie down where we were and hope that we should not be seen before nightfall. Each of us took a turn at keeping watch whilst the remainder slept. We were disturbed only once—by some inquisitive Arab youths, to whom we made a display of our revolvers whilst we answered their questions. They did not appear to be greatly impressed by our arms, but they eventually took themselves off and for the rest of the day we were undisturbed.

Immediately it was dark we started off again and soon reached the lowest part of the valley, which was very marshy and flooded in many places. Towards midnight we came to a stream that had overflowed its banks and was now about five hundred yards wide. We had no idea where the actual bed of the stream was nor how deep it might be. To go up or down stream in order to find a possible ford was not to be thought of, so we decided to cross in single file, each man holding on to the man in front of him. I led the way and suffered agonies of uncertainty in so doing. Water-snakes were very common in that part of the country, and that knowledge served to increase my fears. Imagine what it would be like in England if one were suddenly called upon to cross an unknown

stream, in the middle of a dark night, fully clothed and
weighted down by a heavy pack, and my fears can then be
understood. Very slowly we waded across, until for about
twenty feet we had to swim before touching bottom again. It
was with sighs of relief that we reached the other side in
safety. We were now in a very sorry state, as everything,
food included, was soaked through. To make matters worse
it began to rain, and when dawn came we were a very tired
and wretched party. As we could not see any villages, and it
was still raining, we continued to march for another two
hours, and then, from sheer exhaustion, lay down and
endeavoured to rest. We were shivering with cold so we
huddled together in line, with an Indian at each end. When
one side of us was throughly chilled through, we all turned
over and tried to warm that side, and so on until about
ten o'clock, when the rain ceased and the sun shone forth.
Then we stripped to the skin and laid out our clothes and all
our gear to dry, and—what was even better—managed to get
a few hours' sleep in comparative comfort. Just before sunset
we re-packed our rations, etc., and moved off again. Our
greatest torture that night was from our torn flesh. The rain
had soaked it and the sun had dried it, until to move our faces
or knees was agony. A liberal smearing on of vaseline eased
the pain somewhat, but it was many days before we could
walk or chew with comfort. Nothing caused us any alarm
that night, and we were greatly cheered when daylight came
and we saw the hills only a short march away. At their foot we
could see scores of nomads' tents, and to get up to the pass
without being caught was going to be a stiff proposition. We
continued to march until we considered that we could get
through the Arabs and into the pass before the dawn of
another day, then we lay down and slept.

It was dark before any of us awoke, and it was with the
greatest difficulty that we were able to find water to fill our
skin bags. That accomplished we pushed forward, going

slowly and making as little noise as possible. In less than an hour we were within hailing distance of the tents, and we sat down and discussed ways and means of proceeding by them. We hated to separate, but for us to have attempted to pass them in a body would have been madness. For Micky and me it was not so bad, as we were old hands at that sort of thing, but the others were not so placed and were inclined to be nervous at the thought of being left alone. It was decided that I should go first and Micky stay with the remainder until each one had got through safely. I crept away from the party and advanced towards an opening in the line of tents. Not a sound did I hear as I passed silently by the goat's-hair tents of those nomads, except the thumping of my own heart. Safely through, I lay flat in the grass and awaited the remainder of the party. One by one they arrived, without attracting any attention, and, with light hearts at our good fortune, we commenced to scale the hillside to reach the pass.

The going was extremely rough, and we were only just in the pass when daylight came. We pushed on, determined to get through before we halted for the day. On our left, buried in the hills, was a large village of the Yezidis (Devil Worshippers), but we got out of sight of it without being observed. We got safely through the pass and on to the third stage of our journey—the desert. As there were several tracks running parallel to the hills, we continued on into the desert in order to be safe from any likely travellers.

When we halted we once more unpacked our rations and laid them out to dry, for they were beginning to turn mouldy. Then we all lay down to sleep in a fold of the ground, not bothering to keep a watch. We were so tired that we slept all that day and far into the night before any of us awoke. That did not disturb us, as we had plenty of rations for the remainder of the journey and we reckoned that a good sleep would do us much good.

So far we had been extremely lucky and began to anticipate

a triumphant entry into Baghdad. Little did we dream what the future held for us.

Greatly refreshed by our long sleep, we collected up our rations and then lay and discussed the manner in which we should complete the journey. We decided to ration the water at half a pint per man per day, as we had no knowing when we should be able to refill our water-skins again. It was decided also that, for the time being, we would continue to march only at night, in order to minimize the risk of being seen by Bedouins. It was too late to start that night so we continued to chat until dawn.

Before the following day was far advanced, the heat became intense, and it was with the greatest difficulty that we refrained from drinking more than our ration of water. We covered up the water-skins as well as we could, to prevent evaporation of the water and cracking of the skins. It was with feelings of great relief that we watched the sun slowly sinking that day, and once more prepared to march.

All through the night we pushed steadily on, halting every two hours for a break of ten minutes. The burning sun during the day had the effect of making us terribly sleepy that night, and we scarcely spoke a word the whole time we were marching. We continued to march until sun-up and then lay and endured another day of shelterless agony. It was impossible to sleep with the sun well-nigh scorching the skin off us, and gasping with thirst.

During the afternoon of that day we discovered to our consternation that one of the skins had been badly leaking, and was almost empty. That was very serious, as the ground over which we were travelling was hard and dry, covered here and there with camel thorn or prickly scrub, but giving no promise of likely water-holes. It was impossible to decrease our ration of water still further, as we were, even then, hardly able to talk for the want of it. Another obvious truth dawned upon us. If we continued to march at night we should be unable to locate water unless it lay directly in our path. We were between the Devil and the deep sea. Deciding that the risk of capture by Arabs was to be preferred to death by thirst—with all its attendant agonies—we determined to march that night until midnight and then rest until dawn, when we would resume our march in daylight. We carried out that plan, and I, for one, was pleased to think that I should not have to lie and grill all day in the burning sun.

Disaster overtook us on the very first day that we changed our time of marching. About nine o'clock in the morning we saw coming towards us, on the far horizon, a single dismounted Arab. I was greatly alarmed at seeing only one Arab and told the party that, in all probability, he was one of a party and was coming to investigate. We halted and lay watching the Arab draw near. I was busy making up a yarn to tell him, should he become inquisitive, as he was almost bound to do. We did not fear him, as any one of us would probably have been his physical superior, but we did not want to use violence unless it was absolutely necessary. With almost incredible speed he came to within thirty paces of where we lay, before he slowed down and then raised one of his arms outwards, making his *kaftan* fly out like a sail.

"A signal," I muttered, and got to my feet to interrogate friend Arab. He appeared a typical specimen of his kind, neither Bedouin nor Fellaheen, but of a race that the British "Tommy" aptly called "Desert Rats," dressed in filthy rags held in place by a belt containing a varied assortment of cartridges, prominently displayed.

"Salaam aleikum," I greeted him.

"Aleikum salaam," he replied.

For a few minutes he carefully scrutinized each member of our party in turn, uttering not a word; then suddenly, "Where are you going?" "To Mosul," I lied, then, in answer to further questions I told him of what we were doing according to the plan I had made up. He merely grunted occasionally and then, when I concluded, said that he was journeying to Balad Sinjar, and would get on his way. Still very suspicious, I asked him to break bread with us. He did so, and I noticed his eyes light up when we displayed a well-stocked pack of food to him. When he had eaten, he blessed us in the name of Allah and continued on his way for about a hundred yards, when he surprised us by running off at right angles to the way he was going. His action clearly indicated treachery, and we lost no time in getting on the move again. In less time than it takes to tell, two more Arabs appeared on the skyline, bearing down directly on to us. We changed our course in order to avoid them, and two more appeared in our direct front. We began to feel very anxious and wondered how many more there might be. Keeping straight on we made for the pair of cut-throats to our front. As we bore down on them they let up a yell and ran to our flank. In a few minutes we were being pursued by about forty of those desert vermin. They very speedily overtook us and split into two sections, one ranging itself on our right flank and one on our left. At first they contented themselves with hurling camel-goads and knobkerries at us, which we picked up and hurled back, often with much better aim than they. All the time they were yelling and keening at the top of their voices. Suddenly, one of the band sped away in front of us, and, kneeling down, fired into the midst of us at a range of about fifty yards. We did not waver from our course, and several of us actually laughed, as we did not hear any whistling bullet.

Drenched with perspiration we kept up that fantastic race, determined to stick out to the last. I gave orders to retain all the knobkerries they threw at us; they might prove useful. We began to realize that we should have to come to a halt, as the pace we had set and the weight we were carrying were proving too much for us. For another quarter of a mile we kept it up and then suddenly halted, at a word from me, and, dropping our packs in a heap, formed a circle and drew our revolvers. The band of desert rats came within forty paces of us and encircled our party. I gave instructions not to fire until they came close enough to ensure a hit every time. For a few minutes they stood and shouted at us to hand over all our possessions. We did not reply, but stood waiting their next move. It was not long in coming. Step by step they closed in on us, until a bare ten yards remained between us.

What a vile-looking crowd they were, vultures every one of them. One cross-eyed villain, bolder than the rest, came within striking distance and brandished his knife in the face of the man next to me—Corporal Grant, D.C.M., of the Royal Flying Corps. Aiming his revolver full at the Arab's bare chest, the Corporal pulled the trigger. Click! Nothing happened. Hastily twirling the barrel he tried again, with the same result. With a curse he hurled the useless weapon in the face of the now grinning Arab. Fearful of the result I ran up to the half-stunned Arab and fired at his heart, with the muzzle of my revolver held close to his body. The same click of the striker hitting the cap of a dud cartridge. Reversing my weapon I brought the butt crashing down on the bandit's head, then dashed back to my party. The whole of that little drama had taken only a few seconds and was over before the rest of the unsavoury crew could intervene. I told the rest of my party to try their revolvers. They did so, only to find that their ammunition was like ours—dud. Undoubtedly, the frequent soakings it had been subjected to as we forded the swollen streams in the Nisibin valley, coupled with the fact that it was for the most part made-over stuff, had rendered it useless. We were absolutely in the Arabs' power and to fight meant suicide. Eight against forty were too great odds, so I shouted out for the Arab leader. The ruffianly crowd ceased their cries and gesticulations and shouted for one Abdul. Abdul came forward, and I asked him what he wanted. "Floose" ("Money") was his terse reply. We had a few coins among us, and those I tossed into the sand among the rabble.

In a flash they were fighting and scrambling after the coins, regardless as to how we might act. Had we only had a couple of Service revolvers we could have attacked and beaten them in those few minutes. I was greatly tempted to rush them with the knobkerries we still held, but it was perhaps the best policy that I adopted—standing still. The scramble over I demanded Abdul to allow us to go our way, pointing out that we had "broken bread" with one of his party. That he would not let us do, saying that he must search us all as he was certain that we had more money than we had given them.

So far the Arabs had kept at a respectful distance from us, and it was apparent that they had no useful firearms among them and that they were afraid to come among us. Each one of them had a nasty-looking knife, and I had visions of a frightful end should they wait until dark before attacking us. In my many adventures in those bad lands I had often resorted to bluff to get myself out of a tight corner, and I decided to try it then.

Telling my party that I was going among the Arabs, I instructed them to make a concerted attack, using the knobkerries they still had, if I was seriously molested. I then walked boldly up to Abdul, the leader. One dirty brute grabbed me by the arm and brandished his knife under my nose, but I shook him off. Facing Abdul, I derided him for attacking eight harmless men, and for his lack of breeding in not observing the customs of the Arabs by attacking those with whom one of his number had broken bread. Abdul promptly knocked me down and drew his knife. I got to my feet and faced him again, still bluffing that I was not afraid of him or his gang, when really my heart was like water. At that point the Arab who had given them the signal intervened and said that if we gave them all we possessed no harm would come to us. Abdul agreed to that proposal, so I bargained for enough food to get us to the nearest village, our clothes, and the water-skins. They would agree to nothing of the kind, so I said that we should fight until we were all killed, and in so doing a good many of their number would be killed also. That seemed to impress the remainder, for they all began to talk at once, crowding round Abdul and the Arab scout, who were having a fierce discussion. Eventually, it was decided among them that, providing they could search us for any money we might have concealed, my conditions would be accepted. I returned unmolested to my party and told them what I had arranged, urging that to resist would surely mean our death. They readily agreed, and we suffered ourselves to be mauled about and very thoroughly searched. We were given a small amount of food, one valise, and the leaky water-skin, which was less than half full. Realizing that nothing could be gained by further parley, we left the Arabs to fight over our property—which they had already commenced to do—and made off in the direction of the Tigris.

As soon as we were out of sight, we sat down, and, regardless of consequences, partook of a much-needed drink. Then we took stock of the few rations we had. It was found that with very strict rationing we might make the food last for five days, probably allowing us to reach the Tigris if we made a bee-line to it. At that point Micky surprised us all by announcing that he had managed to hang on to the compass, although he had lost the watch. That was good news, and he fully deserved all the compliments we paid him. Our greatest concern was for water. Unless we speedily came across that vital liquid we were going to be faced with a very desperate situation, as we had only about four pints between the eight of us. Still, all things considered, we were lucky to be in a position to need water.

That night we slept and in the early dawn set out to reach the Tigris—our only hope.

The day was fearfully hot and we suffered a terrible thirst. For six days we staggered along on our ill-starred journey.

Our tongues filled our mouths and our lips were cracked and swollen. We had been four days without a drop of water, with the tropical sun beating down on us unmercifully, when we sighted the precious fluid. I had been feeling very groggy for some time previous to that, and the excitement of the discovery was too much for me and I collapsed. After a short rest I was able to continue, and, with the fear of death in my heart, I pushed ahead of the party, in order to reach the water before I collapsed again. Imagine my horror and disappointment when I reached it and found it to be luke-warm and SALT! I shall never forget those first few minutes of terrible realization. In despair I awaited the approach of my comrades. So great was their thirst that they would not believe me when I told them the water was salt, but all of them tasted it, thereby increasing their thirst unnecessarily.

On the sixth day we came upon salt water twice more, and on the last occasion we had the utmost difficulty in bringing round one of our number who was driven to madness by the sight of it and gulped down a fair quantity of it before we could stop him.

On the seventh day we sighted an Arab encampment, and, not caring what our fate might be, could have shouted for joy had we been able. The Hindu member of our party chose that moment to become slightly insane, and we had difficulty in holding him down until the poor fellow had recovered somewhat.

Long before we reached the encampment the Arabs sighted us, and thirty or forty of them came out to meet us. They were Bedouin and entirely without mercy. I implored them to give us water before they killed us, as I had some sort of fancy that I could die quite happily if my thirst were assuaged. Not until they had stripped us of all our clothing—with the exception of our shorts—would they listen to my pleas for water; then they led us to it. The precious liquid was the fast diminishing remains of a pool that only contained

water for a short time after the rainy season. There are many
such in the region outlying Mosul. It was covered with green
scum and alive with water-vermin, but we did not care about
that. We fell into it and drank and drank again, getting very
sick in the process—to the great amusement of the Arabs,
who sat and watched us. When we could drink no more we
continued to sit in the water and speculate what next would
be our fate.

In ones and twos the Arabs got up and walked away,
apparently not caring what happened to us now that they
had taken all we possessed. Soon, only one old greybeard
was left, and he bade me get up out of the water and go to
him. Wonderingly I seated myself beside him. Looking to
see that none of the other Arabs was near, he pulled from
out his burnous our compass. Thrusting it into my hand he
said, "Make it go." I said, "It is not a watch, and will not
go." "Then what is it?" he asked. There was a poser indeed.
How could I explain a compass and its workings to a wild,
untutored Arab. I made a desperate attempt to do so but
failed, and the old man put it back among the folds of his
cloak. Next he demanded that I show him where we had
concealed our arms. His demand was backed up by threats
as to our ultimate fate if they were not produced. Apparently
he conceived that we were Turkish deserters and had hidden
our arms. I told him of our first encounter with Arabs and
said that they had taken our rifles. After a long argument he
left me and I returned to the pool.

Before long, another Arab returned and began to talk to us
in a sympathetic manner. I inquired of him the way to the
Tigris or the Turks. He was rather vague about either, so I
promised him fabulous wealth and countless camels if he
would lead us to the English. He became very interested at
that, and said that if I was an officer he could do what I asked
for fifty camels and a bag of rupees. I assured him that we
were all officers, and would give him double what he asked if

Other Ranks of Kut   Y

he would get us away. A long discussion followed and he finally led us from the pool. In a few moments we were hopping around in agony, for we were walking barefooted among camel-thorn. With the greatest difficulty I managed to keep just behind our guide, who soon became disgusted at our inability to walk barefoot without such a fuss as we were making. I shouted to the remainder that I would follow the Arab to his particular encampment—whither he said he was going—and for them to follow on as fast as they could.

For about two miles I plodded along painfully in the wake of the silent Bedouin, until he halted on the summit of a low rise. When I came up to him he said that he had changed his mind and would only take me, as the others could not walk and we should all be caught before we could get very far. I refused to go unless he took us all, so he pointed out some tents in the far distance, and told me to take my party there before sunset and he would go and get camels for us to ride. He left me, and I sat down to pick thorns out of my feet. It was not long before Micky arrived, followed at varying intervals by the remainder. I told them what the Arab had said and proposed that I should try and reach the encampment before sunset, and that they could follow on more slowly. To that they agreed, and, with barely two hours to do it in, I set off.

Regardless of pain, I did my best to reach the tents before sunset, but was unsuccessful. My feet and legs were lacerated and full of thorns, and I was consumed with hunger. Hunger had been forgotten during the time of our great thirst, but with the thirst gone we realized that we had not eaten for several days. I reached marshy ground, so concluded that in all probability there would be a tributary of the Tigris somewhere near.

Night had fallen before I arrived at the first tent, and, throwing myself down in the opening of it, implored food from the inmates. Without hesitation I was given a large bowl of *libn* by an Arab woman. It was from camel's milk, but to me it was delicious. Without asking me any questions the woman told me to clear out. I cleared out and stopping at the next tent—placed some distance from the first—started to tell a tale of woe. I was very promptly and firmly told to go elsewhere. I wandered from tent to tent, trying in vain to enlist assistance for myself and party, though I received several more bowls of milk. In despair I lay down near to one tent and decided to await the coming of the others. I had been there only a few minutes when a silent figure glided up to me and threw over me a tattered sheepskin coat. It was a Godsend, as I was beginning to shiver with cold, and I could have kissed the hand that gave it; it was a girl's. I was in the act of dropping off to sleep when I heard a woman's voice, coming from the tent against which I was sheltering, bid me go into the next opening. Wonderingly I went, and was told by the still invisible woman that I could sleep among the packs and saddles. I lost no time in making myself as comfortable as circumstances would allow and was soon fast asleep. During the night I was awakened by an old Arab, who was apparently on guard and needed company. He asked me scores of questions and finally advised me to join the Bedouin and become an Arab. I fell asleep again as he was enlarging on the beauties of Arab existence.

Just after sunrise I awoke and received a bowl of milk from a woman who, together with three others, was sitting just outside the tent. I drank it gratefully and then went out into the sunshine. To my great relief and joy I saw Micky approaching. He told me that the others were not far off and had all received milk and a few ragged garments from an Arab under whose tent they had spent the night. Thanking the woman who had been kind to me, I accompanied Micky to where the others were seated outside one of the tents. One of them was profusely tattooed, and the Arabs were closely inspecting the designs on his arms and body. They were inquiring how and where it was done, etc., when I arrived, and the man concerned was relieved when I came to tell them, as he knew no Arabic. Having satisfied their curiosity, I asked the Arabs whether they would help us to get safely to the British. Almost with tears I pleaded our cause, pointing out that we should soon die if we were to go on a journey without food or water. They were sympathetic, but beyond telling us the way to the Tigris, would not help us more than they had done.

Where would it all end? We were in a terrible predicament, with no alternative but to push on as best we could.

Bidding the friendly Arabs good-bye we set off in the direction they had indicated. Our route lay away from the marshy ground and among small hills that were strewn with flints. We used the rags we had received to bind around our feet, to protect them from further injury. Despite our many handicaps, we managed to cover a good distance that day and our hopes began to rise. The heat of the sun was terrible, and our bodies became huge blisters, which burst and eventually festered. For three days we journeyed in that manner, with only the sun and stars to guide us, but there was no sign of the river we were seeking. We hoped, if ever we did reach it, to swim down to the British by night stages.

During the morning of the fourth day three dismounted Arabs came into view. They speedily reached us and I told them our story. They were young, fierce-looking devils, and, I gathered, fanatically religious. After calling down curses upon us in the name of Allah and the Prophet, they announced their intention of leading us back to the Turks, who, they said, were within a few hours' march. Leading the way, they commanded us to follow them or be instantly killed. For half an hour we followed them, whilst Micky and I plotted on our chances should we show fight. We did not so much mind going back to the Turks, as we were in a terrible physical condition, but to be taken by three dirty Arabs was gall and wormwood to our souls. The remainder of the party were unwilling to fight, and we could not blame them. They had not had the ups and downs that we had had, and their experiences had proved more than enough for them.

We reached a water-hole and there the Arabs stopped to drink and allow us to drink. When we had slaked our thirst and were sitting down resting, one of the Arabs asked me if I were prepared to become a Moslem. I said I was; I was prepared to become a Buddhist if it meant any advantage to us. I repeated the formula, "There is no God but God, and Mohammed is His Prophet," after the Arab. Then I was told to interpret the words to my friends so that they also could repeat them. I suspected some trickery and, instead of repeating the formula, told them to gabble something or other after the Arab and be on the look-out for trouble. They all repeated the words as best they could, and when they had finished were amazed when the Arab hurled his knobkerrie at the nearest Englishman. Micky and I were watching for just such an occurrence, and we immediately jumped on the unready Arab, yelling to the others of our party to fight like hell. The Arabs did not expect that sudden resistance, as we had hitherto been so docile. The fight did not last very long, for we were desperate men and did not care whether we killed or were killed.

One Arab managed to get away and was soon lost to sight. The other two were quickly dispatched and no doubt proved tasty morsels for the vultures. I was greatly alarmed at the escape of the one, as I knew that he would bring others along to exact vengeance.

We lost no time in getting on the move again and resolved to travel all night, as it was tolerably certain that we should be pursued. The member of the party that had been hit had to be assisted most of the time, as he had sustained a nasty cut on the top of his head. For hours we stumbled on, keeping a sharp look-out for any signs of pursuit until nightfall, when we felt more secure. We were still heading for the Tigris, guided by our very imperfect knowledge of certain stars. All night I was haunted by thoughts of what daylight would bring; whether we should have shaken off the Arabs, who, I was convinced, were bound to be looking for us.

It would be during the darkest hour that precedes the dawn that the next calamity occurred. Micky and I had kept together all night, talking about our slim hopes of ever getting out of the scrape alive. He suddenly stopped to replace the rags around his terribly lacerated feet, and I stopped with him, whilst the others went on ahead. All at once I noticed the dim outlines of figures moving towards the party, who had apparently not seen them. Clutching Micky's arm I whispered to him to look. "My God! Arabs!" he cried. With a yell of warning to the party to run, Micky and I dashed off as hard as we could. We were thoroughly frightened and ran until we could go no further and dropped into a small fold of the ground. Huddled together we lay and shivered until sunrise before we got to our knees and took a look round. Gone were friends and enemies alike; we were alone on the desert. Our position was now hopeless. We had not the faintest notion where we were, and we were without food or water. Getting to our feet we started off due east, knowing that somewhere in that direction lay the river. We did not care if we were caught by Turks, or how soon; in fact I think that we rather hoped that we should soon come up with a Turkish outpost or patrol.

During the morning we came upon ruins—of STONE! We were amazed to see how large and well preserved they were and wondered what place it had been, especially as it had been built of stone. Little did we dream that we were at the site of el-Hatra and within a comparatively short distance of the river. Outside the ruins were perfectly obvious signs of the recent advent of disciplined cavalry. Were they British or Turkish, we wondered? We came to the conclusion that they were British and, as I subsequently discovered on reaching England, we were right. A fairly rapid stream ran near the ruins, in a rocky bed, and we feasted royally on watercress that grew in it and marshmallow that grew on its banks. As we were getting to our feet, preparatory to recommencing our march, we espied a solitary Arab coming in our direction. Emulating the feat a of famous king of old—in England—we slipped into the stream and stood with only our heads above water, and those we hid under the weeds that overhung the stream. The Arab passed without seeing us, but we remained where we were for a long time before we dared venture out and get on our way again.

For three days we continued to wander along that stream, not daring to leave it as it provided us with food—of a sort— and drink. The ground was undulating and covered with camel-thorn and patches of coarse grass. We lived solely on weeds. Towards the end of the third day we came across camel-tracks and decided to follow them. Micky was now in a very bad way, and I was only a little better. Our marches became shorter and our halts longer. By noon of the fourth day we were almost exhausted and actually lay down to die, but dying was not so easy and after two or three hours we had recovered sufficiently to be able to stagger on once more, determined to "carry on" until we dropped. Just before sunset that day we sighted an encampment and, with hopes once more ascending, we pushed on towards the tents. We reached the first one and simply dropped in our tracks before it. Several Arabs were sitting around a fire outside, and three women were inside, one of whom quickly brought us *libn* and a cloth of dried dates. Not a word was spoken as we slowly munched the dates and drank the *libn*, watching as the woman spread a sheepskin beside the fire for us to sit on. Poor old Micky was "all in" and lay on the skin and fell asleep. I very much wanted to do the same but was kept answering a lot of questions, until, to my relief, there was a great shouting and bustle in the camp, announcing the return of the camels from the grazing ground, and the Arabs went off to assist in watering them and left me to sleep.

It was dark when next I awoke, and the Arabs were sitting round the fire, quietly chatting. I sat up and saw that Micky was still asleep and that the women were silently regarding him. Noticing that I was awake, one of the Arabs called me to sit by him, and when I had done so he began to question me very closely as to who we were, where we had come from, etc. I had previously told them that we were Germans who had been attacked by Arabs as we were making our way to the "Compania" at Mosul. That was the first time that I had ever denied my race, and I did it because when I had told the three Arabs who had attacked us that we were English they had immediately commenced to abuse us. One old grey-beard was the chief questioner, though I gathered that he was not the owner of the particular tent that had given us sanctuary. He asked me whether I had ever been to Baghdad and seen the English there. I told him that I had been to Baghdad before the English arrived and that I had seen plenty of Englishmen elsewhere.

"By God," he exclaimed, "the English have everything: money, machines, guns, and rifles, and the Germans will soon be finished."

That was a new line, and I hardly knew how to counter it. However, I said that the Germans had plenty of everything and when the English had been driven out of Iraq they would help the Arabs considerably. All the time we had been talking the old Arab had been beating the ground with a club made of a huge steel nut screwed on to the end of a stick. This he now waved in front of me and said, "Do you know what that is?" pointing to the nut.

"Yes," I answered, wonderingly.

"Well, that came from Baghdad, off a 'trombil' (automobile) belonging to the English. They have hundreds of such 'trombils' and will soon make short work of the Germans."

The old man continued to laud the English, and I came to the conclusion that I had made a bad mistake in saying that we were Germans, so, regardless of possible consequences, I determined to retrieve my mistake. Interrupting the old man I said, "We are both Englishmen, but I was afraid to tell you so before as we are escaped prisoners of war."

Very calmly the old man said, "I knew it all along and was wondering how soon you would admit it. Didn't I tell you that I had been to Baghdad and had seen the English? I have heard them talking together, and their talk does not offend the ear, whereas the Allimani (Germans) speak from the belly and make noises like the frogs in the gardens."

Then he turned to the other Arabs and said, "Didn't I tell you?"

My confession brought more questions, and I was kept hard at it until the evening meal appeared. Micky had been awake for some time, and I told him that we were once more Englishmen. The meal—to which we were both invited— was of rice and *libn*, and for once in a while we managed to compete with the Arabs in putting away huge quantities of it.

There was very little talk after the meal, and the visiting Arabs crept silently away to their own tents whilst Sultan— our host—gave instructions to his women to put skins for us to lie on in that half of the tent where the packs and saddles were kept—normally the males' part of the tent.

For a time Micky and I discussed the situation and our good fortune at coming across friendly Arabs before we had starved to death. Then we dropped off to sleep, not caring greatly what the morrow might bring forth.

When we awoke the next morning we found that the tent had been struck over our heads and was already being loaded on to waiting camels. At our heads was a bowl of dried dates which we speedily consumed. When it was seen that we were awake, one of Sultan's wives collected the skins we had lain on and packed them on to one of the camels.

All the encampment was being moved, and everywhere were snarling camels being loaded with tenting and utensils. For the most part the women seemed to be doing all the work and I wondered what the men found to do all day. Beyond cheery greetings nothing was said to us about our accompanying the tribe or anything else. I told Micky that our best plan would be to follow them as best we could and trust to their hospitality to feed us for a few days, and hope that we might get nearer to the river as they continued their grazing circuit.

At last all was ready and, with much *whushing* on part of the Arabs, the snarling, gurgling, camels lurched to their feet and the tribe moved off. To my surprise, very few of the males rode, but strode along beside their own string of camels. The women and children rode in panniers formed of the camel-skin watering troughs and bundles of tenting. On the flanks of the tribe rode a few Arabs on horses, with rifles resting across their knees.

For an hour or two we managed to keep up with Sultan— who was shod with rope shoes—but as the sun rose higher the hot sand began to play havoc with our feet and we found great difficulty in keeping up. After passing through a patch of camel-thorn that tore the skin off our shins and filled our legs with thorns, I asked Sultan whether he would let us ride on a camel. He laughed at me and said that it was not usual for men to ride like women but if we could mount a camel on the move we could ride. I told Micky what we had to do, and we commenced to make ourselves look foolish by attempting to mount the swaying beasts.

Had we been in decent condition, with something on our feet, we might have succeeded without much trouble, but, as it was, all we did was to raise a laugh among the Arabs by our fumbling, ineffectual attempts.

Sultan had pity on us at last and showed us how to mount in two different ways. One by grasping the tail of the camel and using the hock of its hind leg as a step as that member swung back for a fresh stride. The other was to vault into the curve of the animal's neck and climb up from there. After one or two attempts I managed to climb on to a camel that was being ridden by one of Sultan's wives and two of his children, using the first method. Micky tried the same way but was unsuccessful, but eventually got on to another camel by the neck route. It was a tremendous relief to be riding, and we were able to look round and contemplate our novel experience. There seemed to be hundreds of camels scattered all over the "blue," and, whilst they were all going in the same direction, the manner of the going was by no means orderly. I looked to the head of the tribe and to the rear, and it seemed as though we were moving in a huge circle. There was not a sign of a landmark, merely a vast shimmering waste, and I marvelled at the sense of direction that the Arabs must have possessed.

During the afternoon we arrived at the next grazing ground—though I could see very little grazing—and the work of pitching camp commenced, the women again doing most of the work. The camels were driven off to graze by the youths of the tribe, and were soon lost to sight. We helped the women as well as we could, to show our willingness to repay, by labour, the good Sultan. If we did little that was useful we at least caused a good deal of merriment among his womenfolk by our inexperienced attempts.

In an incredibly short time the whole tribe was tented and silence reigned. Sultan's wives smeared butter on our lacerated legs and lay on their stomachs whilst they hunted with needles for thorns in our torn flesh. Those women were undoubtedly unprepossessing and very lousy, yet they had hearts of gold and we were very grateful for their kind administrations.

During the late afternoon the adult males of the tribe gathered at Sultan's tent and engaged us in gossip. They tried to persuade us to show our prowess with the rifle, but, not wishing to lose face by a display that would in all probability have been less skilful than theirs, we excused ourselves by saying that we were both artillerymen and were not used to the handling of rifles. They were a happy crowd and indulged in a good deal of horseplay. I was able to amuse them by a display of ground acrobatics and wrestled with one of the younger ones.

For several days we continued as guests of Sultan, until a proposition he made to me one night caused us hastily to leave. He suggested that, as I spoke Arabic and was an acceptable fellow, I should marry into the tribe and settle down with them. As an inducement he offered to divorce his first wife and then I could marry her. A most unappetizing offer as she was a wizened and much-tattooed lady of shrill voice and uncertain temper. I had a great admiration for Sultan, but I could not see my way clear to fall in with his proposition, and, not wishing to be pressed further in the matter, that same night we faded away into the "blue."

It is illustrative of Sultan's assessment of us that, on an occasion that we were bathing in a stagnant pool with him, he answered a query by a visiting Arab as to whether we were Islami or Nosrani (Mohammedans or Christians) by saying that we were neither, but Ingleezi, and his guests.

Two days after we had left him we came up with another section of the same tribe—the Shammar—and we stayed with them for several days. In the household of our host was a girl of about ten years of age, and she took a very lively interest in us, searching for hours for edible roots for us as we were always hungry, and occasionally stealing a handful of dates for us from the meagre stock in the harem quarter of the tent. During those few days we were constantly being urged to catch up with that section of the tribe that contained the Sheikh—one Abdul Azziz—who would no doubt help us to get to the English. When we left that section we endeavoured to find the elusive Abdul Azziz, and many a hardship we suffered in the attempt. We always seemed to be a day behind him, and at last began to doubt the existence of such a man.

Not all the Arabs we came to were as hospitable as the first and second lots, but on no occasion were we ever maltreated. We had to beg our way along and received anything from one date or an ear of barley to a good feed of rice and mutton washed down with *libn*. Sometimes the women "shooed" us away from a tent, but we only passed on to the next, and it was rare that, sooner or later, we did not come upon some kind soul that gave us something. Our arrival at an encampment was always heralded by the snarling and snapping of the watch-dogs as they circled around us, trying to snatch a morsel from our skinny legs. Only once was either of us bitten, and that was one morning when we were watching our host of overnight preparing to move on. Then one huge brute rushed at me from behind and bit me behind the left knee. It was only a small affair, but for a day or two I was anxious as to the result, knowing that the teeth of those animals were usually fouled with carrion and likely to cause tetanus to the bitten. Micky was bitten by a scorpion the same day, but neither bite could have been serious as neither of us had any after-effects.

At last we wearied of the constant trekking without any definite destination, and with our precarious way of living, and decided that we would once more head in the direction of the Tigris, which we knew lay somewhere in the east. For three days we slouched along, without food or water and half crippled from festering legs. On the fourth day we sighted a village of mud huts. As we neared the village we noticed a rough track that passed through it, going north and south, and we conjectured that it was a road between Mosul and Baghdad, though we had no idea how near we might be to either place. On the outskirts of the village we accosted an Arab and begged for food and water. He led us to his house and gave us a bowl of *libn*, saying that we should have food when the evening meal was cooked. In answer to his questions, I said that we were escaped prisoners of war and wished to get to Baghdad. He would not believe me but insisted that we were deserting Turkish soldiers! As he was friendly enough I did not argue the point but let him assume what he would. After we had quenched our thirst he led us to an empty room and told us to shoot the bolt behind us and remain quiet until he came for us that evening. We did as he bade and then sat and discussed the position, as we were not altogether sure that the Arab would not return with an escort of Turkish soldiers for us. Deciding that the prospect of getting food was worth the risk of recapture we lay down and were soon fast asleep.

We were awake that evening when the Arab came for us and told us that it was safe to come out, and we followed him to where an old woman was setting a large dish of *pilaff* on to a carpet-covered dais. He told us to sit on the ground and wait until he had eaten, when we should have what was left. It was agonizing to have to sit and watch every mouthful he ate, we who had had nothing whatever to eat for the better part of four days, but, at long last, he handed the dish down to us and we lost no time in devouring what he had left. For the next hour I endeavoured in vain to enlist his aid to help us reach the British lines. He persisted in regarding us as Turkish deserters and, beyond offering to let us sleep the night in the empty room, would not help us. That night we went to the room, ostensibly to sleep, and when we thought the coast was clear crept out and wandered away into the darkness.

For several more days we wandered on, going roughly south by east, getting an occasional meal but more often going without, so it was with a certain amount of relief when the end came to our long spell of freedom.

CHAPTER SIXTEEN

ONCE MORE IN TURKISH HANDS

WE had reached an area of stony ground and small hills one afternoon, when we spotted an encampment due east and bore off in that direction. As we neared the camp we saw that it was composed of both goat's-hair and canvas tents. Thinking that we had by chance stumbled upon that section of the Shammar with which rode the Sheikh, we hurried cheerfully towards it. Before we had reached the first tent we were roughly seized by two Arabs and prodded into a run. They drove us towards a marquee set up in the middle of the encampment and pushed us inside, saying as they did so, "More deserters."

We found ourselves standing before a dapper little chap dressed in the Effendi style. I immediately explained to him that we were not deserters but English prisoners of war. I had seen the kind of treatment meted out to deserters from the Turkish army and had no hankering after the same. The Effendi was a cheery sort of chap and gave us cigarettes to smoke and told us to sit down whilst he took our particulars. He did not bother us with many questions and in a very short time had sent for an escort of Arabs to take us away. Our little jaunt was over, and now we were on the way to pay the price, whatever that might be.

For an hour we marched due east and then I recognized the locality. We were within easy reach of the Tigris at Kalat Shergat! Had we only known, how differently the story might have ended. We spent that night in the ration depot where I had sprained my ankle a couple of years before. A Yuzbashi had received us and had regarded us silently for a few minutes after he had read the note sent to him by the Effendi. We were put into a large room near the gate, and a sentry was mounted over us. We received neither food nor water and the sentry only answered my pleadings with a curt "Sus" ("Silence"). I had seen a doctor in the room that housed the Yuzbashi, and I told Micky that it would be a good plan to try some sort of stunt in order to interview him if food were not given to us. So, when night had fallen and all hopes of an evening meal had vanished, Micky started to emit some appalling groans until the sentry was moved into asking what was wrong. I told the *askar* that my friend was very ill and, unless he was taken to the doctor, would most probably die! The *askar* was sceptical and refused to interest himself further, but changed his mind when Micky redoubled his efforts, and shouted for the Onbashi in charge of the guard. After hearing what I had to say, that worthy disappeared, soon to return to bid me help Micky to the doctor's room. The doctor was a young, pink-and-white specimen; scented and prettily dressed, but amiable and pleasant enough. He addressed us in Turkish and told Micky to sit down. I interpreted for Micky and asked the doctor to examine him. Surprised to find that I was familiar with his language he started to engage me in small talk until I drew his attention to the fact that Micky was ill! We had to make some attempt to keep up our pretence. Speaking through me Micky complained of violent pains in the stomach and a bad headache, but the doctor said—after his examination—that he could find nothing much the matter with him. I said that perhaps the pain was caused by slow starvation, as we had had no food for many days. That was the point we had worked up to and we waited anxiously for the result of my suggestion. I added that we were soldiers and were doing no more than our duty in trying to escape, and there was no reason why we should not be fed now that we were prisoners once more. The doctor agreed—much to my relief—and sent for the Yuzbashi. That officer was told the story and said that he would have food sent to us when we returned to our room. The doctor was keen to hear more of our adventures and kept us talking for over an hour, giving us a handful of cigarettes to smoke meanwhile. The Yuzbashi proved to be a decent sort too, and assured us that we should be all right when once we got to Mosul, where he was sending us the following day. We returned to our prison and a good feed of *burgrll* (boiled wheat and mutton) washed down with water. After another cigarette and a laugh at the success of our ruse we lay down on the bare floor and slept peacefully.

Next morning we joined a party of sick Turks who were returning from the front to Mosul. As we were leaving —seated in a ramshackle old *arabah* containing a dozen or more wretched *askars*—the doctor came to wish us good-bye and good luck, and he gave us each a small bag of rasins and a few more cigarettes.

Jolting along a dusty road in the hot sun was unpleasant enough for us but it must have been a positive torture for the sick Turks, though they did not complain, perhaps because they were glad to be away from the sunbaked wilderness that was their front line. By the time we had reached Hammam Ali we were so sick of riding in the bone-shaking conveyance that we vowed to walk the rest of the way into Mosul. After a night spent in a filthy hovel we continued on into Mosul, on foot as we had vowed we would.

At Mosul we were taken to a prison in the middle of the town and closely questioned by an ancient Chaoush. From there we were taken to the town baths and once more endured the agony of having the hair torn off our bodies. By this time the sole wearing apparel that I possessed was the ragged sheepskin that I had received many days before. The remains of my shorts I had used to tie round my feet. Micky was in rags of the raggedest. Before we entered the bath-house we had to strip so that our rags could be fumigated, and goodness knows they wanted that treatment. Unfortunately for me, hide will not stand being fumigated, and when I returned from the bath I found myself the possessor of a skin very much shrunken and as hard as a board! The only way I was able to cover my nakedness was to tie it round my middle with a piece of string that the bath attendant found for me. I must have presented a singular appearance even for that country of singular sights.

From the baths we were taken to a large *sokiet* in the town, near the right bank of the Tigris. That place appeared as though it might at one time have been a caravanserai and was a two-storied building surrounding a spacious courtyard. A gateway gave on to what had once been a garden but was now a latrine of a vileness known only to the Turk. An Onbashi and a party of soldiers occupied the two rooms under the domed entrance but all the other rooms in the building were occupied by ragged humanity of every race and creed, overflowing onto the cobbles of the unswept courtyard. Immediately on arrival we were inoculated, by a young man who may or may not have been qualified to perform the operation. I appealed to the Onbashi for something to cover my naked body and he very kindly gave me an old shirt that was holed and patched, and very much "alive." The latter fact did not worry me at all, as even had it been a brand new one it would very soon have been in the same state.

Water was brought to the inmates in two baked-clay jars carried by a diminutive donkey. There was not nearly sufficient water in the jars to afford a drink to a quarter of the number of men and the result was that as soon as the donkey appeared in the yard, there was a wild scramble for water and the biggest and strongest prisoners got it. We had nothing that would hold water so it was useless for us to join in the scramble, though we were just as thirsty as the remainder. In desperation I went to the Onbashi's room and begged for a drink, explaining our plight. Much to my surprise he took us into the *askars'* room and gave us a drink of ice-cold water and a cigarette apiece. We chatted for a time and then he told me that any time we wanted a drink we could get one for ourselves from the *askars'* supply. Further, he promised to get us a tin or something that we could get our *kurrawanna* in that evening. He told the *askars* who were in the room what he had told us and ended by saying, "These men are English soldiers, not lousy dogs like the remainder."

That night, and every night for the next week, we slept on the cobbles of the courtyard, using mud bricks for pillows and without covering other than the rags we wore. Twice more we were inoculated—against what, we had no idea—and many times we were questioned by various *katibs* about our movements since we left Nisibin. At the end of a week we were taken to a civil prison in the heart of the town. Before the place had been a prison it had been a mosque and we were put into one of several tombs that faced into the courtyard. The tomb was about six feet wide by eight feet long, though two feet of the length was occupied by the brickwork of the actual grave. The roof was curved and about five feet high in the centre, so that we could not stand upright. The entrance was closed by a gate of iron railings. Truly a remarkable prison cell.

We had not been in that vile place many minutes when the Chaoush in charge of the prison shouted, "Ho! Ingleezi! Sisim emsharilar shimdi gelior" ("Your friends are coming now").

We peered through the bars of the gate, and to our great amazement saw several others of our party of escapees being shepherded out of a similar "cell." Our gate was opened and the others pushed inside and the gate clanged to and relocked. For the time being we took no notice of the lack of space but excitedly exchanged experiences. They told us that they had evaded the attack of the Arabs and had eluded them in the darkness only to be recaptured the next day by a posse of mounted Gendarmes. One of the Englishmen and the Hindu—that same Englishman who had almost succumbed at the salt lake and the Hindu who had become slightly crazy shortly after—had been taken to hospital at once, as they were seriously ill from exposure to the sun. The rest of them had been beaten and cursed by the local Commandant before being slung into prison, where we had now found them. They were all very much the worse for wear and terribly despondent. Beyond receiving starvation rations they had not been ill-treated in prison and had not been put to work. They listened open-mouthed to the recital of our adventures and stated that, all things considered, they had not had such a bad time as we. That was a matter of opinion and was certainly not shared by either Micky or myself.

When evening came we were allowed out of the tomb to eat our watery *kurrawanna* in the courtyard, where we sat for an hour before being bundled back. Five Englishmen and one Sikh in a space six feet by six! It was ghastly and sleep was impossible in that fetid atmosphere. For the most part we were naked and the sweat from our bodies was sufficient to dampen the beaten-earth floor. For two weeks we endured the torture of that close confinement and semi-starvation, keeping madness at bay by gnawing bones that the Chaoush gave to us as our share of meat. For bread we each received a handful of crumbs, gritty and black; crumbs that had once been loaves of millet and rye until the banging about in the ration sack had broken them up, lacking, as they did, the consistency necessary to keep them whole. After the first night, for some unknown reason, we were not allowed out of the tomb except for sanitary purposes, and then only once a day, so by the time we did eventually get out we could not stand upright, and were almost too weak to walk.

In that state we were taken to the village of Eski Mosul (Old Mosul) and handed over to an old Yuzbashi. When our escort had gone that officer told us, in passable English, that he had just returned from India, where he had been since he was taken prisoner at Qurna in 1914, when the Vali of Busra had surrendered to our Force. He had been exchanged and very much regretted the fact! We had no cause to regret it as he proved to be a very decent old chap and gave us far more rations than we were entitled to—if one could consider himself entitled to anything in those days. True the rations were nothing to get excited about, coarse flour and dirty lentils, but to us they represented a feast. The Yuzbashi got a woman of the village to make our flour into *chupatties* and to cook the lentils for us, and for the first time for many a long day we ate a really satisfying meal, a meal that was to prove a painful one for Micky. We slept that night in the yard of the ration store and without a guard. The old Yuzbashi apologized for his inability to give us more than he had done, and was very sympathetic with us in our trouble. The next morning we started on the long trek back to Nisibin.

In prison we had discarded the rags from our feet and were now barefoot, and before very long we were made painfully aware of the fact. As the sun rose higher in the sky and the sand became hotter and hotter we began to jump about like cats on hot bricks, much to the delight of the solitary *askar* who was our escort. A bare body was less painful than bare feet so I soon tore my shirt to pieces and bound up my feet. Micky did the same but the others dared not do so as their backs were still festering from the effects of the last exposure.

Our way lay along the route of the proposed railway—recognizable by the metre pegs—and towards evening we came to a small camp of Indian prisoners, where we stayed the night. A Eurasian Assistant Surgeon was in charge and gave each of us a pair of baggy cotton drawers from his meagre stock of clothing. I threw away my sheepskin and felt quite well dressed when I had donned the drawers, though I was still half naked.

Micky had been suffering terribly from gastritis as a result of over-indulgence in hot *chupatties* and half-cooked lentils, and by the time we reached Tel Zioane—thirty-five kilometres from Nisibin—he was almost too ill to continue. At Tel Zioane was a German transport camp and I was successful in persuading one of the drivers of a heavy lorry to give us a lift into Nisibin. The second driver of the vehicle was optimistic enough to demand payment of us after we were well clear of the camp, but in answer to my protests the other driver told him to shut up and leave us alone. Micky was driven frantic with pain, aggravated by the jolting of the lorry, and attempted to throw himself over the tail-board. I clung to him and sat on him for the greater part of the journey, much to his rage but all for his good.

At Nisibin we were taken to the Commandant's office where we were cursed and had our ears boxed before we were put into the village prison. There we found another party of would-be escapees, who, emboldened by our long absence and thinking that we had got safely away, had tried to do the same. They had not been out of camp twenty-four hours before they were caught by mounted police who had been sent to get them. The leader—a naval Petty Officer, recalled as a reservist from the Metropolitan Mounted Police at the outbreak of hostilities—was given a terrific thrashing with the usual whip, and his body bore eloquent testimony to the severity of his punishment, being one huge bruise from his ankles to the middle of his back, a bruise that was purple, blue, and horrible green.

We might have received the same treatment had not our escort given the Commandant a note from the Commandant of Mosul saying that we had already been punished. Despite that, we were destined to spend another two weeks in prison before the Commandant was satisfied that we had been punished enough!

It did not take me long to get on good terms with the Onbashi of the prison, and I was allowed a good deal of latitude, even to being allowed to sleep outside the cell that we were all supposed to occupy. I also persuaded him to leave the cell door open so that the others would not feel their confinement so badly and so that they could sit at the door and look outside when they felt like it.

We had absolutely nothing to do, and time dragged horribly. The first party were taken back to work for the Company after we had been there three or four days. I asked the Onbashi to find me some sort of a job that would take me out of the prison if only for a few hours a day. He found me a job—and what a job! Provided with a leaky kerosene oil can I had to carry water a distance of about six hundred yards and lay the dust in the road under the verandah of the Commandant's office. The dust was ankle deep and I could make not the slightest impression on it. Still, I was outside the prison, and could see what was going on and didn't care what I did or how foolish was my job. On my second day outside I saw a huge white dog running around the bazaar with a pack of scavenging pariahs, and I thought that I recognized in it my dog Winnie that I had handed over to one of our Sergeants before I left. I gave the peculiar whistle to which I had trained her, and sure enough it was my dog all right. She came bounding up and almost knocked me down in her excitement and pleasure at finding me again after all those weeks. The Sergeant told me subsequently that he had tied her to his bed with a stout rope on the first day after I had gone, and when I did not return she had turned so savage that he had been unable to approach her. She refused all food offered to her and on the second day had gnawed through the rope and bolted. The *askar* who accompanied me on my watering job made to beat her off with the butt of his rifle, thinking that she was attacking me. He could not understand a dog retaining that much affection for a man. Mohammedans rarely touch a dog, however fond of them they may be, and I have rarely seen an Arab show any affection for one. When I returned to the prison the *askars* had great difficulty in preventing her from following me inside. I explained the situation to the Onbashi, who was good enough to let her remain at the door, and he even fed her with *kurrawanna*. Every day after that she trotted by my side as I carried water, or lay gazing into the prison when I was inside. She was rarely absent from the door, but it so happened that on one of those occasions I was taken from the prison for good, and it was many weeks before I saw her again.

To my great bitterness Micky and I were parted when the time came for us to leave prison. He was sent to the Company's headquarters in the foothills and I was sent down the track to a place called Ghir Ghiro, fifty miles below Nisibin.

I was very depressed as I trudged those fifty miles with only a garrulous *askar* for company. Life would be very dreary without Micky, I thought, and I wondered what I should do until I got used to being on my own. I knew that I should not find his like again although I was bound, sooner or later, to chum up with someone else.

It took two days to reach the camp on the rail-track—five miles south-east of Ghir Ghiro village—and the site of a railway station. The village itself was built on one of the numerous Tells that are a feature of that part of the country; mounds that concealed the ruins of towns of a dead civilization.

CHAPTER SEVENTEEN

WITH THE "COMPANIA" AT GHIR GHIRO

I FOUND on my arrival at Ghir Ghiro camp that the English there only numbered about ten, the others being Armenians, Greeks, Albanians, and Arabs. There were several substantial buildings already completed and occupied—offices, stores, and workshops, etc.—whilst the personnel were housed in tents of all descriptions, the Britishers being in two large bell-tents of canvas.

I reported at the offices and was interviewed by the German engineer in charge, who sent me to report to the Armenian foreman carpenter. He told me that I should live with the other Englishmen and would be employed as a carpenter along with one other Englishman—a man of the Norfolk Regiment.

When I went over to the bell-tents—free at last from my *askar* escort—the English prisoners there did their best to make me welcome and feel "at home," giving me a liberal helping from their evening meal. They were anxious to hear from me all the news of what was happening at Nisibin and whether I thought the end of the war was in sight. Strangely enough, I had never given much thought to the progress of the war hitherto. I had lived a life for many months that called for concentration on where the next meal was coming from, and the possibility of getting safely to wherever I was bound. The war, and all it stood for, was something well in the past and seemed to belong to another age. It was impossible for me to contemplate the miracle of freedom, when I should no longer go hungry or be able to move from place to place without doing so at the risk of my life—if I decided to go alone or on my own initiative. However, I was able to tell my new companions tit-bits of news that

I had gleaned here and there, of how things were going on the Palestine front, the front that seemed to display the most activity at that period.

From them I learned all there was to know about life at Ghir Ghiro. They all had "staff jobs" except one, who did the cooking for the remainder and looked after the two tents in the daytime, and all seemed fairly contented with their lot. I was informed that an English Medical Officer of the Kut Garrison lived in the sick quarters of the camp and looked after their interests as much as he was able. All of them were of the Kut Garrison, as were the sprinkling of Indians employed in various capacities on the camp.

After many hours of yarning we lay down on the ground outside the tents and went to sleep. Enough old bits of blanket and sacking had been found to provide me with a bed of sorts and—after my rough experiences in the matter of sleeping—I was very comfortable. It was long before I slept, as I missed Micky and was feeling very sorry for myself. Actually I was a thousand times worse off than before my attempt to escape; no pal to joke with, no prospects of another attempt to escape or anything else to break the monotony of a dire captivity.

For two or three weeks I worked as a carpenter, but without interest or enthusiasm. After work hours I had made friends with the native element in the camp, particularly the Armenians that worked in the offices, and the result of the latter friendship was to lead to a different occupation, one that gave me a fresh interest in life and altered my whole outlook.

All the food stores for the camp were bought, as far as possible, from the surrounding villages and tribes. Meat was bought on the hoof, and, like the flour, raisins, beans, and chopped straw—to feed the live meat—had to be weighed on the Company's scales before payment for it was made. The job of check weighman was being performed by an Armenian of the office staff, who, in addition to thinking that the job was below his dignity as a *katib* (clerk), was afraid of his contact with the tribes and villagers with whom the Company dealt. When he discovered that I could speak Arabic and understood the jargon of the Bedouins, he recommended me for the job to the German cashier, who was in charge of the office staff. I knew nothing of all this until the job was offered to me and when it was I readily accepted. That was the commencement of a bloodless but wordy vendetta between the office staff and the shop foreman, who did not want to lose my services, carpenters being a rarity in that part of the country.

I saw in that job the certainty of a break in the monotony of my existence and the possibility of a break-away from the camp. It was an easy matter to learn the system, and, so far as actual work went, was a very easy billet for me. The livestock as well as the produce was handled by coolies and I simply checked the amounts as they registered on the scales—in kilos—and entered the totals into a ledger. The stock was paid for at so much a kilo, according to the class of goods, and in hard cash as the natives would not accept paper-money. I put the total amount of goods supplied on to a slip of paper, together with the name of the seller, and signed. That slip was presented to the cashier, who paid out at once on seeing my signature. I soon saw a way of making money at the expense of the enemy, even if it were not strictly honest, remembering that all was fair in love and war—at least that was what I had always been taught! I adopted a very friendly attitude towards the Arab of each village who dealt on behalf of his community—usually the headman—and what I expected soon came to pass. One of them said to me one day that he was delivering fifty sheep the following day, and, if I was agreeable, he could make it worth my while to be easy on my figures! After a good deal of verbal fencing I agreed to help him on a fifty-fifty basis.

The following day the sheep were duly driven in and put on the scales. To the actual weight of each animal as shown on the machine, I added two kilos in my book, which made a difference in the total purchase price of about Lira 3 (nearly £3). I told the headman the amount of extra that I had given him, and he, according to plan, sent a villager to me the next day with half the amount. It was all very simple!

At that time stores were being bought in in great quantities, both for the current supply for all the employees and staff and for storage for the winter, so that I speedily found that I was accumulating a fair amount of money. I improved on my system and "double-crossed" both the Germans and the Arabs by telling the latter that their stock weighed less than it actually did, so that after I had increased the amount I got two thirds of the loot.

The Germans were so pleased at the way I was handling the job that they promoted me to stock-controller, and I used to visit the villages and tribes and negotiate sales. I was given a revolver and supplied with a mount and an escort, for my protection, by the camp Commandant. I had a hut built and kept a servant, which was in keeping with my improved status. My servant was a young Armenian girl, daughter of the temporary wife of the Turkish Commandant. Her mother told me that the German engineer, as well as several other Germans, had been trying to get her as a temporary wife but she would not let her go. As I was an Englishman—therefore someone she could trust not to harm the girl—she would let her come to me subject to the Commandant's permission. I got the permission easily enough as I had already made friends with the Commandant by pandering to his immense liking for arrack. In fact, I had more than once joined him in a carousal!

Apart from business I was a very frequent visitor to the neighbouring villages, particularly to the village of Ghir Ghiro, inhabited for the most part by Kurds. During the feast of Ramadan of that year I attended the celebration at Ghir Ghiro in full Arab dress, much to the delight of Oman Aga, the Kurdish headman. He benefited greatly from my association with him and he showed his appreciation by making that feast a very enjoyable one for me. When the wandering minstrels gave their turn and the bard had sung innumerable verses lauding the virtues and greatness of Oman Aga, that worthy said something in Kurdish and the bard put a in few verses about the *Ingleezi* and *el Longa!*

Towards the end of the summer the great influenza plague swept across the country and I became a temporary victim; our M.O. had very little with which to combat it and he had many patients in the camp. My native friends brought presents of fruit every day, and at one time I had over twenty huge water-melons in my hut.

Abdul Hamid the Fifth, Sultan of the Turkish Empire, died during the period I was at Ghir Ghiro, but very little notice was taken of the event, even by the Commandant and his soldiers. The Armenians rejoiced in secret, as to them he was one Turk the less.

About that time my German friend Adam Renner and two of the others from the "House on the Hill" were posted to this section of the line and we renewed our acquaintanceship by a "binge" on new wine and old *raki*—a terrible combination. They were very jubilant over the news of the big German *putsch* on the Western front and readily accepted my bet of Lira 5 that the Germans would never enter Paris as victors. I knew little or nothing about the state of affairs but I had supreme confidence that the British could not be beaten!

One exciting incident happened in the camp one day, an incident that might have had serious consequences for me. In order to get more head room and greater coolness, my English companions had dug a three-foot-deep pit under their tents. One day I was sitting on the steps of one of the pits talking to the cook, who was busily engaged skinning beans ready to cook for the evening meal. (Those beans were an inevitable part of the day's menu; huge, dried field beans with skins like leather that took two days' soaking before it was possible to remove them, and each bean contained a weevil.) The rest of the men were at work. The tents had been pitched a few yards from a small stream, and in the wall of the pit nearest to the stream were several holes like rat-holes. As I was talking a snake suddenly glided out of one of those holes. I yelled a warning to the cook which startled the snake and it turned and glided into another hole. I jumped from the steps to the floor of the pit and managed to put my foot on the tail of the reptile before it could get away. The cook had promptly dashed up the steps! I called to him to get me his skinning knife, which he had dropped just out of my reach. Armed with the knife I pulled at the tail of the snake with my free hand. I had hoped to snatch it from the hole and kill it before it had time to strike, but with my first pull only a couple of feet of it came out, so I held it again with my foot. The perspiration dripped off me and I wondered how much more of the snake was left in the hole, and whether to give a hefty pull or only a short snatch. I trembled with indecision and regretted interfering with the reptile. For several moments I stood, not daring to risk another pull. I knew that if I cut it in two as I had it it would kill it, but I was anxious to make sure—a feeling most men have when dealing with snakes. Bracing myself for another pull I yanked the thing out and made a wild slash with the knife, cutting off its head just as it fastened its teeth in my stocking. For all I knew it might have been a perfectly harmless reptile, even so I was greatly relieved to see it decapitated as I sat down to recover from the excitement of the moment. It was just over four feet in length, brilliant yellow with a line of red spots running the length of the body on either side near the belly. I took it to our

M.O., who said that it was a dangerous variety and advised that all the holes in the pit wall be stopped up.

One other incident I must mention—though a much more pleasant one—to show how it was possible for men of the "other ranks" to work up to positions of trust that carried many privileges, even as prisoners of war, given the right opportunities. I had a great urge to revisit Nisibin now that I had money enough to get me a good time, so I applied for a week's leave! Without any trouble at all I received a written pass from the Commandant, and a pass from the German engineer that permitted me to travel on any transport belonging to the Company. I rode into Nisibin on one of the heavy lorries and reported to the headquarters of the prisoners' administrative section—where Sergeant-Major Leach used to hold sway. I was given a bed there to use during my stay and invited to have my meals with the small staff of Britishers who worked there. That week was a very full one; a week of glorious memory. The first day I hunted the bazaar until I found Winnie, my dog. I did not doubt that my hunt would be successful if she were still alive. From that day she never left my side during the time I was in Nisibin. Drunk or sober—and I was very drunk more than once—that pariah dog was at my heels, my devoted guard. I visited the English camp and swopped yarns with my old friends there, and bought what luxuries I could get from the station store—still being run by the same British N.C.O. At the end of the week the only conveyance I could get back to Ghir Ghiro was a fully loaded *arabah*. I was unable to bribe the *arabanchi* into allowing my dog to ride, principally because of the protests of the one other passenger besides myself—an Effendi going to Mosul by stages. So Winnie had to follow as best she could the whole fifty miles, and a pretty tough journey it was for her. We started early in the morning, and, with a short halt at midday, completed the journey by the evening of the same day. At times the *arabanchi* whipped his team of four flea-bitten, bony horses into a gallop that threatened every moment to shake the crazy *arabah* to pieces. On those occasions my dog was left well behind, but it was not long after we had once more settled into a walk that she would come loping over the horizon. By the time we reached camp her pads were swollen and bleeding and she was almost exhausted. She soon became a favourite of the other Englishmen, but would not tolerate an Arab anywhere near her. By day she slept in my hut but all night long she lay at the entrance, outside, fully awake, and growled threateningly every time anyone approached within yards of the place.

After my return from Nisibin and during my next visit to Oman Aga I discussed with that Kurd the possibility of escape. He was definitely pro-British and promised to help me in any way that he could. On a subsequent visit we went more into details and it was eventually settled that, after the crops were in, he would supply me with an escort and a mount, and that I should be taken to the British lines via Kurdistan. I was secretly exultant that before very long I should once more be on the move, my only regret being that it would be impossible to get Micky along to join me. My plans were not to bear fruit, for before the end of September all the prisoners of war at Ghir Ghiro were ordered by the Commandant to be ready to leave the camp.

Two days later, greatly excited and wondering what such a sudden move could portend, we were marching out of the camp under an escort of *askars* and going in the direction of Mosul. That night we camped under the stars beside the dusty track that passed for the main road. We discussed the situation with the Indians, but they could not give us any idea of what was afoot, and the escort would not answer questions. Within a day's march of Mosul we halted at a

ration depot for the night and there I was told, by one of
the local soldiers, that we were going to the Mosul front
to help dig trenches, as the Turks were preparing to make a
great attempt to stem the advance of the British. I told my
companions, both British and Indian, the news and we
debated what was to be done. None of us were now the
servile and broken-down wrecks who had passed this way
two and half years previously and we decided that we must
refuse to go any farther. The Indians promised to back us
up in any action that we English might take.

The following morning the Chaoush of the escort came
to us and commenced the usual "Yellah-ing," and, when we
took no notice of him, he became greatly excited and struck
one of the Indians. In an instant there was a great outcry
and the Chaoush was surrounded by a threatening crowd of
us. The Yuzbashi in charge of the ration depot came running
up in answer to the shouts of the askars, who had commenced
to load their rifles. I told the officer what had happened and
of our decision not to proceed farther. To my amazement,
he was most reasonable and said that he would send a
soldier into headquarters at Mosul and ask for instructions!
Meanwhile we could remain where we were, he said, if we
promised to behave ourselves and not quarrel with his men.
This was something new indeed, and I pressed our advantage
and asked for extra rations, saying that we were used to being
properly fed by the Company and could not submit to being
starved by the army. Further, I asked that all orders from
himself to us be given to me for transmission to the remainder
to prevent friction between us and the escort. He granted
both requests and we settled down to await results.

Something bigger than we could guess was behind that
change of front on part of the Turkish officer, but none of
us had an inkling of what it might be.

Late that afternoon the Yuzbashi called the escort together
and talked to them earnestly and excitedly. Undoubtedly,

news of great importance had been received, but we were out of earshot and could only gaze intently at the little knot of soldiers and wonder what would happen next. Whatever the *askars* had been told they did not tell us, but there was a distinct change in their demeanour towards us and they became quite friendly, addressing me servilely as Chaoush Effendi!

The next morning we were told by the Yuzbashi that we were being sent back to Ghir Ghiro. Beyond that he told us nothing.

Arrived back at Ghir Ghiro we found everyone excitedly talking in little groups. I endeavoured to find out what was taking place but the only answer I could get to my questions was, "Bir shey yok" ("Nothing"). We were not put to work immediately, as we expected, so I sent a coolie to the village with a request to Oman Aga for a horse, and, when it arrived, galloped off to visit him to see what I could learn. He told me that the Turks were on the run both in Palestine and Mesopotamia and that we could expect their collapse at any moment! That news was so unexpected that it staggered me and I could hardly believe it to be true, though the changed attitude of the *askars* seemed to point to the truth of it. After a hasty meal with Oman Aga, I galloped back to camp and told the rest of the prisoners, then went in search of my German friends. I found that they were on continual duty at the telephone, but they would tell me nothing. They were obviously very worried and their manner was enough to confirm the news that I had received from the Kurdish headman.

The next day we went back to our various jobs, though I am afraid very little work was done. At sunset I was told that I was wanted at the German Mess, and, when I got there, I was asked by an engineer if the English would like to purchase from him a case of assorted spirits! He had arrived at Ghir Ghiro on his way to Mosul and had been recalled to Nisibin. The fact that I was being asked to purchase spirits, when officially it was forbidden for prisoners of war to do so, was another indication that something important was in the air. I came to a rapid decision and offered a price for the whole case, which was accepted. The case was carried to one of the bell-tents and I told the rest of the English prisoners what was in it, saying that the end of the war was undoubtedly in sight and we had better celebrate! They were only too willing to join in and we rigged up a table and seats in one of the tents, in preparation for the carousal. Chipped enamel basins and empty food tins were for the most part our drinking vessels, but we were not fussy over that. We emptied the case and found that there was whisky—labelled Scotch!—German "Steinheiger," cognac of sorts, peppermint, vermouth, and several bottles of stuff that we could not recognize. All of the bottles were placed at one end of the table in front of me and I proceeded to pour a tot out of each bottle into the various drinking vessels. Cocktails! We drank that night cocktails that were more potent than any that have ever come out of America, before or since! We called the stuff alternatively "Barbed Wire" or "Fixed Bayonets," and either name was appropriate.

That was no dainty party but a real "binge" by near a dozen hard-bitten men of the "other ranks" who had nothing to gain and little to lose whatever happened. It can be imagined that, drinking that horrible mixture, the party soon became boisterous—to say the least of it—and we began to sing at the top of our voices. The night wore on and one by one the members of the party dropped into unconsciousness where they sat, thoroughly drugged by the foul brew. Three of us were left when the last bottle was emptied, and I announced that I was going to get some *raki* from the Company's store. Staggering out into the darkness I made my way to the quarters of the German cashier and pounded on the door. After a few minutes, during which I continued to pound the door, it was flung open and the German stood there brandishing a revolver! I was beyond caring; mad drunk actually, but with a clear impression of what I wanted and what I was doing. I demanded a chit for three kilos of *raki* and pushed by him into his room, an action that would, under normal circumstances, have brought me a severe flogging, if nothing worse. He no doubt thought that discretion was the better part of valour as he wrote me out the chit and pushed me outside. I went over to the store and woke up the storeman—who slept on the premises—and he served me without question, despite the fact that it was in the early hours of the morning. Seeing a *raki* glass on his table I picked it up, and, clutching the three bottles, I reeled over to the tent, only to find that the other two "survivors" had vanished. For a time I sat drinking alone, then made my way to Adam Renner's room, taking with me a full bottle and the glass. He had just come off duty from the telephone and was getting into bed, but he joined me in one drink "for old times' sake." When I insisted that he help me finish the bottle he picked me up bodily and put me down outside and locked the door against me! I went on to the telephone office where the other Germans were on duty—both old friends of mine—but they would only take one drink and then urged me to go away. Wearying at last of being alone I decided to go to bed. When I got to my hut I found the door fastened on the inside and my dog alternatively growling and whining. I peeped through a crack in the door and saw someone sleeping on my bed. Bursting open the door I found the sleeper to be one of my party, so without ceremony I rolled him on to the floor and took his place on the bed and was soon fast asleep.

I was still half drunk when I was awakened a few hours later to learn that all the prisoners of war had to leave for Nisibin without delay. In a maze, I parcelled up a few

belongings and joined the others, who were all more or less
in the same state as I was. Then we started for Nisibin, with
only one *askar* as an escort. How I managed to get through
the first day's march I have no idea. With my head on fire
and no water to quench a raging thirst I paid dearly for my
overnight's carousal.

CHAPTER EIGHTEEN

CONCLUSION

ON the second day we arrived at Nisibin and went into camp on the banks of the irrigation stream near the station, where we found all the prisoners of war from the surrounding camps of the section concentrated. I asked for news of Micky and was told that he was one of a dozen picked men that the Germans had kept back at headquarters, to act as an escort for them should they decide to leave the district via Mardin. The next day I set off—without permission—to visit and, if possible, to join Micky and his party. Half way to the foothills I was arrested by the Commandant, who was making his way back to Nisibin from a visit to the Germans. I was handed over to a posse of Gendarmes, who were camping in a small ravine, and was taken back to my camp astride a camel!

At the station the Germans were hastily handing over all the stores to the Turks. The British prisoners employed there were handling the goods, and, as some of them carried them back into the warehouses after being checked, others were doing a roaring trade at the back doors—unknown to the Turks—selling all they could at any price they could get, and to all comers! Shovels were going for one piastre and metal wheel-barrows for two. Grain and other produce was sold for similar cut-throat prices, and, until they were detected, the prisoners had the time of their lives. When a Turkish soldier eventually caught them at it they simply "downed tools" and ran off, never to return. Everywhere was chaos and I have often marvelled that the native population of Nisibin did not attempt wholesale looting.

The climax to the excitement came when a train, comprising carriages full of German engineers and other officials, among whom were two Nursing Sisters, and wagons containing their baggage and sundry loot, was held up by Kurds before it got to Ras-el-Ain. All the passengers were stripped of their clothing and the goods wagons emptied and the train-driver was ordered to take the train and passengers back to Nisibin. All the passengers—including my old friend Adam Renner—looked white and badly scared as they left the train, wrapped in blankets supplied by the Commandant. They were taken by *arabas* to headquarters and left the next day by convoy with the rest of the Germans there, going to Angora via Mardin and Sivas. Micky and the rest of the English escort went with them and I saw him no more until I reached Port Said.

A few days after that incident two armoured cars, flying small Union Jacks, arrived from Mosul, bringing with them Lt.-Col. E. H. Keeling, M.C., who was to make arrangements for us to leave the country. That was our great moment and we were mad with joy.

Several of the more obnoxious of the Commandant's soldiers were badly man-handled by their victims among the prisoners, and the Commandant made himself very scarce.

A train was got ready for us, and after several false starts we commenced the journey to Aleppo and freedom. Several bright spirits had made, during the period of waiting for the train, a large Union Jack, and at every station where we stopped everyone wearing anything approaching a Turkish uniform was forced to salute "The Flag." It was their way of obtaining redress for the cruelties and indignities to which we had been subjected. At a station about twenty miles out of Aleppo we were told that we should have to walk the rest of the way, as there was no fuel left for the two engines that were pulling the train. Walk for lack of fuel? Not on your life we didn't. Doors were wrenched off their hinges and window-frames from their sockets and were smashed up for fuel in no time, and the drivers ordered to proceed! We had done all the walking we intended to do in Turkey.

At Aleppo we were housed for two or three days in the Turkish barracks on top of a hill outside the town, under the kindly eye of a Colonel of the 5th Cavalry Division—the advance guard of General Allenby's victorious armies. The only water available for drinking purposes was in a well sixty fathoms deep, in the barrack yard, and, on the very day that we arrived there, the brand-new rope that had been supplied by the Division for drawing the water had been stolen. We were told that until the R.E.s arrived there would be rather a scarcity of water, as there was not another rope to be had long enough to reach. I offered my services in an attempt to recover the rope, and, accompanied by an English and a Sikh military policeman, I set off on the job. I tackled the small boys who were crowding round the outside gate first, and from them I got my first clue, the name of an Arab seen leaving the barracks early that morning carrying a bundle. They told me where that Arab lived, not a stone's-throw away, and there I frightened his womenfolk into an admission that the man we wanted had found such a rope and had gone to the bazaar to sell it. An Arab who had heard the women tell us that commenced to curse and swear at them as we were leaving, so we took him along with us, suspecting that he might know something about the matter. As we were passing through the bazaar, another Arab shouted to the one we had under arrest, telling him not to give any information. Unfortunately for that second man he was unaware that I could understand Arabic, and we arrested him also! In the street of shoemakers we were just in time to catch the man we were after, in the very act of selling the rope to one of the shopkeepers. He was with another Arab, who appeared to be having a lot to say about the price to be paid for the rope, so we took them both along. We arrived back at the barracks with the four prisoners and the missing rope in a little over an hour after we had left, a job of police work of which I am secretly proud!

The Colonel was very pleased to get the rope back, but he confessed that he knew of no appropriate punishment for the thieves, saying that he was not used to a job of that nature. There was a golden opportunity not to be missed, so I suggested that he could do worse than allow four of our party, who had suffered terrible things at the hands of the Arabs, to whip them. After some hesitation the Colonel agreed to that, on condition that a Corporal of the Military Police was present to see that the punishment was not excessive. I chose the four men for the job and they were supplied by the police with leather belts, and the whipping duly took place. It was a thorough punishment but not brutal, and after it was over I gave the culprits a little lecture on how to behave now that the British were in occupation of the town, pointing out that had the Turks caught them under similar circumstances they would have been tortured and shot. Which was most probably true.

That same afternoon we each received a couple of pounds and were turned loose on the town, to do and go where we liked. How we spent the cash and the next two days is another story, but I have no doubt that some of the officers of the Light Armoured Motor Batteries (L.A.M.B.s), who joined us the first night, can remember something about it!

From Aleppo we were taken to Homs by rail and then, as the rails had been torn up, we travelled on to Tripoli in motor-lorries. At Tripoli our rags were burnt and we were immersed in a tank of creosol, after which we received as much clothing as we could carry—on our person or off it.

We spent two days in the camp outside Tripoli and I managed to elude the Military Police and get into the town, where I met an Australian soldier who had broken arrest and together we had a great time.

From Tripoli we were taken by boat to Port Said, there

to wait for over a month before we could get a ship to take us further on our journey home. When at last we did get away the sea voyage ended at Taranto, Southern Italy, where we entrained for Calais. Two or three days' wait at Calais for a storm to abate and then we crossed to Dover. When we did make the Channel crossing, a good many of us wished that we could have walked it, even to the goad of "Yellah, yellah!"

A short wait at Dover and then we went off to Canterbury, where we had our first glimpse of the amazing efficiency of the War Machine, and thence, once more repatriated, to our various homes, three months after the Armistice with Turkey had been signed.